From Homebreakers to Jailbreakers

Southall Black Sisters

---

edited by Rahila Gupta

ZED BOOKS
London & New York

From Homebreakers to Jailbreakers was first published in 2003 by
Zed Books Ltd, 7 Cynthia Street, London N1 9JF, UK,
and Room 400, 175 Fifth Avenue, New York, NY 10010, USA

www.zedbooks.co.uk

Designed and typeset in Monotype Joanna by Illuminati, Grosmont
Cover designed by Andrew Corbett
Printed and bound in Malta

Distributed in the USA exclusively by Palgrave, a division of
St Martin's Press, LLC, 175 Fifth Avenue, New York, NY 10010

A catalogue record for this book is available from the British Library
Library of Congress Cataloging-in-Publication Data available

ISBN 1 84277 440 9 (Hb)
ISBN 1 84277 441 7 (Pb)

Contents

I am an activist. It pays the rent for living on this planet.

Alice Walker

Acknowledgements

We would like to thank the countless women that we have met in the course of our work whose courage and resilience have lit the way for us. The names of many of the women who appear within these pages have been changed to protect their anonymity, so we are not able to acknowledge them individually here.

We would also like to thank Rohit Sanghvi whose cautious legal opinion on libel involved us in many hours of careful checking of our facts and sources, Nira Yuval Davis for sharing her insights on transversal politics, Sue Shutter, Navita Atreya, Wesley Gryk, Nick Blake, Raza Hussain, Alison Stanley and Duran Seddon for their advice on immigration rules, Charlotte Cole, Charlotte Gascoigne, Penny Warburton, Graham Smith, Mark Daniels and Julia Bard for their help with the preparation of this book and Steve Woodhouse and Raju Bhatt for tolerating SBS's disruption of their daily lives.

Foreword

Baroness Helena Kennedy QC

Working as a lawyer in the British courts for the last thirty years, I daily see women at the receiving end of a justice system which fails them. This is not the result of a conspiracy of men in horsehair wigs but a reflection of laws, which were essentially made by men without much reference to women at all. In addition, there remains in place a set of attitudes which support the survival of the status quo.

Law in most of the UK is a composition of case law, which is created by the judges over hundreds of years, and statute law, which is passed in Parliament. In neither process is there a significant place for the voice of women, let alone those from ethnic minorities. There are still very few women in the judiciary, particularly at a senior law-making level, and in Parliament the slowly growing numbers cannot redress policymaking dominated by male priorities. Women's issues are too often treated cynically as a vote catcher, as long as they are not too controversial. Black women in our society are particularly disadvantaged because there are so few people in high office to champion their cause or give voice to their experience. In every area they experience multiple disadvantage because the marriage of gender and race is such a powerful discriminator.

Southall Black Sisters has played a significant role, enriching feminist activity and providing truly important insights into an experience outside the reach of white women. I am very conscious of my own indebtedness to the extraordinary women at SBS who have acted as my mentors over the years. They have taken me on a journey of learning and shown me the meaning of courage. Alliances between people committed to justice are more important now than ever before, and we would be unwise to ignore the warning signals contained within this important book.

In recent years feminist activity has focused increasingly on the courts, with a move away from demonstrations and direct activism of the 1970s and early 1980s. We have seen some remarkable victories like the extraordinary shift in provocation laws, which mean that the old definition of 'sudden' loss of control is now capable of incorporating the slow-burn experience of battered women, who only kill their partners in despair after years of abuse. We are even seeing changes occurring in the field of rape, still a crime with a scandalously low conviction rate, despite so many years of campaigning.

However, in their determination to win justice for women some feminist groups fall into the trap of demanding a reduction of defendants' rights, which would not only in the end have damning consequences for women as defendants in the courts but undermine the justice system as a whole. One of the lessons I have learned in the courts is that justice for women cannot be secured by reducing justice for men. There has to be some other way. The victim lobby grew out of the women's movement, when feminists threw the spotlight on law's failure to deliver for women, particularly in the area of violence against women. The marginalising of the victim in rape and cases of domestic violence, the ready dismissal of their experience, the failure to bring the reality of women's lives into the courtroom, all led to the development of a powerful campaign for victims' rights. However, that campaigning has in recent years been mainstreamed and hijacked by the law-and-order lobby to make inroads into the rights of the accused – male or female. It is a lesson in unforeseen consequences! For this reason I feel strongly that feminism has to take a hard look at itself and not only ask where it is heading but also who its bedfellows are.

Why I have long admired the SBS is because it does not shy away from the difficult questions, especially as they affect the black community. The women there have led the way on domestic violence as it impacts on ethnic minority communities. Shame is a common experience of abused women, and one which has contributed to the long silence on this issue. But that sense of shame is even greater amongst Asian women, who feel that to expose the violence of their partners is to open their community to scrutiny and yet more negative stereotyping. The mantra that such behaviour should be kept within the 'family' has meant enormous suffering for too many women. Giving voice to the treatment of women in the ethnic minority communities has frequently meant vilification for the Southall Black Sisters, especially from their own people. That is always a particularly painful experience for any political activists, but these extraordinary women have steadfastly resisted the pressure to which they have been exposed.

SBS timeline

23 April 1979	Hundreds arrested and injured in police operation to stop mass protest against National Front presence in Southall. Blair Peach killed by Special Patrol Group officers. Defence campaign followed.
November 1979	Founding of Southall Black Sisters.
January 1980	Chix strike, Slough. Many Southall women on mass picket.
1980	Anti-virginity tests campaign.
1980	Mrs Dhillon and her children set on fire by her husband. SBS protests.
1983	GLC (Greater London Council) funding received. Southall Black Women's Centre established.
May 1984	Krishna Sharma found hanged at home. Demonstration outside the house. Slogans 'They say it's suicide; we say it's murder', 'Black women's tradition/Struggle not submission'. Links set up with other campaigns on domestic violence.
June 1984	Dispute in Brent refuge starts. Management locked out. Demand to run projects separately.
1984	Miners' strike support activity.
October 1985	Balwant Kaur murdered by her husband in Brent Asian Women's Refuge. Campaign to ensure her husband's conviction.

1985	Refuge demands conceded.
1986	Gurdip Kaur campaign initiated in Reading following the murder of an Asian woman. Pickets and demos. Husband and brother-in-law conspired to murder. Brother-in-law charged with murder, got off with manslaughter. Charges against husband dropped.
July 1986	National demonstration of women against violence against women organised by Network of Women.
August 1986	Helped to produce film, *A Fearful Silence*, on domestic violence in Asian communities with Azad Productions.
October 1986	Split in Southall Black Women's Centre.
March 1987	New centre established in the name of Southall Black Sisters.
1987	Anti-deportation campaign, 'Josephine & Peter must stay'.
May/June 1987	Dominion Centre campaign on safety of women workers.
November 1987 –January 1988	Save SBS campaign. Funding threatened. Council lobbied. Slogan 'Where will women go?'
987/88	Ealing FAB campaign (Fight the Alton Bill, which was an attempt to restrict women's access to abortion).
July 1988	Launch of single homelessness campaign.
9 March 1989	International Women's Day meeting called 'The resurgence of religion? What price do women pay?' SBS and Labour Party, Southall Women's Section issue statement in support of Salman Rushdie.
23 April 1989	March and rally on tenth anniversary of Blair Peach's murder by police.
6 May 1989	First meeting of Women Against Fundamentalism.
27 May 1989	Women Against Fundamentalism picket religious Muslim demonstration demanding an extension of blasphemy laws. Demands include a secularization of the British state, no state funding of religious education and abolition of the blasphemy law. Slogans 'Our tradition: struggle not submission', 'Religious leaders don't speak for us', 'Blasphemy laws police dissent', 'Fear is your weapon/Courage is ours'.

1990 — Publication of *Against the Grain: A Celebration of Survival and Struggle*, narrative on the first ten years of SBS history.

January 1991 — Set up the Save Our Schools Campaign with local groups, teachers and parents in Southall to prevent two schools opting out and becoming Sikh-only schools.

May 1991 — Helped to launch 'Remember Vandana Patel Campaign' with local Asian women's groups.

1991 — Launch of the Free Kiranjit Ahluwalia campaign, a woman who was given a life sentence for murder for setting her violent husband on fire in a final act of survival.

1992 — Kiranjit is released and her original conviction is quashed and reduced to manslaughter.

1992 — SBS gives evidence on how the one-year rule in immigration traps newly married women in violent situations to the Home Affairs Select Committee's inquiry into domestic violence.

1992 — SBS is awarded the Martin Ennals Civil Liberties Award by Liberty.

May 1992 — Memorial held for Abnash Bisla, killed by her husband. SBS also demonstrates outside the husband's house with a number of other Asian women's groups.

1993 — Pragna Patel, a member of the management committee, wins two Cosmopolitan Achievement Awards: in the Public Service category and as the overall winner for the year.

1993 — SBS forms Alliance Against Communalism and for Democracy in South Asia with a number of local groups in Southall and Brent in the wake of the destruction of Babri Masjid in India by Hindu fundamentalist and Hindu and Muslim riots. Aims to fight communal forces in South Asia and the UK.

1995 — SBS starts a campaign against the one-year immigration rule and wins Advice 2000's 'Challenge Award' in 'recognition of our efforts to gain justice'.

1995 — SBS sends a delegation of women to attend World Conference on Women in Beijing.

1995	Successfully appeals in the case of an Asian woman with mental health problems who killed her child; her conviction for murder is reduced to manslaughter.
February 1996	SBS makes a submission on immigration, asylum and domestic violence to the UN hearings on the International Convention for the Elimination of Racial Discrimination.
February 1996	Memorial for Imtiaz Begum and her four children, killed by her husband/their father in Birmingham and Bristol. Works with local Asian women's groups.
1996	SBS starts campaign to free Zoora Shah, a woman serving life for the murder of her abuser, Mohammad Azam in Bradford in 1992.
1997	SBS secures a first ever conviction of a husband in a marital rape in the Asian community. Members of his family are also sentenced for abusing his wife.
June 1997	Publication of Circle of Light, the story of Kiranjit Ahluwalia's life, co-written with Rahila Gupta, a member of the management committee.
April 1998	Zoora Shah loses her appeal against her conviction for the murder of Mohammed Azam. SBS continues to explore other legal avenues including representations to the Home Secretary to reduce her twenty-year tariff.
October 1998	The conclusion of an internal review of SBS management and administrative structures results in SBS moving from a collective structure to a hierarchy.
1998	SBS is nominated for the Ethnic Minority Charity for the Year by the Ethnic Minority Media Awards sponsored by NatWest Bank.
March 1999	The House of Lords delivers a historic judgment in the Shah and Islam case: women who fear gender persecution should be recognized as refugees. SBS had advised one of the women and her legal team.
June 1999	The Home Office announces concessions on the one-year rule for abused spouses/partners subject to a probationary period following discussions with SBS.
August 1999	SBS is invited to join the Home Office Working Group to inquire into the issue of forced marriage.

1999	SBS, along with five other women's organizations, are the beneficiaries of money raised by a 'V-Day' charity event – the first celebrity readings of Eve Ensler's *Vagina Monologues* in the UK.
1999	Hannana Siddiqui, joint co-ordinator of SBS, is nominated for the Emma Humphries Memorial Prize.
1999	SBS supports the Lufthansa Skychef workers, most of whom are Asian women, sacked for going on a lawful one-day strike in protest against new working practices.
January 2000	Southall Black Sisters Trust is set up.
2000	After representations to the Home Secretary by SBS, Zoora Shah's sentence is cut from twenty to twelve years.
2000	SBS begins work on the case of Morgan James Smith in conjunction with Justice for Women and Liberty. The case involves the House of Lords deliberating on the defence of provocation under homicide law. Their conclusions reinforce the crucial advances made on the law of provocation in the cases of Ahluwalia, Thornton and Humphries.
June 2000	Flowers laid outside the house of Jaspal Sohal, a local woman killed by her husband, who was later convicted of her murder.
June 2000	The Home Office Working Group on Forced Marriage produces its report. SBS resigns from the Working Group over the issue of mediation.
July 2000	SBS celebrates its twenty-first anniversary.
2000	Pragna Patel is nominated for the Emma Humphries Memorial Prize.
2001	SBS makes a presentation on the intersection between race and gender at the preparatory meetings for the UN Conference on Racism, Racial Discrimination, Xenophobia and Related Intolerance, and oral evidence to the UN Commission on the Status of Women, 45th Session, in New York.
2001	SBS submits research to the Home Office on the operation of the concessions to the one-year immigration rule since they were announced in summer 1999.

June 2001	Written and oral evidence is given to the United Nations Working Group on Contemporary Forms of Slavery in Geneva.
2001	SBS publishes *Forced Marriage: An Abuse of Human Rights* to mark the first anniversary of the Home Office Working Group Report, *A Choice by Right*, to assess government progress. It makes a number of recommendations for future action.
November 2001	Kiranjit Ahluwalia wins the Asian Woman of Courage award and SBS is given a Lifetime's Achievement Award organized by Media Moguls.
2002	SBS is involved in AWAAZ, a loose network of individuals and organisations, formed in the wake of the Gujarat genocide of Muslims, to oppose religious fundamentalism in the UK and Indian subcontinent
July 2002	SBS seeks a judicial review of a coroner's decision not to hold an inquest and not to recognise SBS as an interested third party after the collapse of a criminal trial against the husband of Nazia Bi, who was burnt to death with her child. This was the first time a voluntary organisation challenged a Coroner's Court in a domestic violence case. Although the High Court refused leave for judicial review, SBS continues to campaign on issues raised in the case.
October 2002	SBS successfully helps a young Asian woman secure the first annulment of marriage in England and Wales in a forced marriage case.
October 2002	Hannana Siddiqui wins the Women of the Year Award from GG2 – Garavi Gujarat newspaper.
November 2002	Home Office minister Beverley Hughes announces further reforms to the domestic violence concession of the One Year Rule and incorporates it into the Immigration Rules following consultation with SBS.
November/ December 2002	SBS holds a historic series of regional consultation meetings with black and minority women and women's groups to start a national initiative on violence against black and minority women.

December 2002   SBS holds a vigil and a public meeting to highlight the issues of race, child abuse and state accountability following the death of Victoria Climbie. The event is jointly organised with the Family Foundation Group in support of the Victoria Climbié Family Campaign and acts as a memorial to Victoria. It is also the first meeting to examine the role of Ealing Council in Victoria's case.

February 2003   Hannana Siddiqui nominated by the government's Women and Equality Unit for the Asian Women's Achievement Award.

I

Some recurring themes:
Southall Black Sisters, 1979–2003
– and still going strong

Rahila Gupta

I would like to introduce Southall Black Sisters (SBS) with the blurb I wrote for a fundraising event organised by Eve Ensler, an American feminist, in 1999 called *The Vagina Monologues*. This was based on Eve's interviews with hundreds of women on their feelings about their sexuality and, on this occasion, performed by celebrity women actors ranging from Kate Winslett to Melanie Griffiths from across the Atlantic.

> Southall Black Sisters was set up in 1979 to meet the needs of Asian and African-Caribbean women. Since then we have helped thousands of women facing violence and abuse at home. Apart from providing welfare services and support, we have run campaigns to highlight and bring about changes in the social, political, economic and cultural constrictions that have led women to our door. We have sought to liberate women from these constrictions on their individual freedom.
>
> In the last year alone (1998), three workers dealt with 1200 cases. Every woman escaping violence presents complex issues – we need to find a refuge space and decent housing, to help with the legal battles for custody of the children, to unravel the complicated welfare benefits system, to safeguard their immigration status, to support children who may have been abused and perhaps damaged forever and to open doors for women locked away by their lack of English, lack of family and community support and

lack of self-confidence. In an under-resourced organisation, this takes it toll on the workers too.

No matter how much our heads have been bowed down in casework, we have continued to campaign and pursue ground-breaking legal decisions. We have made headway with our campaign against the One Year Rule, an immigration rule which obliges non-British spouses to remain in violent marriages or face deportation. We also campaigned on behalf of Zoora Shah, an Asian woman who poisoned her abuser after 12 years of sexual slavery and violence and was convicted for murder with a tariff of 20 years. Her case goes before the Home Secretary this month. He will review her tariff, favourably, we hope.[1]

And finally, to end on our very own vagina story. One of our earliest campaigns was against immigration rules that forced Asian women to hold their hymens up for inspection by officialdom. Were these women virgins? Because if they were not, then the arranged marriage that was their passport to this country could not be genuine. We soon made that a 'no-go area', so to speak.[2]

SBS was one of the first black women's groups to tackle sexual oppression. To mark our tenth anniversary, we published a collection of articles, *Against the Grain* (1990),[3] written by the SBS collective, which looked back on the issues that we had to confront in the early years. In 1989, we lamented the irony that SBS was a child of Thatcher as our existence at that point coincided exactly with the years of her office. Thatcher's policies redefined the centre so completely that the whole political agenda shifted irrevocably to the right. Now we register the transformation of Thatcher's image from populist dictator to a comic irrelevance with disbelief. Even her own soundbites reflect this change. The famous 'The lady's not for turning' became the self-deprecating 'The Mummy Returns' when she was wheeled out in the 2001 general election by a William Hague desperate to reverse Tory fortunes. How did this happen when the Thatcher project had appeared so difficult to demolish and had left us defensively campaigning against cuts, when the only notable success appeared to be the poll tax campaign? Could this be an attempt to underplay her legacy and thereby deflect attention from the debt owed to Thatcher in both substance and style by Blairite New Labour?

This collection of essays was meant to mark our twenty-first anniversary, a reflective pause to look into the future through the prism of the last decade of the last millennium, but in true SBS style (lack of resources) we have got there just a little too late. It is not easy for activists to sit down and record their work, but in this age of information overload you need to record in order almost to prove that you exist. There have been huge changes in the political landscape and our own fortunes since *Against the Grain* that need to be flagged up and analysed, but there have also been recurring themes. From the moment we were born, we owed equal allegiance to our dual identity as black women. But it is a moveable feast that defies attempts to be pinned down. Both black women and men who continue to be involved exclusively in the anti-racist struggle see feminism as the Trojan horse of the anti-racist struggle and believe that campaigning against male oppression in our communities is tantamount to betraying the anti-racist struggle. This book sets out to map that difficult juncture where race and gender make competing claims. It also examines the resurgence of religious fundamentalism and the continuing popularity of multiculturalism, as a vehicle for delivery of services to and development of state policy towards minority communities, both of which remain deeply problematic for us.

We have had a tendency to write off the 1990s as an apolitical period, in which the children of Thatcher appeared to be focused on self, career and materialism. Even political campaigning focused on individual cases as a way of raising awareness of wider political issues – as if individual pain was the only point of entry into an understanding of a systemic disorder. The race uprisings of 1979 and 1981 in Southall, Brixton, Handsworth and Bristol crystallised around dissatisfaction with the police or against the National Front (much like the Northern cities in 2001). But in the 1990s the same issues were raised to the forefront of public consciousness through individual cases involving racial justice, the most prominent being that of Stephen Lawrence.

Many battles were fought in the courts. Increasingly, the arena of political change moved from the streets to the courts. Take our campaigns to free Kiranjit and Zoora. At the heart of these campaigns was our attempt to appeal successfully against earlier court judgments. Although this was accompanied by wider political campaigning to raise awareness of violence against women, which was critical in influencing the courts to take account of gender in their interpretation of current law, the fact remains that the main forum for change was the courtroom. When the Human Rights Act came into force in 2000, it provided us with a whole new framework of concepts and tools with which to push for women's rights. Of course, even this Act falls short in its vision of equality: the right to work or to live free from poverty, for example, is not enshrined within it. And from many of the cases brought under this Act, we have noticed in George Orwell's memorable words that 'some are more equal than others'; the human rights of some, usually the more powerful vested interests in society, are more important than the human rights of others. This is an area that is examined by Pragna Patel in her chapter, 'Shifting Terrains'.

Towards the end of the decade, though, we did see a return to campaigning on the streets. There is a new generation of activists that has taken on the bigger battle – against multinationals and global capitalism – a battle that, in the early 1990s, appeared impossible to contemplate let alone wage. Poverty has returned to the heart of the political agenda in a way that we have not seen for a long time. Although these protests are being criticised for a lack of direction and for being too unwieldy because of the disparate groups that form part of the membership, they have forced the issue of global inequalities to the forefront. Even schoolchildren came out in their thousands to protest when Britain was poised on the brink of war against Iraq in spring 2003. The new era of brutal American imperialism, which breathtakingly uses the 11 September attacks on New York and Washington as an excuse for its actions, is being challenged by mass global protest.

Genderquake?

It has also been a period in which we have felt as if we were operating in a vacuum, at least in terms of feminist politics. At the end of the 1980s we were debating whether there was such a thing as a feminist *movement* left: today we are hard put to find examples of feminist activity. There was no better visual metaphor of this than the numbers of women we were able to mobilise in our two campaigns on behalf of battered women who kill. The pickets we held outside the High Court for Kiranjit Ahluwalia in 1992 were large and well attended, but the crowds who turned up for Zoora Shah in 1999 were much smaller, although there does seem to be a hunger for political action out there. When we mobilised support in 2000 for the submission we made to the Home Office Working Group on Forced Marriage, we found that a large number of women turned up for a hastily arranged meeting and more than thirty-five women's groups became signatories. There are many women's groups doing very good work on the ground and much feminist academic pondering about the state we are in, but we could name the number of politically active feminist groups on the fingers of one hand. There were brief spurts of activism around the Kiranjit Ahluwalia and the Vandana Patel campaigns and against 'bounty hunters' active within Asian communities in Huddersfield. Turkish women led demonstrations through Haringey, London, an area with a large Turkish population, following a spate of sudden deaths of local women, and African women protested against female genital mutilation in Brent.

Generally speaking, the 1990s saw a decline in younger women becoming involved in women's groups. More women, including black women, moved away from the voluntary sector and into the mainstream. Despite the glass ceiling, women moved higher up the corporate hierarchy with some entering senior managerial positions. More black women joined professions such as medicine, the law, journalism, academia and the entertainment business. Women in the voluntary sector expected higher wages and better conditions of work without the same level of commitment to or understanding of the issues displayed by previous activists. Indeed, some women's refuges and services have closed down or been taken over by housing associations or larger women's groups like Refuge because of their inability to continue the struggle to obtain adequate funding and maintain control and support at a grassroots level. Muneeza Inam explores this area in her chapter on 'Taking or Giving Refuge?' The professionalisation of women has 'depoliticised' the women's movement, and turned domestic violence into an industry. The 'value for money' strategy that underpins government funding has turned safe houses into hostels.

It has become fashionable to assert that we are in a post-feminist phase, which is generally taken to mean that women today are reaping the benefits of campaigns waged by an earlier generation of feminists. However, Hannana Siddiqui in her chapter on 'Black Feminism' presents evidence that the fruits of that harvest are unevenly distributed. If post-feminism means a backlash against feminism, then we are certainly suffering the whiplash effect of that. Every success comes with its own distorted curve, every silver lining with its own cloud. Pornography is no longer considered oppressive to women but something that women can use and turn against men. For example, an American feminist has left the ivory tower of academia behind and embraced lapdancing as a career because it is the ultimate expression of female sexual power! American academia must be more oppressive than we realised. A new club called CAKE, which has been very successful in the USA, is about to hit Britain. It looks to feminism to provide it with its rationale that

> sexual equality hinges on the freedom for women to express themselves as publicly and as theatrically as possible.... The aim of CAKE is to prove that women can be as aggressive and forceful in their sexuality as men; enjoying watching and participating in pornography and sex shows such as stripping just as lustfully as the other half of the population.[4]

When economic powerlessness is taken out of the equation for some women, it allows for a more fluid situation to develop where they feel free to take up whatever interaction they want with men and not feel the same pressures to conform. However, the ideological bombardment continues. For example, women may have gained more control over their reproduction, choosing to have children when it suits them, and as lone parents, because they now have the economic power to do so. However, the newspapers are full of surveys purporting to show how the children of lone parents will grow up to be low achievers, be overrepresented in the criminal ranks, have broken homes themselves, be drug or alcohol driven. As if that wasn't enough to scare single women considering a family, we see stories of 'irresponsible single mums' who go off on holidays leaving their children alone at home. Virginia Bottomley, a Conservative minister, in a speech on the importance of nuclear families in 1993, said, 'Without them individuals are like a frantic whirl of atoms, attached to no one, responsible to nothing, creating a vaporous society.' So, there you go, single mums – not just responsible for vapid children but also for a vaporous society.

The same applies to the public recognition of sexual abuse of women and children. When feminists were quoting anecdotal evidence in the 1970s and 1980s to assert that nearly one in four women had been sexually abused at some point in their lives, they were condemned out of hand for men-bashing – until Esther Rantzen set up Childline in 1986 and found that the statistics supported feminist claims. Interestingly enough, the moment sexual abuse of women and children came to be seen as an endemic problem, false memory syndrome reared its ugly head in an attempt to discredit those grown women who were beginning to come to terms with a history of abuse. Feminists have condemned the failure of the criminal justice system to treat rape as a serious crime and institutionalised sexism which blamed women for having 'asked for it' in the way they dressed or behaved. Just as we began to see a shift in those attitudes[5] we saw the sudden emergence of date rape as an issue – the papers were filled with individual stories where the lines of responsibility were blurred, where the issue of consent became one of 'honest belief': perception rather than objective reality. These debates muddied the waters, introduced doubt and reversed the positive steps that had been taken to make it easier for women to report rape to the police and be taken seriously.

There has also been a sea change in attitudes to marriage – it is no longer seen as an institution that oppresses women – especially when diehard feminists like Gloria Steinem begin to get married in their sixties. The myth of the new man has gained sufficient currency to make it seem possible that women can negotiate greater equality within marriage, and the government tax and benefits regime continues to favour married as opposed to cohabiting women. The decade started with the owner of Suman Marriage Bureau in Southall being given the Mother of India award for services rendered, and ended with SBS being invited for the first time to sit on the Home Office Working Group on Forced Marriage. As it becomes more acceptable in British society to use dating agencies and other forms of 'arranged' meetings, the opprobrium once poured on arranged marriages in Asian communities has now moved to forced marriages. However, in Hannana Siddiqui's chapter on forced marriage, 'It Was Written in Her Kismet', we see that the distinction is often a spurious one as many women experience subtle pressures that 'force' them to agree to an arranged marriage.

When we argued at the appeal court in 1992 on behalf of Kiranjit Ahluwalia (see Timeline), that she was unable to leave her husband because Asian women were the vehicles of family honour or *izzat* and that divorce would be an unacceptable stain on it, little did we realise how this notion would be used to explain bizarre behaviour by an Asian woman nine years later. In 2001, a Bangladeshi refuge worker, Saira Rehman (31) married Charles Bronson (48), a notorious white prisoner who had spent twenty-two of his twenty-seven years in prison in solitary confinement because of his violent behaviour. She explained to the *Daily Mail*[6] that because she was a divorcee her *izzat* and that of her family were stained. We had obviously failed to appreciate just how peculiar Asian culture could be, that the state of marriage is infinitely preferable to being a single woman regardless of the suitability of the candidate.

Throughout the 1990s we saw a growing public awareness of domestic violence. This has been the mainstay of SBS work, not so much because we chose to work in this area but because that was the recurrent issue which women brought to us. Anita Johal's chapter, 'Struggle Not Submission', looks at changing attitudes to domestic violence in the Asian community and wider society. What is the resultant impact on the mental health of the women who have lived with such brutality? Hannana Siddiqui and Meena Patel, in 'Sad, Mad or Angry?', explore how medical models of treatment have been used to deal inappropriately with women where timely social welfare intervention would have sufficed. How are the children affected? What are the issues that confront black children who have experienced violence in their families? This is a question picked up by Meena Patel, in her chapter on black children, 'Silent Witnesses', an area to which we have not paid enough attention — again a question of resources. When television soaps run a storyline, as *Brookside* did in 1993, about battered women who kill, or as *Coronation*

Street did in 2001, on forced marriage, they are reflecting a national concern and ensuring that the issue gets a wider airing. Both story-lines have been developed hot on the heels of campaigns that we have run or been involved in. Justice for Women and SBS together raised the profile of women who kill through their campaigns to release Sara Thornton, Amelia Rossiter and Kiranjit Ahluwalia in the early 1990s. The Zero Tolerance Campaign run by local authorities was also successful in raising awareness around domestic violence.

Of course, the media are always looking for a new angle, and state institutions in their skewed attempts at balance have began to talk about the violence perpetrated by women on men (of which there is a small percentage) because they do not understand the gendered nature of violence. Growing public condemnation of violence against children and the strength of the anti-smacking campaign have created a climate of decreasing tolerance towards violence in society and consequently violence against women. This is not a view that can be objectively justified. A day at SBS would certainly make it hard to hold on to such optimism. Besides, proper statistics on domestic violence are not available and an increase in reporting of domestic violence can be attributable to a number of things, including the fact that there is less stigma attached to it.

The demand for better monitoring of domestic violence has led to more studies and surveys worldwide. As there is no standardisation of record-keeping and as definitions of domestic violence vary so widely, it is difficult to know what we should make of the picture that is emerging. From our own experience it is becoming obvious that domestic violence manifests itself differently in different communities. On an anecdotal level it appears that while forced marriages may be prevalent in all South Asian communities, abduction is more common in the Pakistani and Bangladeshi communities, who take their girls abroad, while the Indian community forces girls into marriage with boys already settled here. Dowry abuse also appears to be more common in the Indian community. The Foreign Office said that more than 90 per cent of its forced marriage cases originate in Bradford and Tower Hamlets, home to the Pakistani and Bangladeshi communities.[7] More worryingly, it appears that on a global level the percentage of women experiencing violence varies from country to country. According to research by

Lori Heise, there are societies where gender-based abuse does not exist, and surveys from a wide range of countries show that between 20 and 50 per cent of women interviewed have been beaten by a male partner.[8] What are the differences between societies where 20 as opposed to 50 per cent of women experience violence?

This leads us onto very controversial ground indeed. One of the very useful sacred cows of feminism has been the assertion that domestic violence cuts across race, class, religion, age and so on. It underpins the theory that patriarchy uses violence extensively to subjugate women, but it also acts as an effective counter against racism which seeks to portray men of particular backgrounds – that is, black men – as more barbaric. If these statistics represent a half-accurate picture, then it is important to raise this question in the proper context so as to pre-empt racists from using this as a stick with which to beat minorities. It is not an issue of racial or ethnic differences. It is a question of the economic, political and social development of a society, of the levels of democracy and devolution of power within communities. Lori Heise found that low-violence cultures share key features that include female power and autonomy outside the home, strong sanctions against interpersonal violence, a definition of masculinity that is not linked to male dominance or honour, and equality of decision-making and resources within the family. The work of SBS is concerned precisely with the development of such a culture.

Of course, a lot more research needs to be carried out in this area of different forms and different rates of domestic violence in various communities. The question of differential rates of violence is a sensitive one, which we raise tentatively as the opening shot in a debate that needs to be conducted among feminists. I have also highlighted the contradictions and the reverses in order to emphasise exactly how uneven the gains of feminism have been and how some of these debates seem to be a million miles away from the daily struggles of the women that we see at the centre.

The race equation

There appears to be a similar unevenness in the struggle towards Britain becoming a non-racist society. If you're feeling optimistic, you might agree with Miranda Sawyer when she observes that 'There are many nooks and crannies in Britain that the *Daily Mail* and Diet Coke ads cannot reach.'[9]

Historically British society's attitude to immigration has been the gauge of its deep-seated racism. For all its rhetoric of anti-racism, the Labour Party has had a shameful record on immigration legislation. And yet a survey in the *Guardian* (21 May 2001) on public attitudes towards refugees showed a slim majority (51 per cent) of the public in favour of letting in unskilled economic migrants and skilled immigrants even if there was no shortage of skills in the British economy. This figure shot up to 70 per cent when the question related to support for migrants who could fill the skills gap here. This is a small but significant change to which we can cling hopefully. 'State racism contaminates civil society', says Sivanandan.[10] Yet it is civil society that appears to be ahead of the state in its attitude to immigration.

Other surveys of British social attitudes show that the younger population is less racist. Of course, racism is not about individual attitudes but about institutionalised racism. The existence of this had long been recognised and the CRE (Commission for Racial Equality) had been an ineffective tool through its powers of formal investigation into the direct and indirect discrimination resulting from institutional policies. It is, however, the Macpherson report that has put the concept on the map. The brutal killing of Stephen Lawrence by a group of white thugs and the bungled handling of the investigation into his murder by the racist police force sparked off the longest period of soul-searching in British society that we have seen. Although the Macpherson recommendations were aimed specifically at the Metropolitan Police, the media, the NHS, education and other state institutions began to explore their hearts of darkness as a result. It was a moment of hope for black people. Of course, the rank and file of the police force continue to dismay us – Duwayne Brooks, the young man with Stephen Lawrence on that night, has been stopped and searched countless times by the police. Stephen's father, Neville Lawrence, and Bishop Sentamu, an adviser to Macpherson, have also been stopped and searched. If the Macpherson report had been such a seminal moment in British history, as has been claimed, we would have expected the faces of those individuals connected with the Lawrence case to be etched on the hearts and minds of every single police officer in this country.

However, this debate on race has still not opened up a space for our experiences as black women, as Pragna Patel argues in her chapter on policing, 'The Tricky Blue Line'. Women, who need to use the police to investigate and prosecute perpetrators of domestic violence and sexual assaults, find that the racism of police attitudes is compounded by their sexism. When we see posters in police stations today proclaiming 'Domestic Violence is a Crime', an early feminist slogan, it may look as if the battle has been won. But we need to go behind the PR to separate the wheat from the chaff. As far back as the early 1980s, bell hooks complained about the failure of the American feminist and anti-racist movement to recognise the specific struggles of black women.[11] When public debates allude to racism, they implicitly mean black men, and when they allude to feminism, they implicitly refer to white women. The inability to understand the faultlines that lie at the intersection of race, gender and class is a blind spot for both policymakers and campaigners. Take the CRE and the EOC (Equal Opportunities Commission), institutions set up to tackle racism and sexism. Black women fell between two stools: turned down by the CRE because their cases were muddied by sexism and turned down by the EOC because their cases were not straightforward ones of sexism alone. Although we have been banging on about this for ages, it was only in 2001 that the UN began to get to grips with the race/gender conundrum. Pragna Patel was invited to address the preparatory UN meetings for their conference on racism in 2001 in South Africa. The women's caucus felt 'that most governments' understanding of intersectional analysis or what they conceive to be "multiple discrimination" is still limited to the idea of additional grounds for discrimination, rather than simultaneous interaction of discrimination as it relates to the multiple layers of human rights violations and inter-connected identities'.[12] Similarly, the Civil Rights Movement, set up in the wake of the Stephen Lawrence case, did not include the demands of black women in its agenda, arguing that the space that had been opened up for anti-racist campaigning must not be cluttered with other issues.

A positive outcome of the Macpherson report was the Race Relations Amendment Act, which came into force in 2001. It places a positive duty on all public services to promote equality in every area of work. Immigration, however, is noticeably excluded from its provisions. It makes a mockery of Labour's much-vaunted attempts to introduce joined-up government. This is explored at greater length by Poonam Joshi in her chapter, 'Jumping through Hoops', on the work that SBS has done around immigration. As the UN Committee on Elimination of Race Discrimination made clear in 2000, racism is indivisible – there cannot be a trade-off between fair treatment of minority groups already here and those who are newly arrived.

Despite the changes brought about by the Macpherson report, our cities burned with the anger of dispossessed Asian youth – Oldham, Burnley, Leeds and Bradford. There is a worrying rise in the popularity of fascist parties like the British National Party in these areas, where they achieved their best general election results. Nick Griffin, the leader of the BNP, appeared on *Newsnight* in June 2001 and was famously let off the hook by Jeremy Paxman's sudden toothlessness. The BBC defended its decision to interview him as an 'attempt to get to the truth'. The media now talk to racists where once they would have been starved of 'the oxygen of publicity'. The BNP's arguments are becoming more sophisticated. They no longer talk of forced repatriation but only of voluntary schemes. They seek to capitalise on traditional Hindu–Muslim tensions by alleging that Muslims have been carrying out an ethnic cleansing policy and getting rid of other religious groupings from the subcontinent in northern British cities. A news report on Sunrise Radio on 6 September 2001 reported that Hasmukh Shah, leader of the World Council of Hindus, had been approached by Nick Griffin to make an anti-Muslim pact. The report did not tell us how Hasmukh Shah responded to this approach. But, as a Muslim interviewee said, after 150 years of colonial divide-and-rule, Asians should know better than to have any truck with the BNP. Some people may have played readily into BNP attempts to fragment the Asian identity into its religious/nationalist components. Although there have been attempts by both liberal and conservative sections of British society to demon-ise Islam, especially in the post-September 11 climate, the appropri-ate reaction to this is neither the proud assumption of a Muslim identity nor the abandoning of the anti-racist platform in favour of the anti-Islamaphobia platform. Attempts by members of Stop the

War (against Afghanistan) Coalition to express their solidarity by saying that 'we are all Muslims' or by fasting during Ramadan or wearing the hijab will only further squeeze the public secular spaces. It is more critical than ever now to enlarge those spaces.

The process of adopting religious identities is fraught with division. Adopting a Muslim identity does not automatically unite vast chunks of the minority population. Somali Muslims are not welcomed with open arms in Asian mosques. In Oldham, Muslims fight Muslims and much work is being done to bring warring factions of Bangladeshi and Pakistani Muslims together. After the showdown between police and Asian youths in Leeds, a youth counsellor, Shakoor Haider, said to Burhan Wazir, the *Observer* reporter, 'you know we're different here from other Muslims. We're Mirpuris – we have different principles and ideals from other Muslims. I didn't see any Punjabis or Sindhis here last night. So how can they say we were all British Asians?' Young British Asian fans at a cricket match at Lords did not like the tag 'British Asian' because it lumped them 'unfairly', they thought, with Indians, Sikhs, Kashmiris, Sri Lankans and Bangladeshis.[13]

The journalist Faisal Bodi, one of those who identifies as Muslim, rather than as Asian, nevertheless presents an interesting analysis of the development of reclusive and defensive communities in order to explain why Oldham, Burnley and Bradford exploded so spectacularly in 2001.[14] He considers the role played by racist housing policies, which ensured that Asians were segregated in the poorest estates in town; and the economic decline of the cotton mill towns, where whites moved out in search of greener pastures but the Asians stayed behind. This analysis was echoed in Herman Ouseley's report on Bradford published in 2001.

Segregated schooling has also been responsible for stoking tension in Oldham. The National Secular Society has warned that an expansion of church schooling would lead to racial conflicts. In this context it is difficult to understand Tony Blair and New Labour's enthusiasm for religious and specialist schools. What is even more amazing is Lee Jasper's (special adviser on race to Ken Livingstone) call to Afro-Caribbean churches, business and parents to set up their own schools. Whilst it is true that the educational system has spectacularly failed black children, segregation is not the way forward. The educational system must be made to deliver to all its pupils. In any case, the underlying thrust of denominational schools is to churn out model wives, mothers and daughters. Communal autonomy is traded off against women's autonomy and has not been given the prominence it deserves in these debates. This is an issue explored in greater depth by Sukhwant Dhaliwal in her chapter, 'Orange is Not the Only Colour'.

The question of identity is not merely an issue for us but has also provoked soul-searching among the 'white tribes' since the devolution of Britain into England, Wales, Scotland and Ireland. What is less frequently discussed is the way in which this has robbed the minorities of statehood – we could say Black British but we cannot describes ourselves as Black English, especially when Englishness is equated with the Anglo-Saxon race. According to Gary Younge, the label 'black' is redundant; its definition as a political colour is no longer useful because the experiences of racism of different sections of what encompassed black are so different.[15] But although the landscape is becoming more fractured, there has always been a differential impact – for example, immigration law has always been more of a problem for Africans and Asians, whereas education has been an important issue for Caribbeans. Black was not simply a way of describing the experience but it allowed for united action against the state. We at SBS have had to fight for the retention of the term 'black', and increasingly so in this period of fragmentation.

Nairobi to Beijing

Avtar Brah, a founding member of SBS, wrote about her visit to the United Nations Conference of Women in Nairobi in 1985.[16] White women failed to address racism or imperialism, while black and Third World women worked together at the conference to challenge white feminists and Western governments alike. Although some progress has been made since Nairobi, the black women's movement in Britain has been weakened by internal splits, political differences and the process of depoliticisation.

Many of the early groups, such as the Birmingham Black Sisters, the Brixton Black Women's Centre and OWAAD no longer exist. SBS has worked with African women's groups such as Forward and Akina Mama Wa Africa to protest against female genital mutilation and the one-year immigration rule. Other minorities such as the Chinese, Latin American and Turkish are developing services, although they have not been as active in political campaigning. Except for the occasional moment, there is little joint work between these groups. Camden Black Sisters, for example, only includes African-Caribbean women in the term 'black'. SBS, too, has worked largely with Asian women, although this reflects local demand and expertise, rather than a desire to limit our scope. However, in 2001, a group of Asian and African-Caribbean women formed the Network of Black Women in Birmingham, which is being funded by the Home Office Social Exclusion Unit! In 2002, in order to remedy the lack of a national network of black and minority women and women's groups, we began such an initiative focused on the issue of gender violence.

In 1995 an SBS delegation attended the fourth United Nations World Conference on Women in Beijing. There was less unity among black and Third World women, where the primary division was along religious lines, a development which reflected the situation back in Britain. Muslim and Christian fundamentalists in particular were well organised and vocal. Major demonstrations were held by Iranian women, clad in black burkas with militant chants about Islam. We worked with Algerian women who condemned atrocities committed by Muslim extremists against women and human rights activists in their country. At one point the two groups clashed in a street demonstration. More moderate Islamists based in the USA held meetings demanding recognition of Islamic law in Western countries, claiming that this gave Muslim women better rights to property and children upon divorce when compared to civil law. When challenged, they argued that failure to do so amounts to religious discrimination. They also stated that Islam itself called for sexual equality, and that a patriarchal interpretation of the religious text was to blame. They demanded that Islam be reinterpreted along feminist lines.

Some women in Britain took on the mantle of 'political Muslims' because of the rise of Islamophobia, while others, like Rana Kabana, espoused the virtues of the veil for empowering women and covering up class differences! There is a clear need for more unity between different black and minority women's groups in order to build a vibrant and stronger black women's movement.

Black and white, unite and fight!

The slogan, 'Black and white, unite and fight!' common to the anti-racist movement has not, unlike other slogans such as 'Self defence is no offence!' been appropriated by the women's movement. Despite temporary alliances, the relationship between black and white feminists has been tense. Although SBS and other black women have successfully worked with white women, such as Justice for Women and Women Against Fundamentalism, the priorities of white feminists have not always been the same as black feminists. At times, our aims are also in conflict. Our most successful attempt at coalition politics to date has been our work with Women Against Fundamentalism. This is explored more fully in my chapter, 'Walls into Bridges'.

There have been ideological differences too. Some black women have argued that feminism, especially white feminism, has developed a critique of the family which is problematic for black women. They argue that the black family is a site of resistance against racism. This view in turn has been problematic for SBS because we recognise that the extended family, like the nuclear family, black or white, can be an arena of sexual oppression. In fact, the extended family places additional burdens on women because they are at the bottom of a complex hierarchy of a large number of relatives. Some white women have been reluctant to take up issues such as religious fundamentalism or forced marriage and dowry violence for fear of inciting racism or upsetting cultural sensibilities. This fear has been easily exploited by some black women playing the race card and engendering guilt. Racism within the white women's movement, however, is a real problem. Many, for instance, have been less than robust in supporting black women in our campaigns against immigration and asylum laws, such as the one-year rule and restrictive interpretations of gender persecution. Many have also ignored the need to deal with racial attacks and discrimination or the disproportionate number of African-Caribbean women and foreign nationals in prisons. Audre Lorde sums it up well:

Unchallenged, racism ultimately will be the death of the women's movement in England, just as it threatens to become the death of any women's movement in those developed countries where it is not addressed. Feminism must be on the cutting edge of real social change if it is to be a true movement.... We do not exist in a vacuum. We are anchored in our own place and time and we are part of communities that interact.[17]

Some recurring themes

Our relations with the state have changed. As a political entity we always imagined ourselves to exist outside of it and our interests to be opposed to it although as an organisation we relied on the state for funding to carry out our welfare and advice services. As a minority group we felt that the state constructed us as being outside the scope of their provision. But today we look for points at which to intervene and influence state policy so that it meets women's needs without being co-opted in the process.

Almost all areas of SBS work have been complicated by the ideology that underpins state policy towards minorities – that is, multiculturalism and the delivery of state services via the mechanism of multi-agency forums. To avoid repetition, I have attempted to define these concepts and establish their parameters here, although the application to specific areas such as policing may require a specific discussion of it in that chapter. Multiculturalism – as an aspect of institutionalised racism, which impacts on gender inequality – has not received the attention it deserves from anti-racist activists or commentators. But on the ground it remains one of the most pressing challenges that we face in our day-to-day struggles for freedom. At its best it is a laudable attempt to promote racial tolerance and respect for cultural diversity; at its worst it challenges neither the structural basis of racism nor inequality. Indeed it bypasses the need for local democracy because it relies on self-appointed community leaders who historically have no interest in social justice or women's equality. The problem lies not merely with the multicultural approach but with the way in which the notion of 'community' is constructed.

Through the politics of 'multiculturalism' the state more or less enters into an informal contract with the more powerful leaders in the minority community. In practice community leaders maintain power over family, cultural and religious affairs of the community, with the effect of concealing power relations between men and women and legitimising women's subordination within minority communities. Without understanding how the process of such dis-empowerment occurs, our understanding of institutionalised racism in this country can only be partial, and the strategies which flow from such partial understandings can be seriously deficient and even dangerous. This classic multicultural view – predicated on notions of fixed and homogeneous (as opposed to dynamic and changing) concepts of minority community culture and religion – dictates social welfare policies towards Asian and other minority women.

There are changes taking place even on that front. We have noticed a growing readiness on the part of the government and other agencies to intervene in minority communities on issues such as forced marriage in order to protect the interests of women. When Mike O'Brien justifies this intervention by invoking his brand of *mature* multiculturalism, 'Multicultural sensitivity is not an excuse for moral blindness' (see Chapter 4, 'It Was Written in Her Kismet'), we realise that our critique of multiculturalism has been taken on board. The language of multiculturalism is also being displaced gradually by the language of cultural diversity. But is this anything more than a purely semantic development? In an Arts Council policy document,[18] Tony Bennett defines cultural diversity: 'The shift from homogeneity to diversity as the new social norm requires a re-thinking of the processes, mechanisms, and relationships necessary for democratic policy development in diverse societies.' What kind of democratic mechanisms? In our experience, this is the question on which this bright new world runs aground. Culture, as seen in the new language of cultural diversity, is not just defined in terms of race and religion but is linked to attributes such as gender, sexual orientation, age or income levels. In recognising difference within communities, it is an advance on multiculturalism although there is a danger of atomisation in that some definitions of cultural diversity point to the truism that no two people are alike. Worryingly, it dispenses with the notion of equality and replaces it with equity, in much the same way that multiculturalism displaced notions of racial equality with respect for cultural differences.

The other issue that has proved to be the bane of our lives is the current preference for government to deliver social policy through multi-agency forums. There appears to be very little disquiet on the part of other feminist and left organisations in the way that this works in practice. The multi-agency approach is borrowed, with some modifications, from models developed by the police and other agencies in the USA, Canada and elsewhere. Multi-agency work, in essence, is about the coming together of a range of state and voluntary sector agencies, professionals and increasingly the business community, in formal arrangements within a specific locality to develop a common strategy on a range of issues. Since the 1980s, domestic violence, racial violence, drug abuse and juvenile crime have been singled out for multi-agency work. Such initiatives are likely to be led by the police or local authority, and those led by voluntary groups will usually involve police and local authority participation.

It needs to be stated at the outset that our scepticism about multi-agency work is not about the idea per se. In fact, in areas such as mental health and child protection, it is vital that the expertise of different agencies, working cooperatively, is harnessed to ensure efficient delivery of services. We have long recognised the need for a coordinated strategy on domestic violence, particularly at the national level. Any such coordinated strategy would also serve to illuminate the interconnectedness of different power structures, including racial and patriarchal structures. Unfortunately the reality of the multi-agency approach as we see it is very different. The only outcome of the recommendations of the Home Affairs Select Committee on Domestic Violence in 1993 appeared to be a circular encouraging multi-agency initiatives at the local level. It ignored the many substantial recommendations made by women's aid and other groups on safe and improved housing, full access to legal aid, reform of civil legislation and other proposals. The document was circulated for consultation, but SBS refused to endorse it because it ignored the need for resources and for reform of immigration legislation, which has a devastating impact on black women with insecure immigration status fleeing domestic violence.

In some cases, funding was tied to the formation of local multi-agency projects. In the early 1990s there was a series of projects on domestic violence funded by the Home Office. SBS's own proposal – a research project to investigate the links between mental health and domestic violence amongst Asian women – was one of the projects approved for funding. However, we eventually pulled out when it became clear that one condition of funding was the formation of a local multi-agency initiative which involved engineering a false consensus on the complex politics of race, domestic violence and mental health with a number of state and voluntary-sector groups with whom we had little in common. There was also a stipulation that the Home Office was to retain 'ownership' of the project. Any publicity pertaining to the project had to be first 'approved' by the Home Office. These conditions would have severely compromised our autonomous voice, especially in relation to the state's failures.

Many of the multi-agency projects, including those that are held up as models of good practice, may be well-intentioned attempts to do a good job in constraining circumstances. But they appear unable to move beyond multi-agency jargon such as 'sharing information', 'partnership', 'openness', 'facilitating', 'networking' – terms which are meaningless in the absence of real changes. Even Labour-controlled local authorities do not offer women comprehensive housing options, rehousing due to homelessness, or eviction actions against violent perpetrators holding joint tenancies. Nor do we see much evidence of multi-agency forums lobbying central government to bring about changes in housing, immigration and other legislation, which constrain local authority delivery of services. In this light, multi-agency forums amount to nothing more than a formal recognition of domestic violence, giving the appearance that 'change' is occurring in 'partnership' with many organisations, including the police and women's groups. Questions remain as to the long-term impact of multi-agency work in all localities and whether the benefits are conferred on all sections of the community in equal measure.

It is our view that the multi-agency approach, with its emphasis on consensus-building and co-option, accommodates a multicultural perspective. Precisely because the multi-agency model gives centrality to liaison with so called 'community' leaders, other more radical voices are delegitimised. One of our strongest criticisms is that the police and the entire criminal justice system, notwithstanding the multi-agency project, actually disempower women from minority communities in very specific ways.

Changes in Southall

Although SBS's reputation has become national, we still serve mainly Southall and the surrounding West London area. In that sense, and because Southall is one of the oldest Asian conurbations, changes in Southall obviously impact on our work, and some of those have been outlined below. In 1992, Southall got its first Asian MP, Piara Khabra, a man who had once tried to get SBS closed down. He had established his power base through the Indian Workers' Association, which over the years had lost its radical roots and become representative of business interests. At one point Khabra had acquired the unenviable reputation of having made the fewest interventions – none – in Parliament in a whole year. However, when SBS acquired a national reputation with its Kiranjit Ahluwalia campaign, Khabra became quite sympathetic to our work. He managed to get re-elected in 2001, but with very little visible campaigning in Southall, on the pro-Labour apathy that seemed to have swept the nation and earned Britain the reputation of being a 'democracy in drag'.[19] However, he appears to have achieved little for Southall. Southall is in the top 7 per cent of the most deprived areas of the country, suffers from higher unemployment than the rest of Ealing and West London, is home to 7,000 of the borough's 12,000 refugees, and 50 per cent of the population does manual and semi-skilled work. Seventy per cent of the population is from an ethnic minority background.[20] Although unemployment has fallen since 1991, full-time manufacturing jobs and service-sector jobs have been replaced by part-time jobs and self-employment.

During the 1990s there has been a rapid development of Asian media in print, radio and television. Sunrise Radio, based in Southall, is extremely popular with Asian audiences and has proved an effective means for us of reaching Asian audiences nationally. There is however a strong editorial bias in favour of employers and against workers. In 1999, when the workforce of an airline catering company based in Hounslow, Skychef, went on strike, a large majority of whom were Asian women, they found the reporting to be biased in favour of the management. A trade-union delegation was sent to the radio station to protest, but to no avail.

Southall has been home to diverse religious communities from the subcontinent and increasingly to different racial groups from Somalia and Eastern Europe. Mixed communities, such as those of Southall, allow secular traditions to flourish and provide more breathing space for women. We have seen how little space there is for negotiating freedoms in more tightly knit communities, like the East End of London or Yorkshire and the Midlands, where the structure of the community allows it to police the morality of its women collectively in a way that would be unimaginable in Southall. The secular traditions of Southall have been at threat from increasingly entrenched religious forces. The attempted sale of Southall Town Hall was a salutary lesson on the role that local government can play in encouraging divisiveness in the community. Originally the Conservatives wanted to sell it off to the highest bidder. This turned into a battle between Hindus and Muslims, who wanted to convert it into either a temple or a mosque. In 1994, a charity worker, Ali Khan, went on hunger strike to stop the town hall being sold and causing strife between Hindus and Muslims. Eventually it was taken over by the Single Regeneration Budget.

In *Against the Grain*, we explored how the growth of religious fundamentalism in the aftermath of the Salman Rushdie affair had a detrimental effect on women's struggle for self-determination. We wanted to broaden it out to include Jewish, Hindu and Christian fundamentalisms. We set up a group, Women Against Fundamentalism (WAF), in 1989 to combat the dangerous communal/religious trends that threatened to tear our communities apart. The group went online in 1999 as a compromise solution, as many of its members were active in their own communities and were unable to devote time to WAF, but is beginning to stir again in the post-11 September climate. This area of our work is explored in greater detail in my chapter on alliances, 'Walls into Bridges'. Given the current state of Islamaphobia, we decided to highlight our campaigns against the equally pernicious Hindu fundamentalism in 'Rama or Rambo' by Pragna Patel.

Internal changes

Our hard-fought campaign to get Kiranjit Ahluwalia released from
life imprisonment in 1992 catapulted us into national consciousness.
This success brought us much needed recognition for our work but
it also engulfed us in a ballooning caseload without the relief of
extra funds. In the same year Ealing Council cut almost every other
voluntary welfare service in the area except us, partly because SBS
had acquired a national reputation and a tendency to turn up with
a large contingent of noisy women and children to council meetings whenever our grant applications were being discussed. Recently
the council has entered into three-year funding contracts with local
organisations, which has brought a measure of stability although it
is by no means a guarantee of continued funding.

We have been the victims of our own success. New clients and
other professionals and organisations have very high expectations
of us. It is only when they visit us and see the state of our offices
and the number of workers, that they are shocked by the level of
our achievements with such poor resources. Through much of the
1990s, we struggled on with only three core workers and an occasional fourth depending on the success of our funding strategies.
With the departure of Pragna Patel from the ranks of the workers
to that of the management committee in the early 1990s, we found
ourselves in the unfamiliar situation of having to recruit new workers
after a period of stability, when Hannana Siddiqui, Meena Patel and
Pragna Patel had worked well together for a number of years. We
blamed the professionalisation of feminism for our difficulties in
recruitment.

To ensure that we continued to provide a high level of service, in
terms of both quantity and quality, to retain the expertise that we
had built over the years, to attract and nurture new workers we set
in motion a root-and-branch review of all our structures and
methods of working in 1996/97. External consultants were brought
in to advise us. The collective set aside time to focus on future
prospects so that we could go into the millennium with confidence.
SBS went from being a collective to a hierarchy although it retained
a collective method of working and a democratic ethos in decision-
making. This was as much a reflection of the changing political

realities as of internal pressures. The problem with lines of responsibility and unequal allocation of work in collectives without adequate compensation of money or status became a particular issue when new workers who lacked similar levels of commitment were recruited. Currently we have a very committed team of six full-time workers and three part-timers. Whether this has happened as a result of tightening up our structures or whether the global picture has changed is hard to say.

We may have spread ourselves too thin and taken on too many issues. We are expected to have an opinion on every subject. Although politically we would argue that there is no such thing as a woman's issue, diverse interests can lead to a loss of focus. Our work in schools has suffered consequently. We have not only faced a dilemma about areas of work to concentrate on but have also had to tread carefully in this minefield of race and gender oppression. All the chapters in this volume attempt to examine how we have responded politically and practically, groping instinctively towards a solution and, in time, using political experience. We don't pretend to have all the answers. Under Labour, the doors of government have been more open to us. But this has raised the knotty question: how do you work with the state and retain your critical edge? When Hannana Siddiqui explores the dynamics of the Home Office Working Group on Forced Marriage and her resignation over the issue of mediation (See Chapter 4, 'It Was Written in Her Kismet), we have to ask ourselves whether the strategy was successful. Have we lost the opportunity to influence government policy again? Is it possible to talk to government without being co-opted? We will continue to seek answers and to refine our responses. Meanwhile it appears that in the last decade we have carved out a niche for ourselves in the psyche of grant-giving bodies. After years of underfunding, in 2000/01 we embarked on a funding drive which was so successful that we are still reeling. At the moment our future looks more secure than it has ever done before.

I would like to end with a small anecdote as my contribution to the crystal ball exercise. Minutes of an SBS meeting in April 2001 noted that Benazir Bhutto had expressed an interest in visiting us but we had turned it down. No further comment was recorded, providing us with much hilarity, as we went over the minutes at the next meeting. What would future generations of students/academics make of this? Would they infer that this was an everyday occurrence because we treated it with such nonchalance? Or was this SBS's brush with the mainstream? We complain bitterly of being marginalized, but each time we are invited to join the mainstream we worry whether this means we have lost our radical edge. We had a further brush with the mainstream in November 2001. At an awards ceremony organised by Media Moguls, the publishers of glossy magazines *Asian Woman* and *Asian Bride*, where the chief guest was no less than Cherie Booth QC, SBS was given a lifetime achievement award, and Kiranjit Ahluwalia the Asian Woman of Courage Award. We wondered if the comparison with Hollywood actors who are given a lifetime achievement award when they have one foot in the grave was too ominous for our liking. The award was presented by Scary Spice Mel B. Girlpower meets feminism! Now there's a subject for our next book.

Notes

1. Zoora Shah's tariff was reduced to 12 years in 2000.
2. Brochure for *The Vagina Monologues*, 1999.
3. Southall Black Sisters, *Against the Grain: A Celebration of Survival and Struggle*, SBS, London 1990.
4. Amelia Hill, 'Manhattan's Women Find Power in Sex', *Observer*, 17 June 2001.
5. As far as we know, SBS secured the first conviction for rape in marriage within the Asian community in 1997.
6. *Daily Mail*, 3 June 2001.
7. Lucy Ward, 'In Sickness and in Stealth', *The Guardian Supplement*, 6 November 2001
8. Lori L Heise, 'Overcoming Violence: A Background Paper on Violence against Women as an Obstacle to Development', unpublished, 1995.
9. Miranda Sawyer, 'Don't Fence Us In', *Observer* magazine, 18 March 2001.
10. Ambalavaner Sivanandan, 'How Labour Failed the Lawrence Test', *Guardian*, 21 February 2000.
11. bell hooks, *Ain't I a Woman? Black Women and Feminism*, Pluto, London, 1982.
12. Women's caucus, *Newsflash no. 1*, UN Conference on Racism, Racial Discrimination, Xenophobia and Related Intolerance, Durban 2001.
13. Burhan Wazir, 'Born in Manchester but Loyal to Lahore', *Observer*, 24 June 2001.
14. Faisal Bodi, 'Ghettos in the North', *Guardian*, 25 June 2001.
15. Gary Younge, 'The Many in One', *Guardian*, 28 June 2001.

16. Avtar Brah, 'Journey to Nairobi', in S Grewal et al., eds, *Charting the Journey*, Sheba, London 1988.

17. Pratibha Parmar and Jackie Kay, 'Frontiers: Interview with Audre Lord', in Grewal et al., eds, *Charting the Journey*.

18. Arts Council of England and the Council of Europe, 'The Shared Space: Cultural Diversity and the Public Domain', Report from a working seminar, Arts Council, London, February 2002.

19. Sawyer, 'Don't Fence Us In'.

20. Southall Regeneration Partnership, *Single Regeneration Budget Delivery Plan Year Four* 2000–2001.

2

Struggle not submission:
domestic violence in the 1990s

Anita Johal

I am writing this from a personal perspective as SBS provides the first insight I have had into the progressive black feminist movement. Although I have always considered myself progressive, this was more a personal struggle for identity, autonomy and freedom against the oppression justified by the patriarchal value systems of my community. I experienced this at first hand in my first marriage. I was a student of law focusing on the legal systems of South Asia and UK immigration and race relations law. It was a cruel irony to be studying issues, such as dowry and violence, which I was facing in reality. I did not see some of my friends for two years, because I was not allowed to. When I finally mustered the strength to leave that marriage, my friends said that it was as if I had built a wall around me. It was this experience along with more defined views on racism and politics that propelled me to apply to Southall Black Sisters for a job.

Miraculously, I was offered a position as a caseworker, which left me feeling both euphoric and frightened, as I felt I knew very little and was going to be working with women who had a vast amount of experience. Although the latter was true, I was amazed at the collectivity and spirit of SBS, where I was given the support and space to formulate my political and feminist opinions. A lot of time was taken to explain issues, supervise and encourage. I found it a very nurturing environment and felt I could talk to anyone in the organisation: both the workers and the management committee.

Every day at SBS is unique and unpredictable. We juggle with multifarious issues. It is both exhilarating and exhausting. We could be dealing with an emergency in trying to find refuge space for a woman; obtaining injunctions; collecting her belongings; or getting her child back from the home she has fled. It could be a matter of casework, whether it is liaising with her solicitors, battling with the council, or working with a human rights group in the subcontinent in relation to a forced marriage. A radio station may ring for a comment or professionals may want advice on any given issue. We could be organising a picket in relation to a campaign we are running and be mobilising women for it. We could be working on a policy document or be preparing a training package or a talk for a seminar/conference. We could be running a support group for women to come together and share their experiences and discuss issues that have affected them. We might be helping young women to produce their own track and lyrics, as we did in 2000 when we collaborated with Community Music, part of the Asian Dub Foundation collective. We may be drying a woman's tears because she has just written a monologue based on her experiences to be staged with the help of Kali Theatre.[1]

There has been a year-on-year increase in the number of women we have seen since the early 1990s. This is partly due to growing national and local recognition of our work and partly due to the funding policies of the local authority, which have led to the decimation of the local voluntary sector. The number of women with immigration and asylum issues also experiencing domestic violence has risen sharply. From a personal perspective, I have been amazed by the strength and conviction displayed by the women, which runs counter to popular perceptions of Asian women as passive and subservient. If women are failing to break out of situations of domestic violence, control and oppression, it is not because they are passive but because the state has failed to protect them and because community and family pressure can sometimes be too much to surmount. In terms of the national picture, domestic violence accounts for almost a quarter (23 per cent) of all violent crime.[2]

In this chapter, I will focus on the kind of cases that we deal with, on the changes in community attitudes to domestic violence and to SBS in the last ten years or so. I will also be looking at changes in state policy on domestic violence. Although there has been some heartening progress, we still have a long way to go. In response to the lobbying of women's groups, domestic violence has come to be defined more broadly to include not just physical violence but verbal abuse, mental cruelty, financial control, sexual abuse and imprisonment. But what does this mean in practice? Many state services need proof of violence before further action is taken, and this is still most easily obtainable where signs of physical injury are visible. How do you provide independent evidence of verbal abuse and mental cruelty? A woman has to show clinical signs of depression or provide a witness statement to that kind of abuse – neither of which is easy to come by. Where sexual abuse is concerned, women themselves have been reluctant to talk about it or even to see it as part of a spectrum of violent behaviour.

In 1998, SBS made a leap forward in a case where, for the first time, an Asian woman obtained a conviction for rape, attempted rape and two counts of indecent assault against her husband. She also secured a number of convictions for false imprisonment and assault against him, her mother-in-law, her brother-in-law and her sister-in-law, each of whom had their own defence lawyer, after a three-week trial. There were a total of eleven convictions. The woman herself showed enormous resilience and gave evidence for five full days at the Old Bailey, undergoing rigorous cross-examination by four defence barristers. She required intensive support from SBS in order to face her ordeal in court. SBS also gave evidence in support of the prosecution. We had worked with the police to secure her release from false imprisonment, after she had thrown a note over the garden fence to a neighbour, and helped her through a two-year preparation period before the trial. Understandably, the abuse had traumatised the woman and we had to provide regular counselling. She was also facing deportation, the marriage having ended within the one-year probationary period. The Home Office had refused her application to remain in the UK. Although this woman had not been forced into marriage, she deeply regretted that her father had not been more careful in his choice of a marriage partner when arranging the match. She was devastated to learn that her sister in Pakistan was forced into marriage to cover up the shame caused by her separation from her husband and initiation of legal proceedings against him in the UK. Finally, following the convictions, the Home Office overturned its decision and allowed the woman to remain in the UK indefinitely. Incidentally, the police also wrote to the Home Office in support of her application to remain – a rare example of police compassion.

As far as we know, this was the first rape-in-marriage trial in the Asian community. The case set an important legal precedent by recognising the collusion of the in-laws in the imprisonment and abuse of daughters/sisters-in-law. It also recognised domestic forms of unlawful imprisonment, which are rarely taken seriously and prosecuted, never mind leading to conviction. The trial judge was particularly hostile to the woman and handed out sentences that were disappointingly light despite the jury returning unanimous verdicts on virtually all counts. The CPS appealed to the Attorney General against the five-and-a-half-year sentence imposed on the husband. The Court of Appeal upheld the trial judge's decision because the case involved 'domestic imprisonment', and made an implicit assumption that Asian women are 'tolerant' of marital rape.

Rape in marriage and abuse within the extended family are common features of SBS casework, but much work needs to be done to encourage women to come forward and take action against rapists. Another woman, Sunita Veg from Hounslow, successfully prosecuted a priest for rape. The community, in particular the priest's son, used the classic method of diverting attention from the rape by calling her sexual morality into question. The manager of the gurdwara took the attitude that Sunita Veg was at fault and called her various names, including khunjuri (slag). The Granthi (priest) has come out of prison and returned to the gurdwara without protest from the community, which would, it appears, rather place its faith in abusers than stand up in support of abused women.

And still the death toll rises

In an idealistic sense, I feel outraged that despite the work that SBS has done in the last twenty years, women are still slipping through the net and being killed by violent partners. Of course, SBS cannot by itself prevent all future deaths of women even in the local area. Take the case of Jaspal Sohal. She had four children with a man whom she married contrary to the wishes of her parents. Her husband, Ranjit Sohal, took a claw hammer and killed her with at least twenty blows to the head. He called the police some hours later and said to them 'she was going to leave me and take the children. She can't do that.' He then pleaded not guilty to murder but guilty of manslaughter on the grounds of diminished responsibility, in that he was suffering from a psychotic illness. Due to disputes between psychiatrists, his plea was not accepted and he was tried for and convicted of murder.

SBS involvement meant we were able to push the issue of domestic violence to the fore. We questioned the police about what evidence they would be producing in court. We presented to the police the history of domestic violence that Jaspal had suffered and showed how the murder was part of that continuum. We also encouraged the family to communicate with the police. Jaspal had come to some support group activities. We had noticed injuries and suspected domestic violence. We pushed for a statement to be taken from us. The case highlights that the most dangerous time for women is when they are leaving or about to leave relationships.[3] The British Crime Survey: England and Wales 1999 calculated that 22 per cent of separated women had been assaulted in the previous year by their ex-partner. Domestic violence often continues and may escalate in severity after separation.[4]

The local press had not really picked up on this case until we brought it to their attention. SBS marked Jaspal's life by holding a wreath-laying ceremony, which was attended by many users of the centre and was an emotional occasion. There was coverage of this in the local press. However, there was no great outcry from the community. In fact, the response was quite muted, which shows just how far we have left to go on the issue of domestic violence.

In Hounslow, in October 1995, Jarnail Singh Chera argued that he 'snapped' when he discovered that his teenage daughter, Ravinder, had a boyfriend and was afraid she was going to leave home. He attempted to strangle her to death. She had to be resuscitated and was severely disabled as a result. She was confined to a wheelchair and suffered permanent brain damage. Her father was convicted of causing grievous bodily harm with intent and sentenced to six years in prison.[5] In November 2000, Nighat Ghilani, with a history of domestic violence, sat down in front of a train in Northolt (see Chapter 6, 'Sad, Mad or Angry?') These local cases are only the tip of the iceberg.

Changes in local community

The structure of the community in Southall has changed over the last ten years. There has been a marked growth in African (mainly Somali), Afghani and Eastern European communities. Somali men seem to be concentrated in the Old Southall area, which is a more deprived area than commercialised New Southall. Since I joined three years ago, SBS has seen an increase in the number of refugee women from Africa. We have also had traveller women come in for advice. SBS's client group is truly reflective of the demographic diversity of Southall.

At present, we do not have a Somali-speaking worker, although we aim to fundraise for one. However, even if we cannot find an interpreter, we manage to unravel the problem to some extent; more often than not, the issue is homelessness. We have not been able to assess the level of domestic violence faced by Somali women, partly because of the language barrier. I have taken on outreach responsibilities to forge links with the Somali community. As part of this, I met with the Somalian Women's Refugee Centre, which provides advice on welfare benefits, housing and immigration. They also facilitate training in employment, IT and sewing. I felt that the project coordinator was uncertain as to why very few Somali women asked for assistance with domestic violence, suggesting that there was either a low incidence of violence in their community or that women did not speak out. It was interesting that she did not mention female genital mutilation (FGM), which is so prevalent in the Somali community. She talked extensively about the racism faced by the Somali community in Southall. This seems to parallel the development and structure of the Asian community in the early days when it was preoccupied with issues such as housing and racism; it was only when the families began to join the men and settle down that domestic violence became a concern. Also a number of Somali households appear to be headed by women despite the visible presence of single men in the streets. One woman I spoke to from the Forward project felt that many families were headed by Somali women due to widowhood, separation, divorce or because their husbands were working abroad.

Another group, the Somali Women's Health Project, deals with FGM but only in terms of its health implications, its irreversible physical and mental repercussions, rather than challenging the practice itself. FGM is a means of denying women sexual pleasure and thereby of enforcing sexual morality. There are four main types, as classified by the World Health Organisation; they are practised on young girls between the ages of 5 and 10 within the Somali community as well as other communities. With certain types of FGM, such as infibulation (the excision of part or all of the external genitalia and stitching/narrowing of the vaginal opening – type three FGM), childbirth can lead to the ripping of the vagina and cause a lack of oxygen or fatal distress to the child. Hence there is a high incidence of Caesarean sections for Somali women, as health professionals are not trained to treat them. The health project makes links with hospitals and educates them about FGM.

The project worker felt that, in terms of second-generation Somali women in the UK, FGM was on the decline mainly because it is illegal. However, young girls are still taken back to Somalia, and even in the UK some health professionals are practising it illegally. Interestingly, one of the reasons cited for the reduction of FGM was the exposure of the Somali community to other Muslim communities who abstained from the practice. This took away the religious underpinnings and made it harder to justify as a cultural practice. In terms of other kinds of domestic violence, the project worker stated that in Somali culture women did not talk about their private lives in public as it was embarrassing and shameful unless a woman was considering breaking out of a relationship. Locally, there is much work to be done in terms of FGM, although nationally Forward and the Black Women Health and Family Project have taken a lead.

We hope to be able to provide advice and information on domestic violence in the safe setting of a service provider such as the Somali Women's Health Project. There is also a gap in provision for women from the Eastern European and Roma communities. Refugee women have a particularly hard time of it due to the uncertainty of their immigration status, their lack of knowledge of the language, of systems, of services, and their experience of racism – all of which is made worse by their invisibility stemming from subjugation within their own communities.

Deserving and undeserving

Although high-profile cases such as Kiranjit Ahluwalia have raised awareness of domestic violence and led to large sections of the community condemning it, these changes are undermined by and coexist with a number of regressive trends. There are a number of myths with regard to domestic violence. It is often seen to be a widely prevalent occurrence in another community and fits in with popular prejudice against that community. I got talking to a Sikh taxi driver about the work of SBS and the number of Asian women who come to the centre for help (after I had an argument with him about his persistent use of the term *bhen chaudh* (sister fucker) while talking to someone on his mobile). His response was that it was only Pakistanis who beat their women. Exasperated, I gave him a few home truths. There is also a common view that domestic violence is justified if the woman's behaviour is unacceptable. Another cab driver told me that 'Women are the cause of domestic violence. In India they don't know their rights but here they have started to know and are sticking up for themselves. My wife cooks my roti every day when I say I want it.' When I asked him if he would hit her if she did not make his dinner, he said he probably would, although he never had.

However, in Kiranjit Ahluwalia's case, we found taxi drivers very supportive. The response of the community was very different in her case as compared to that of Zoora Shah. Kiranjit was the archetypal, virtuous housewife who had tried everything in her power to make the marriage work. She was a paragon of the 'fragrant' housewife before she took the desperate step of killing her husband, setting him alight after ten years of abuse. The women of Southall came out in support and demonstrated that they could identify with her plight. In contrast, Zoora and her young children had been abandoned by her husband. A man called Azam befriended her and sexually enslaved her in return for helping her secure a roof over her head. She was in a relationship outside of marriage and the abuse was of a sexual nature. Here the community reverted to the principle that women are still the upholders of *izzat* (honour) and that Zoora had other more 'respectable options' to follow. Even those Asian women at our centre who had experienced domestic violence found it difficult to confront their own prejudices about Zoora, making it clear that we still had a long way to go in challenging attitudes to sexuality and rape within our communities. These issues remain taboo.

We have fought this case through the courts, the community and the media and have brought about substantial shifts in the way in which Zoora is seen. We managed to mobilise support for Zoora from the most orthodox elements of the Muslim religious establishment (see Chapter 12, 'Walls into Bridges'). Naseem, Zoora's daughter, mustered a lot of support from young people in Bradford. Also, the support from younger factions of the community was stupendous when Raha, a conscious clubbing collective, in collaboration with SBS, held an event at the Scala in London. The place was packed out by around eleven o'clock and it rocked all night. Naseem Shah, Zoora's daughter, made an emotional speech and the hall resounded with cries of 'Free Zoora Shah' (See Chapter 8, 'The Tricky Blue Line').

Where a woman's sexual morality does not conform to the values of the establishment, she is unlikely to get community support even if she has suffered horrific violence as a result. Perkash Walia, who was in a relationship with a Hindu priest, was brutally attacked by him when she attempted to leave him. He slashed her in the leg leaving a six-inch scar and stabbed her in the neck. The community did not support her: partly they felt that she 'had asked for it' and partly the status of a Hindu priest in the community alienated all sympathy for Perkash. The police response was inadequate to say the least (see 'The Tricky Blue Line'). The police did not want to interfere with religious or community leaders in the name of multiculturalism. Here was an example of community and state collusion.

When Pal Kaur Dal was murdered in October 1999, the media were more interested in whether she was having an adulterous relationship with her brother-in-law, Kulkarni, who was convicted of her murder. The facts are that Pal Kaur, her husband, children and brother-in-law, Kulkarni, had claimed asylum from Afghanistan.

They were Sikhs. Pal Kaur was found strangled and Kulkarni was charged with her murder. Kulkarni's semen was found on her body at the post-mortem. He had denied the alleged affair to the police, and had done so even when they had told him they had found his DNA on the victim. Later, in court, he admitted to the affair. He said he was frightened and 'ashamed', and did not want his brother or family to find out. It is not known if the relationship was consensual or not but we do know that Pal Kaur was going to move house with her husband and her children and did not want Kulkarni to go with them. The jury found Kulkarni guilty of murder and he was given a life sentence.

Pal Kaur's family was deeply distressed by the press 'sensationalising' the sexual dimension of the case and issued statements to the effect that the conviction vindicated their belief that Pal Kaur had not been having an affair with Kulkarni; evidence presented in court pointed to the fact that he had been harassing her. They described her as a faithful wife and loving mother. Even the police issued statements to that effect.[6] It was as if her death would arouse greater sympathy from the community if it could be proved that her sexual morality was above reproach. The issue of preserving family honour remains central to the community attitude to domestic violence. If a woman brings dishonour to her family, then any violence committed against her can be justified on this basis.

At a seminar on domestic violence within the Muslim community in 1999, the keynote speaker, Dr Zaki Badaawi, Principal of the Muslim College and Chairman of the Council of Imams, stated that 'the justification, perpetuation and acquiesce [sic] domestic violence has no basis in Islam'.[7] He went on to say that women as mothers did not play their part in preventing violence by the way they reared their children. In the same breath as condemning violence, he levelled the blame at the door of women.

In 1992, a Channel 4 documentary followed the activities of a bounty hunter who was being hired by families to track down women who had left home in certain Asian communities in northern England. He would then intimidate them and force them to return to abusive situations. It appeared to be part of a general development where male gangs were increasingly being used to police women, particularly young women and girls. A bounty hunter, Tahir

Mahmood, who calls himself a 'mediator', once told SBS: 'I am only doing what social services want me to do, keep families together.' SBS called for an independent public enquiry into the activities of the bounty hunter and gang networks, as well as into wider issues concerning the needs of Asian women and girls escaping abuse. SBS, together with a number of other women's groups, attended a demonstration organised by the Kirklees Asian Women's Welfare Association in Huddersfield to draw attention to the activities of this bounty hunter. Some of the local women who attended the demonstration were forced to wear the veil in order to protect their identities.

'The black sisters are violent'

In 2000, we had death threats and bricks thrown through our windows. Given our presence in Southall for over twenty years, you would have thought that the community would see us as a very positive and necessary service. Yet the subheading above has been taken from a quotation from a religious leader expressing his opinion of SBS. Is it possible to argue that there has been a shift in community attitudes and, if so, to what extent? We have very little time to take stock of how the community sees us and the work that we do. We usually make an assessment of this through the support we receive in our campaigns or in the media. For the purposes of this book, however, I called a few institutions in Southall to get a response and was extremely depressed by how negative and ill-informed their opinions were.

A mauhlvi (priest) at the Central Jamir Masjid, a mosque in Southall, who thought he was speaking to a student, when asked about SBS said: 'Very bad, very upset. When Muslim girls run away, they stay with them [SBS] and we can't go near these houses. The black sisters are violent and there are men there. They are rough and they want to fight you.' I asked if he had had any personal experience of this or if this was what he had heard. He replied: 'a few years ago, a girl left home and we went to Norwood Green. We took our solicitors but they [SBS] did not want to know us. They told us to get lost.' He continued 'I don't know if this is right or not but I have heard that they put the girls on the business.' I asked what he meant by that and he replied that SBS 'put them on the game'. I asked him if he seriously believed that and he said he was not sure, but he was 'one hundred and fifty per cent sure there were men there and they came out swearing'. I asked him what a woman should do, then, if she were facing violence. He said she should see a social worker not the black, green or white sisters!

On dialling a number which I thought was that of a temple, I accidentally got through to Suman Marriage Bureau. Not one to miss an opportunity, I asked the man who answered what his thoughts were on SBS. 'No comment' was the reply. I probed a little further and asked him whether it was because Suman Marriage Bureau felt they were trying to 'make' families whereas SBS was trying to 'break' them? It did not take much for the onslaught to begin. He said that women went to SBS after any argument and SBS advised them to divorce their husbands straightaway, whereas a community leader would have tried to patch it up. He said, 'as far as the community goes you will hear that view'. I questioned him on the arranged/forced marriage problem: did families who used the Bureau put pressure on women to accept the proposals? His response was that forced marriages were wrong and the Bureau advised parents not to force their children.

The Southall Church of God said that they understood that SBS helped battered women but they had also heard they 'spoiled' Asian women and encouraged them to break from traditions. A woman once came to the centre looking for her sister and asked me where we were hiding their women.

I met with the secretary of the Islamic Educational Institute, who was initially evasive of the direct questions that I put to him about SBS but took the opportunity to promote Islam. Eventually he said that if women's rights are being abused, then women should stand and fight. I felt that this was a progressive attitude. He went on to say that the mosque had resolved problems where men had abused women. Promising, I thought. However, this apparent liberalism soon evaporated when he said that SBS did not try and conciliate as they always sided with the woman and encouraged her to abuse values and break up families. He said that SBS was playing a negative role in the community by taking one issue and publicising it. 'They [SBS] try to make the organisation prominent by fighting for women's rights but they don't reconcile [sic]'. He said SBS adopted

Western views: 'SBS are not only family breakers but community breakers.' He observed that even the Western media recognised and appreciated the Asian family structure. I asked how it was possible for SBS to break something that was already broken. As far as he was concerned, SBS was an 'extreme' organisation. He did not believe that the violence against women was so severe that it merited interference. The police 'interfere' here but they would not do so in our countries of origin. I asked what recourse women had in those countries. He responded that violence did not exist there, as 'in front of relatives, violence hardly occurs'. I stated that women also faced violence from the extended family as it was not just the male partner who abuses. He said he had come across two or three cases a month of women complaining about their marriages, sometimes for no justifiable reason.

However, all is not doom and gloom. A man at the Ramgharia Sikh temple said he knew that SBS looked after the interests of women. I asked him if he thought they broke homes and he said no, they did good community work. One view from a man at a gurdwara in Hounslow was that the gurdwara should have the confidence to refer a person to a relevant organisation where it did not have the expertise. He felt that the lack of communication with the Black Sisters clouded the issues and promoted a mistrust of each other's motives. He felt that because the response was emotive, judgements on the organisation's merits and what it was offering could not be made. He stated that they liaised with an Asian women's centre in Hounslow.

Although sections of the anti-racist left have also criticised us for being home-breakers or for taking the focus away from the fight against racism, there have been some positive developments on that front too. Balraj Purewal, ex-leader of the Southall Youth Movement may have shared these views about SBS in the 1980s, but as co-ordinator of the Asian Health Agency he invited us to speak on the issue of domestic violence at a mental health seminar in Southall in the late 1990s. SBS was given a good reception. Traditionally male organisations that had previously been hostile to SBS have taken up the issue of abuse within the family. The fact that SBS has begun to influence institutions, or has been invited to sit on the Home Office Working Group on Forced Marriages, may have helped to legitimise our position within the community, particularly for men. We are seen as experts in the field and are approached by solicitors up and down the country for expert reports for women with immigration problems or women who have killed their violent partners.

We have seen an increase in the numbers of men coming for advice and assistance on behalf of their partners, who are falsely imprisoned, being forced into a marriage or abducted, or a relative with an immigration issue. Male clients, however, tend not to accept the advice we give them in the first instance. Some of them morph into Bollywood heroes and attempt to rescue women in true Hindi film style. Inevitably, they fail and come back to us a little more ready to listen. Women clients show greater respect for our expertise.

Making the news

Over the years, we have actively sought media coverage as another campaigning tool. When we were running the Free Kiranjit Ahluwalia campaign, in tandem with the Free Sara Thornton and Free Amelia Rossiter campaigns being run by Justice for Women, we found that the press still tended to go to Justice for Women (JFW) for quotations on domestic violence even where black women were concerned. It was only after direct discussions between us and JFW that they began to refer such calls to us as a matter of policy. When covering pickets outside the courts, the media tended to get a quotation from white women rather than the Asian women, perhaps because an Asian woman might have required an interpreter, which may involve more work for them.

The local paper, the *Southall Gazette*, has generally been good at covering domestic violence and the voluntary sector. They have covered cases such as Jaspal Sohal and featured issues such as forced marriage and some immigration cases. However, a journalist on the paper said that it was predominantly a 'white-led' newspaper, implying that they were more willing to expose certain cultural issues than perhaps a newspaper run by Asian men would be. He also said that publicly few people in the community would criticise SBS but would praise us through gritted teeth.

The Asian media, such as Sunrise Radio, have been ambivalent in their attitude to us. They cannot ignore us because we are regularly in the news. Their news desk will call us and asks for quotations and speakers but ignore us when it comes to their features. The most prominent example was when Kiranjit Ahluwalia was released. Kiranjit was asked to go on air and we suggested that we should go on air with her in order to field specialised questions on the legalities of the case. They refused. What they failed to register was that she was a survivor, not an expert, and although her voice was paramount, she should not be put on the spot with regard to any technical questions. In fact, Avtar Litt, their managing director, fielded the legal questions and, embarrassed himself and the radio station when a law student called in and put him right on some basic legal errors that he made. However, in 1998, Sunrise Community Trust donated £2,500 for our work with women in prison. The money is donated by the general public for the benefit of the Asian community; the trustees decide who the money should go to. We have many requests from Channel East, a British-based television channel. In contrast we have very few requests from Zee TV, which is not British-based. When BBA (British Born Asian) radio station got its licence, we did interviews with them, and with the more recently established BBC Asia Network radio. Again these are part of a young British-based medium willing to embrace issues such as domestic violence.

We get invited by radio stations up and down the country to provide short interviews and quotations on any community- or state-led initiatives on domestic violence. However, in a number of instances, SBS is not given coverage or airtime commensurate with its expertise. We are often invited as the radical voice, lined up alongside a religious leader or conservative community leader, so that the programme makers can ensure that sparks will fly.

The state response

If the state colludes with community leaders, what sort of protection can we expect from the state? The police are or should be at the forefront of that protection. Although we have had instances of co-operation from the police, dealing with them on a day-to-day basis has, more often than not, been difficult. Despite that we encourage women to go to the police. Stories are rife about police inaction or the fact that they are more interested in the woman's immigration status. Women come to us wholly unsatisfied with the response they have had from the police, with complaints such as: 'they did not arrest him because they said there were no marks on my face'. This is a failure of the police to treat the assault as a criminal offence. This feeling is exacerbated when women are constantly being directed by the police to take out civil orders as opposed to pursuing any criminal action. For all the progress that has been made as a result of feminist campaigning, in that domestic violence is now recognised as a crime, the police still see it as something that requires non-criminal action. There is always a danger that where black women are concerned cultural sensitivity or a lack of political will may lead to inappropriate action (see 'The Tricky Blue Line'). They will refer women to a refuge or to an organisation like ours or to solicitors. Even Community Safety Units, whose job it is to ensure that the police take criminal action, tend to get involved in welfare advice or in assisting women to take civil action.

Following a complaint made by us to the police which highlighted their failure to acknowledge the role played by SBS as advocates for women, we had a meeting with the Borough Liaison Officer as well as sergeants at the local Community Safety Unit (CSU). They said that we had a very important role to play and suggested various ways in which we could work together. These included involvement in training of officers and regular liaison with SBS on individual cases. We felt that there was no point in closer consultative status when the rank and file of the police were not doing their job better. Policies on domestic violence that were already in place were not being enforced. The police, as an institution, know what needs to be done, so it is not really an issue of training but a lack of will. Now, if we experience any problems, we contact the CSU and receive a quicker response. If there is a problem it is usually the sergeant who calls us, trying to establish or resolve the issue. But we would prefer not to have to go to the CSU. In any case, the wider public should be entitled to the same immediate attention and service that we, as an organisation, are offered when police realise that we are involved in a case.

Generally, when it comes to dealing with beat officers the response is even worse, emanating from either a complete lack of interest or, at worst, a hostile attitude. Take an example of SBS collecting belongings for a woman with a police escort. On meeting a little way from the property, we were asked if we wanted the police to wait there. I said no, the whole point of a police escort was to prevent any breach of the peace from occurring in the aftermath of domestic violence, which in my mind meant they should take the lead. They then asked if the woman wanted to knock on the door first! When SBS get involved and contact the police, more often than not their proverbial back goes up. When a woman came to SBS to find out what bail conditions were attached to her husband's case, the police wanted to know why she did not go directly to them. They would not co-operate with SBS when we were trying to make inquiries on her behalf. There is a constant attempt by state agencies to undermine our role as advocates.

We assist women in obtaining injunctions, which is a civil remedy, as a method of protection. One of the main problems we have here is with breaches of injunctions. If a partner breaches the injunction and the police are called, the police will not take action unless they can verify the assault with the perpetrator, or they say they do not have the proof they require, even if the power of arrest is attached. If he has disappeared, they believe that no further action is required because the woman is no longer in any danger. A common response from women is 'do they want to see me killed before they will do anything?' As the eligibility criteria for legal aid have become more restricted, women on low incomes find the cost of legal action prohibitive. Injunctions can cost up to £1,000 and it is impossible for these women to fork out that amount when their priority is their homes and/or children. It can be a dilemma for us to advise a woman to go down the injunction route when legal aid is not available. Most of our women, however, are on benefit and do qualify for legal aid. Enforcement of injunctions is variable, but overall we see it as a legal document that can help protect women. Where a woman opts to live in the same area as her abuser, it is particularly important for her to get an injunction. Where men obey the injunction, it makes women feel safer. Where they do not, we may then see the failures of implementation. But injunctions often have a power of arrest attached to them which does place a duty on the police to arrest men where there has been a breach. When the police are unwilling to act, we have to go to court to enforce action and that can be a difficult route, especially as the sentences imposed for breach of injunction are quite light.

Any hopes that some of these issues could be resolved at the Domestic Violence Forum in Ealing, a local authority initiative, were soon dashed. It is still struggling to agree a definition of domestic violence when there are a number of satisfactory off-the-peg definitions available (See 'The Tricky Blue Line' for a fuller discussion).

Are you intentionally homeless?

The next encounter with the state for women escaping domestic violence is with local authority housing departments. Getting them housed can be a long and frustrating process. We generally advise the woman to go to a refuge for her own safety (See Chapter 3, 'Taking or Giving Refuge?'). However, some decide or are forced to seek alternatives – for example, if they have male children over the age of ten or eleven. In such instances, they can seek the assistance of the local authority.

Women fleeing domestic violence have come to us on numerous occasions saying that the local authority has refused to rehouse them. Local authorities do not have a duty to house single women who are homeless. When the borough of Ealing was run by a Labour administration in the late 1980s, single women who were escaping domestic violence were considered to be vulnerable and therefore provided with housing. The Conservative administration scrapped that interpretation of the homelessness legislation, a state of affairs that has persisted even under the current Labour regime. Women have to prove they are unintentionally homeless and in priority need. Fleeing the home due to domestic violence does constitute unintentionality. It is proving priority need which is problematic. Women are considered in priority need if they are pregnant or have children or if they are deemed vulnerable. It is only by proving vulnerability that a single woman has any chance of being housed. Most single women are not considered legally vulnerable, and it is very hard to prove that they are – as cogent medical evidence is required as proof of poor physical or mental health. Under the Code of Guidance, Housing Act 1996, local authorities do have discretion as to how they interpret vulnerability of single people. The boroughs of Hounslow and Hillingdon have been much more proactive in housing single women escaping violence. But even they are cutting back because they believe that they are housing women from other boroughs.

The problem has also been aggravated by the fact that local authorities have sold off most of their housing stock. The housing association sector has become the main provider of housing and it is local authorities that must make nominations to them. It is difficult for us to nominate women to housing associations. Much of the housing that is available to single women escaping domestic violence is in the private rented sector, which is far from suitable due to lack of acceptance of housing benefit, higher rents, poor conditions, harassment from landlords and the lack of support structures such women need.

We have also used the law innovatively to help single women as well as refugee women who cannot be housed in a refuge by invoking the National Assistance Act. When a House of Lords decision in 1998 ruled that local authorities had a duty to help destitute people such as asylum seekers under the National Assistance Act, we used it to gain financial help for women with other immigration problems such as those to whom the one-year rule applied or those who had applied for exceptional leave to remain (see Chapter 7, 'Jumping through Hoops'). We succeeded, until in 1999 the government removed 'destitution' as a reason for providing assistance. What other reason there could be for assistance is hard to see. If the women have children, and if the local authority fails in its duties towards them by not giving them priority treatment, then we can invoke the Children Act and refer them to social services, who have a duty to safeguard the welfare of children. This was particularly useful where women had immigration problems and did not have recourse to public funds. Although responses vary, social services can fund temporary accommodation, food and subsistence until the women's status changes.

Women subject to immigration controls have sometimes been accepted on the same basis as 'asylum seekers' when it comes to benefits and housing, whether or not they have applied for refugee status, although this is not a consistent policy. Such women can get assistance only under the dispersal system run by NASS (National Asylum Support Services). This usually means dispersal out of London. As the unprovoked killing of a Turkish asylum seeker in August 2001 in Glasgow illustrates, dispersal can be extremely dangerous. In certain limited circumstances, dispersal can be challenged but it is difficult because of the appeal system – there is no provision for any financial assistance or housing, pending appeal. This leaves women with little say, taking them far away from support structures, legal representatives and any friends or family. If they are sent to specially designated hostels or B&Bs, these may not offer adequate protection for women escaping violence, leaving them open to being tracked down. However, if a woman can prove that her ex-partner has funds (which may be gleaned from the immigration papers), she can make an application for interim maintenance from her ex-partner, which would enable her to circumvent the dreaded NASS route as well as serve as some sort of retribution. The Home Office is now developing a new system placing asylum seekers in accommodation or removal centres. Whichever department of the local authority we deal with, workers there can be unhelpful or complacent through to downright rude. We are proactive in encouraging the women to use the complaints procedure, which, once again, translates into hostility towards us.

There was a time when local authorities would accept the word of a woman who said that she was facing violence. When the Conservatives returned to power in Ealing, they required a woman to provide evidence such as a non-molestation order. The current Labour administration did not change this policy for several years until SBS and Ealing Women's Aid lobbied them. They have now got rid of the requirement to show proof, but it is still hedged about with qualifications. We have to draw their attention to their duty to provide emergency housing and investigate later. The question of intentionality in housing legislation can become a catch-22 for women fleeing domestic violence. If she does have an injunction and it has not been enforced, they may claim that she has made herself intentionally homeless because she has an avenue of protection and is not using it. If there is no injunction, there may be pressure put on her to go to court before she declares herself homeless. In order to establish housing need, local authorities may contact the perpetrator of the violence to confirm the woman's veracity, and SBS still has to point out that it is not good practice to do so.

Often the most widely acceptable proof of violence after an injunction is medical evidence. But that can be problematic too. The response of an Asian female community doctor in the case of a woman who entered the UK as a spouse of a British citizen left me speechless. The woman's solicitor had requested a medical report from the doctor. When the woman went to the doctor to enquire about it, she was met with great hostility. The doctor said she did not believe her because women often get married just to come into the UK, and once here get jobs and leave their families. The doctor said that in her view, 90 per cent of the fault lies with daughters-in-law and 10 per cent with the husbands. The lack of impartiality and the regressive judgemental view displayed was dangerous, and overlooked the fact that most women, particularly from the sub-continent, due to community pressure, expect to stay married for life. We have registered a complaint against this GP. Moreover, reports to GPs are often the only evidence proving domestic violence, as such women are frightened of reporting to authorities for fear of deportation and of damaging family honour. Nonetheless, women can be reluctant to report to their GP, as breaches of confidentiality have been known to occur especially where the GP is Asian or where women cannot disclose domestic violence when chaperoned to their appointments.

Social services have not shown any real interest in domestic violence. In the late 1980s and early 1990s, they worked a lot more closely with us than they do now. This was partly because they had no Asian social workers in Southall! They would systematically refer women to SBS where there was not a child at risk. They would ask us to get involved in their own caseload around young Asian women. We would have to do a statutory assessment of the women and recommend ways to meet their needs. We were involved in many more case conferences. Social services were also involved in community development. In the late 1980s they set up a meeting involving us and religious leaders on the issue of sexual abuse. It turned out to be an exercise in social services justifying to community leaders the role they play and preventing accusations of undue interference. This meant that they reassured the community that they would not get involved in 'grey' areas, such as parental control over lifestyle issues such as smoking, style of dress or forced marriages – exactly the opposite of what we had been campaigning for. Since then, cuts in their funding have led to social services being very internally focused. Now, women come to us asking for intervention because they are unsatisfied with the response of the social services.

Although we work extremely closely with some professionals, we still come across lawyers who do not appear to have an understanding of domestic violence. I have a client who went to court for the second time to get an injunction, having allowed her husband to return after the first injunction. Her barrister told her off, saying that this was a waste of public funds and she must not do it again. I informed the barrister that this woman had had threats from her husband's family that they would harm her family in India but that, nonetheless, it was a common phenomenon for women to give their partners another try for a plethora of reasons and it was his job to get into court and get her the protection she was entitled to. I am glad to say the woman is safe and happily living apart from her ex-partner. However, it is still commonplace for a woman to ask for protection a number of times and return to her partner. This is the nature of domestic violence and must be accepted by professionals as well as statutory bodies. With the experiences women have of the statutory agencies, it is clear that there is still much to be learnt about domestic violence and that it needs to be treated with the seriousness it deserves.

In conclusion, it is fair to say that SBS is extremely effective at assisting women experiencing domestic violence and successful in its campaigning, policy and developmental work. SBS has fought for the recognition that we are part of the community and are here to stay and here to fight. At a personal level, all the hard work and stress is justified when a woman says to me 'I would never have got through this without you. You are my family: my mother, father, brother and sister.' I have had women and members of their families say that they had not understood the nature of our work and had even undermined it until they got involved. We have worked hard to make women feel ownership of the organisation through democratic, secular, anti-racist and feminist ways of working. This has ensured their long-term membership and loyalty to us. There is still much to be done to tackle domestic violence, particularly in terms of improving the state response, mainstreaming the issues, raising awareness and linking up with the new communities of Southall. With more resources and the influx of new workers, we will continue the battle.

Notes

1. For our twenty-first anniversary Kali Theatre developed work by Asian, Caribbean, African and Arab women and put on an evening of readings which were both funny and poignant.
2. *The British Crime Survey: England and Wales*, Home Office, London 2000.
3. Sue Lees, 'Marital Rape and Marital Murder' in J. Hanmer et al., *Home Truths about Domestic Violence: Feminist Influences on Policy and Practice*, Routledge, London 2000.
4. C. Mirlees-Black, *Domestic Violence: BCS Self-completion Questionnaire*, Home Office, London 1999.
5. 'Jail Sentence "Trivialises" Father's Violence', *Southall Gazette*, 25 October 1996.
6. 'Man Jailed for Life for Strangling Sister-in-Law', *The Gazette*, 2 June 2000.
7. 'Seminar: Domestic Violence within the Muslim Community', *Q News*, August 1998.

3

Taking or giving refuge?
The Asian women's refuge movement

Muneeza Inam

I want to thank the women I met at Brent Asian Women's Refuge. They showed me, through their strength and survival, that it was possible against all the odds to change your circumstances.

This chapter will examine the changes I have experienced within the Asian women's refuge movement over the last twenty years. In particular, it will focus on the impact of the Thatcher years, which saw the introduction of a contract culture and market philosophy throughout the voluntary sector – including the women's refuge movement. As one who has worked extensively in this area – I was a committee member of the Brent Asian Women's Refuge (BAWR) for over fourteen years – and as a member of the SBS executive since 1983, I view the changes in the refuge movement from several perspectives. Through the experience of SBS I can see the difficulties faced by organisations trying to find safe refuge accommodation, particularly for women with insecure immigration status. The refuge movement is in the midst of a crisis. A number of refuges have been forced to shut down while many others, like BAWR, have been taken over by housing associations. Although the number of Asian women's refuges has grown to 24 nationwide, 13 of which are in London, the sector remains grossly underresourced. Nearly 20,000 women and 28,500 children stayed in refuges in England in the year 1997/98.[1] In 2000, 200 women in England and nearly 300 in the UK could not be accommodated in already full refuges.[2]

Challenges facing the movement

Asian women began setting up refuges in the 1970s in part as a reaction to the perceived failure of the white women's movement, particularly Women's Aid, to be sensitive to the needs of Asian women. Asian refuges, such as BAWR, were initially established to ensure that Asian women fleeing violence did not seek help outside the community but were reconciled back into the family home, thus preserving family and community honour. It was only in the late 1970s when women who saw the oppression of Asian women within a feminist and anti-racist context became involved and took over the running of the refuge that BAWR truly become a safe house where women were free to make decisions without the pressure to reconcile. However, even these women fearing the backlash of racism subscribed to the view that we must not publicly challenge our communities and agitate on issues such as domestic violence. In the mid-1980s, some members of SBS and BAWR challenged these orthodoxies. When the residents of BAWR actively supported the Krishna Sharma campaign in 1984, the management committee of the Brent refuge – who were my employers at the time – viewed SBS and our political views and actions as sacrilege and playing into the hands of the racists. We were all very conscious of this dilemma and the need for caution when dealing with the media. However, never for one minute did we think that we should keep quiet about the oppression of women within our own communities. That would have meant colluding with that oppression. In our view, one issue could not be subsumed by the other: race was on a par with gender.

There are many sections of the Asian women's movement even today that are not able to raise openly the issue of oppression of Asian women for fear of being seen to be critical of the community. Those refuges that operate within particularly conservative communities, such as East London or Bradford, find it even more difficult. The rise of religious fundamentalism and the absence of an active, healthy women's movement have further isolated such organisations.

Another contentious issue that has plagued refuges and the voluntary sector as a whole is the extent to which we should involve the women who come to us for help in campaigns to bring about political change. At SBS we have felt that it is absolutely vital to do

so. We found that women felt empowered in the process of campaigning and were better able to place their own individual circumstances within a wider political context as a result of it. It often
helped to take away the stigma of domestic violence when women
saw how widespread the problem was. When I mobilised the BAWR
residents for the Krishna Sharma campaign, the management committee criticised our decision. They viewed the residents as passive
victims who were being manipulated by us, when in reality these
were strong women who wanted not only to change their own
circumstances but those of others. They marched through the streets
of Southall, sometimes passing shops owned by their erstwhile
abusive husbands.

In our view residents should be actively involved in the running
of a refuge. When I became coordinator at BAWR, the old management committee was replaced by residents and some ex-residents of
the refuge who were actively involved in decision-making on all
issues from staffing to policy. This unique involvement of the women
lasted for more then ten years, until the refuge finally fell victim to
the increasing complexities of running an organisation within the
funding constraints imposed by market philosophy on the voluntary
sector. At BAWR we never had the resources or time needed to train
women on the changes taking place within the voluntary sector and
funding environment to enable them to have a meaningful involvement in the decision-making process. In any case it is not easy to
involve women who have escaped violence. At SBS, we have found
that the process takes time and effort and is not always successful.
Management meetings are long enough, and when the proceedings
have to be translated into another language to ensure equality of
access they last even longer. Given the personal problems these
women have to deal with, their role in managing the centre can be
limited. Different levels of understanding and experience have also
to be negotiated. However, it is essential that we continue to find
ways to involve women, particularly those who live in a refuge as
it may be their home for a long period of time.

At SBS and BAWR, we saw our work within a political context.
We felt strongly that an Asian women's refuge should not just be a
hostel. It must also provide an alternative to the community: a place
where women are presented with alternatives and are free to decide

their future without pressure from family and community to reconcile; where they are given practical help and support to enable them to lead independent lives free of violence; where they are provided with a network of support to enable them to sustain independent living and to cope with the isolation of being a single parent, ostracised by the family and community. At BAWR, up until 1997, the support came not only from workers but from residents and ex-residents of the project as well. As a result, a refuge community developed and for many women and children it became sometimes their only source of support, and one of the most stable factors in their lives. A refuge should also campaign for changes in state laws and institutions which disadvantage Asian women and to raise awareness of domestic violence within the community.

What happened to BAWR in the 1990s and particularly since 1997 mirrors the depoliticisation of the refuge movement and the voluntary sector in general. Management committees require voluntary effort and can be notoriously inactive, with the consequence that often the majority of the work is carried out by the same members. To counteract this, there has been a trend of inviting workers of other related organisations, including local law firms, social services, health professionals and women's organisations, to sit on the management committee, who then carry out their management responsibilities as part of their day job. This too can contribute to depoliticisation, as the motives for their involvement are less to do with commitment to the issues that drive a refuge and more to do with representing the interests of another organisation. Often these are professional women who are involved because of the skills they have to offer or the kudos attached to being involved with a refuge rather than any inherent commitment.

It is also harder to recruit new workers who are interested in campaigning and the wider political context in which we work. We have seen the growth of a 9-to-5 working ethos in the voluntary sector. If a woman comes to SBS at 4 p.m., we have found it difficult to get refuges to take her on as they say they will not be able to greet her or settle her in. The selection criteria used by refuges to admit women are also becoming more restrictive. Some refuges refuse to take on referrals by SBS because they believe that the cases we refer are complicated and difficult to unpack. They tend to be

wary of SBS because they find us more challenging. They know that
we will question them if they turn down a referral. Where there are
resource constraints, SBS workers have been happy to offer their
support, either by taking on some of the casework or advising refuge
workers on various aspects of the case. SBS has found that many
refuges do not appear to recognise that women escaping forced
marriages are escaping violence. A lot of refuges are raising the age
limits of women that they are prepared to take on, and yet it is
younger women who are likely to be affected by the prospect of
forced marriages. They feel they cannot deal with younger women,
who may be more vulnerable in terms of possible suicide. With the
disappearance of the collective ethos in the way in which refuges
are run, many refuge workers need to refer every decision, even
minor ones like whether to buy food for a woman when on a long
appointment, back to their manager. Unsympathetic managers can
make things worse. At one discussion at BAWR, a refuge worker
said she did not see the relevance to her work of campaigning
against the rise of fundamentalism. To me the links are inescapable,
as these reactionary movements are manipulating deeply held
religious beliefs to push back even the small gains made by women.
At the heart of fundamentalism is the control of women, restricting
their choices and imprisoning them in traditional roles.

Although the growing recognition of domestic violence as an
issue by religious establishments is a positive development, it has
led to attempts to set up separate refuges along denominational
lines where the emphasis is on providing women with a breathing
space rather than a clean break in order to maintain the status quo.
At a seminar on Domestic Violence in the Muslim Community in
1999, one of the participants felt that refuge providers went against
the grain of Islam by perpetuating certain behaviour and encouraging girls to go to clubs. She was challenged but stated that refuges
were not the answer and that the community should deal with the
issue. She implied that women working in refuges were somehow
outside of the community and that only women acceptable to the
community should take on the role of supporting women. Women
with conservative views are increasingly joining refuges as workers
and management committee members in an attempt to influence
their agenda. We feel it is dangerous to compromise women's safety

by placing an emphasis on reconciliation. A report commissioned by Manningham Housing Association in Bradford in 1998 on the feasibility of setting up a refuge for Asian women found that some earlier projects had closed down because of the lack of clarity in their role. The contradiction inherent in providing safe emergency accommodation to women while at the same time attempting reconciliation with their families led to a breakdown of trust between the project and the clients.

The new funding regime – a blessing or a curse?

The conditions attached to funding have been largely responsible for the depoliticisation of the refuge movement. Funding bodies will generally give money to organisations run along hierarchical lines, so that the lines of accountability are clear. They believe that in a collective the lines can be blurred, but even in hierarchical institutions like housing associations accountability is not always guaranteed. It is transparency rather than structures that is paramount. In addition, the majority of funding bodies will only fund organisations with a charitable status. The Charity Commission will not grant charitable status to organisations involved in campaigning and political work.

Along with many voluntary organisations in the 1980s, when there were massive cuts in public services under Thatcher, BAWR had to fight every year for its survival. However, once contracts were introduced in 1992, the refuge got secure funding for five years. The effect of this was that it became more insular. Workers realised that they now had security to plan, develop and improve the service the refuge provided. They successfully set up a child development project. With more secure funding came greater demands for accountability. While this was necessary, it led the refuge movement too far down the road to professionalisation and did not necessarily bring about a better service. We did make great improvements to the service provided to the women and their children. However, this was done at the expense of our political work. The difficulties of obtaining new funding, fighting over scarce resources, and the market culture within the voluntary sector have got to the point now that refuges are in intense competition with each other.

Some refuges have been taken over by others or by housing associations. What the refuge movement failed to appreciate was how to operate in this new climate without being taken over by it. And this unfortunately is just what happened. SBS, despite its own recruitment problems, has managed both to balance the immediate needs of women coming to the centre and to continue to campaign successfully around issues such as domestic violence, forced marriages, immigration and battered women who kill.

Business goals and market philosophy have got the voluntary sector in a stranglehold. They measure quantity not quality: every bit of help, advice or service provided is now assessed by time and cost, leading to the worship of targets and performance indicators. How do you quantify success? Helping a woman and her children escape violence, supporting them through a traumatic time, exposing women to choices and opportunities and ideas previously denied to them, and enabling them to have greater control in shaping their own lives − all are of assistance. The value of this help to women and their children cannot be measured in terms of hours spent with them and seen in the framework of *value for money*. The obsession with statistics does not sit well with the traditional values of the women's movement and the voluntary sector. Yet, I have seen more and more how the voluntary sector has started to wear these new clothes with ease.

The contract culture which began under the Conservatives has largely continued under Labour. A Labour government funding initiative, 'Supporting People', which came into effect in April 2003, is believed to be even more detrimental to the future of refuges. It will cover the funding of all supported housing services: elderly housing schemes as well as refuges. This will mean that some of the core elements of funding previously given by the Housing Corporation, a government body, to refuges based on the number of bed spaces provided and eligible service charges which are paid by housing benefit will be pooled together with other forms of supported housing funding into one pot − and distributed by the local authority. If relations between a local authority and a refuge are strained, it could affect the refuge's access to that sum of money. Local authorities may favour local schemes rather than schemes where residents do not have a local connection. There are signs that local

authorities will engage in a cost-shunting exercise, cut their social
services budgets by moving clients with high care needs to a scheme
which was originally intended only for those who could cope in
supported housing schemes. There is no confidence that this policy
will be managed effectively. A survey conducted recently on the
needs of the black voluntary sector, as part of the 'Supporting People'
initiative, did not contact sufficient refuges. Refuges will now have
to apply for this money, thus increasing their administrative overload. This further hurdle for refuges to raise core funds will place
other organisations, such as housing associations with their huge
resources, at an unfair advantage. Although some money has now
been made available for refuge provision, this is unlikely to be
sufficient or ring-fenced to benefit specialist, such as black women's,
refuges. The positive aspect of this initiative is that it is not linked
to the individual's income and is given to people who need supported housing. This will help women on the road to independence:
women will be able to afford to go to work without suffering cuts
in housing benefit as under the old system.

Closed to some women

A specific example of how funding criteria have led refuges to
abandon the basic ethos of the movement is their inability or unwillingness to accommodate women with insecure immigration
status and no recourse to public funds. As refuges rely on housing
benefit as one of their main sources of income, these women found
that, with some honourable exceptions, refuges shut their door to
them. Although councils are aware of this and despite their duty to
provide for the children fleeing violence, they are making it very
hard for refuges to get money from social services. Councils tend to
pass responsibility for particular families to other councils. Council
officials will shrug off their responsibilities, saying that further research needs to be done on the extent of the problem even when
presented with the experience of Asian women refuge workers.

The case of a woman from Gujarat who was imprisoned in the
matrimonial home for the duration of her marriage provides a good
example of how refuges have lost sight of their ethos. SBS spent the
best part of a week trying to find a refuge space for her but only

managed to find her an emergency place on a sofa. When we could not find another refuge to move her on to, the refuge worker said they could no longer accommodate her as she had no recourse to public funds. The woman had leg fractures in five separate places as a result of being pushed down the stairs by her mother-in-law. She needed to go to the hospital for medical treatment. As she didn't speak any English or know her way around, the refuge should have sent a woman to accompany her – a befriender. They refused to do so because the woman was not a resident of this country. When challenged by SBS that the two issues were not connected, they said it was policy. SBS offered to pay the expenses of the befriender. The refuge would not even pay the cost of her painkillers. Eventually another refuge took her in. But the woman's partner traced her – not through any fault of her own, as she had not revealed the address of the refuge. They decided to evict her, but instead of finding her another refuge she was taken to the police station and left there from 4 till 10 p.m. She had not eaten or drunk anything that day. The refuge had not bought her any food, and yet one of the issues that she had faced with her in-laws was that of starvation. Finally, she was taken in by Ealing refuge, which had fundraised for women in her position – an example of good practice. She was given a room of her own and a small weekly allowance to meet her basic needs.

Ealing Women's Aid (EWA) had tapped into Women's Aid Federation (WAFE) special funds for women with no recourse, although it was successful only once. In any case, the funding was for four weeks' accommodation only. This source of funding ceased two years ago. Since then, EWA have fundraised themselves with the assistance of a management committee member. They made a grant application to an International Missionary fund, providing case histories, and managed to secure three years' funding at £10,000 a year. Not only can they now provide accommodation for four women a year and money for living expenses but also grants for private accommodation deposits and childcare. This proactive approach should be adopted by more refuges.

Manningham Housing Association in Bradford runs a black women's refuge and they have used the Children Act, which places a duty on social services to protect children, to get their local authority to meet the costs – rent and income support – for women with no recourse to public funds. They worked tactically by threatening to evict one woman until the local authority caved in and came to an arrangement whereby the refuge received a rental income and the equivalent of income support for the woman's living costs. This agreement now applies to all their women with insecure immigration status.

Unfortunately such examples of good practice are few and far between. There should only be one entry qualification for a refuge – that you are a victim of domestic violence. The failure of the state to protect women with immigration problems is completely indefensible – both racist and immoral. And this is precisely why refuges should be involved at a political level, campaigning alongside SBS to change the immigration rules which prevent Asian women from accessing public funds and services.

The housing association sector

The naked impact of market philosophy on the voluntary sector is nowhere to be better seen than the housing association movement. These social landlords were born out of a need to supply decent and affordable housing to the poor and vulnerable of society. They can no longer claim that the housing they now provide is affordable: especially where housing associations are providing temporary accommodation for homeless families. The tenants are charged market rents. This is justified on the basis that on the whole the homeless families receive housing benefit and therefore would not face hardship. The reality is that because of the present crisis in the housing benefit system, particularly in London, many families live under the cloud of very high arrears and the prospect of eviction. The housing associations have not set up any systems to help these tenants through the crisis. Theoretically a woman and her children who have suffered violence and are provided temporary accommodation could be evicted because of arrears caused by delays in the delivery of housing benefit. She could then be put in different temporary accommodation and evicted again for the same reason.

Funding pressure has led the housing association sector to focus on maximising rent collection. A senior manager in a housing association told me that their main priority was 'getting the money in'. When I asked why they did not pursue the local authority for the non-payment of housing benefit rather than the tenants, her response was that they did not wish to jeopardise their relationship with the local authority as they gave them the contracts to house homeless families. In any case, according to her, 'tenants are a dime a dozen; lift up a rock and one will crawl out from underneath'. It seems to me that they are making money from the most vulnerable and are providing a level of service that would be unacceptable even in the commercial sector.

Success in this sector is about the number of properties that are managed and the amount of rent that is collected. Meaningless statistics are trotted out, talks are given about 'value for tenants' when what is really meant is 'value for money' to justify continued funding. The language of the business community is now echoed in the service sector: for example, words such as 'service providers', 'customers', 'clients' and 'consumers'. What is provided is now seen and presented as a product, like washing-up liquid. They talk about selling themselves and about profitability. Given the quality of the homes provided it is clear that truth, reality and substance are sacrificed for presentation and image. The race for housing associations to become larger in order to survive in a climate of reduced government funding has actually led to the collapse of many housing associations, where organisational and management structures have not been able to cope with the rapid growth.

The growing involvement of housing associations in the refuge sector is part of this drive to take on a range of housing services to improve their own competitiveness, to win kudos and to acquire an additional source of income. As far as they are concerned, running a refuge is the same as running any other hostel accommodation. For housing associations there is more profit in running a refuge themselves than subcontracting it to housing agents like specialist black women's groups. But they lack the understanding and the expertise acquired by feminists in dealing with women, especially those who come from religious, conservative communities, or the dangers of pursuit by estranged, violent partners. At an Asian refuge directly managed by a housing association, little or no attention is paid to the security of the refuge; the refuge address is known or is easily accessible to any worker in the organisation. There seems to be no awareness that this could endanger women in the refuge. The emphasis is on rent collection, and staffing levels are poor, with one worker allocated to seven families with differing levels of needs. This leaves women with little English and raw from their experiences to navigate the complexities of getting benefits, legal help and housing on their own.

The adoption by housing associations of the practices of the commercial sector can be seen in the changing relationship between BAWR and the landlords of the property, Network Housing Association. Prior to the introduction of contracts by Brent Council in the 1990s, Network had a hands-off relationship with the refuge. So long as BAWR's finances were in order, and we were accountable for the service provided, Network respected the fact that it was an autonomous women's group with expertise in their field. When BAWR had difficulties coping with changes in funding requirements by the Housing Corporation, Network supported them through the process.

However, in 1992, Network gained the contract from Brent Council to run refuge provision in the borough. BAWR and Brent Women's Aid effectively became subcontractors, answerable directly to Network. Initially their relationships remained the same. But in 1996 there was a change in the management in the special project section within Network. Combined with the cultural changes taking place generally in social housing, there was a noticeable hardening of attitudes towards BAWR. Then in 1997 there was a change of management at BAWR. Given the complexities of running a refuge and a relatively inexperienced management, Network put more and more pressure on meeting targets where the goalposts kept changing. Network did not assist the refuge despite being represented on their management committee. Instead they seemed determined to see the organisation fail. All of this came to a head at the time of the renewal of BAWR's five-year subcontract with Network. Despite the fact that Network Housing brought in independent consultants to carry out a review of BAWR, which stated that 'the service to residents is high quality and is underpinned by good policy and procedures', in 1999/2000 BAWR did not have its contract renewed. Although fundamental changes had taken place at BAWR since 1997, it was still an autonomous Asian women's project. It was the end of an era – the end of the longest running Asian women's refuge in London run by Asian women for Asian women. Despite public protest and demonstrations, Network took over the running of the refuge. In a post-Stephen Lawrence climate, Network Housing's actions appeared to amount to indirect and institutionalised racism. Their draconian style of management has not been experienced by the other non-Asian women's refuge in Brent.

Under Network management, refuge workers did not appear to be familiar with or sensitive to the needs of the residents. One woman with insecure immigration status was advised by a refuge worker that, at worst, she would be deported to India and if she went back to an urban area she might be able to support herself and not be at the mercy of hostile relatives. This advice betrays a complete lack of understanding of how the Asian community regards women who leave their violent partners. Such women are ostracised because they are seen as having brought dishonour to the family name. Indeed, Network found it could not cope with the management of the refuge. Yet instead of handing the refuge back to Asian women to run it, they handed it to an Asian housing association, ASRA, where nearly all the senior managers are men with no more under-standing of the needs of Asian women than Network. Network, like many housing associations that are now attempting to run refuges, seem to believe that it is merely a question of having a good man-ager in place. Directly managed refuges also suffer from the fact that they are at the bottom of everyone's agenda in a housing associa-tion. Refuge staff have to be accountable not only to their own management committee but also to the housing association board.

It might appear that progress has been made in terms of the high awareness of domestic violence. It has prominence given to it in the press, with horrific statistics: for example, every twenty seconds a woman somewhere suffers domestic violence. New state policies have been developed to tackle the problem. And yet we continue to hear of cases like the following. A woman, living in a housing association flat, who had escaped domestic violence found her front door broken down by her ex-partner. When the maintenance de-partment told her that they would not be able to repair her front door for four days (although the standard response time should be twenty-four hours) she was naturally very distressed. Furthermore, she was told that she would have to pay for this, despite having a crime number (which enables the association to claim the expense of the repair from the insurance company). The maintenance team said, in defence of their actions, that they do not treat domestic violence as a crime. In other words, it was not an emergency and the woman was being charged because they had already fixed her window, which her ex-partner had previously broken while trying to break into her house. Women are still being blamed for the actions of their partners or even their ex-partners. The reason why the woman's ex-partner was able to harass and continue to abuse her was because the council and the association had not transferred her to safer accommodation. Although there were empty properties to which this woman could have been transferred temporarily for her own safety, the housing association did not consider this course of action because the housing officer felt that as the women was an alcoholic she would probably tell her partner the new address, although she had never done so before. Even if good domestic violence policies are in place they mean nothing if workers are not trained and monitored.

However, in some limited cases, housing association involvement in a refuge might be helpful. In more conservative communities like Bradford, where the Dehleze refuge was closed down by the community through demonstrations and threats to the workers and residents, being run by a housing association can provide protection. In Bradford, the local authority did not support earlier refuge projects for fear of alienating male members of the community, some of whom were councillors. The council recognised the need to fund refuge provision but, as it was too hot an issue to handle, it was careful to avoid upfront, public ownership of the Dehleze refuge. The climate was such that even the women on its management committee could not reveal their involvement to their families for fear of the hostility they would face from them. Agencies were petrified of referring women, with the consequence that the refuge was not running to full capacity and eventually closed. Manningham Housing Association (MHA) is now running an extremely successful refuge in Bradford. As it was a black housing association run by men with status and legitimacy in the community, many of the councillors who would have challenged a women-only project did not dare tackle these men. Additionally, MHA has access to the kind of resources that allows the refuge to be protected by a high-tech security system and 24-hour staffing. Safety is the paramount issue for women who use refuges. In close-knit areas like Bradford, where the *biraderi* – taxi brotherhood – discovers and circulates the whereabouts of a refuge the day after it opens, no matter how tight the security, it was a particularly important issue. As MHA was perceived by Bradford council to have a strong track record in providing housing to the ethnic minority, financial expertise, credibility and accountable management structures, the new refuge easily won the support of the local authority.

The Newham Asian Women's Project in East London, which runs a refuge and a second-stage hostel, believes that black workers might feel attracted to working at refuges run by the housing association sector because the levels of support and resources that are available simply cannot be matched by independent black women's projects. In the long run, however, there would be a loss of expertise as housing associations are often guided purely by the profit motive. It should be noted, furthermore, that housing associations that directly manage refuges can soak up to 25 per cent of refuge funding on administrative costs. NAWP, according to its former director, Anjum Mouj, is seen locally as a strong organisation, partly because it has been successful in bringing funds into Newham from a range of external sources on a match-funding basis with local authority funding for Asian women's services. This has helped to consolidate its position vis-à-vis the housing association and the local authority. Any cuts to NAWP's budget by the local authority would result in cuts in match funding from external sources and therefore prove to be a net loss to the borough.

Supporting Asian refuges

Recognising the difficult circumstances under which Asian refuges have to operate, NAWP and the Asian Womens' Resource Centre in Brent have set up an initiative called Imkaan – an Urdu term which means empowering through nurture and support – to offer support and training to the beleaguered staff of Asian refuges. Black refuges are often too impoverished to set aside their own funds for staff development. Imkaan also aims to inform and lobby policymakers. It produces quarterly briefing papers on issues of interest to the refuge movement, including one on the politics of the takeover by housing associations and ways of accommodating women with no recourse to public funds. However, Imkaan is itself underresourced, with a small staff team attempting to provide a coordinated voice for Asian women's refuges nationally. These initiatives are important because Women's Aid has failed to provide the necessary leadership and to counter the erosion of values and services occurring in the movement.

The Asian refuge movement is fragmented – lacking in both direction and political vision. A national organisation is needed to consolidate the movement, develop a political agenda and campaign on the issues affecting Asian women both within the community and outside it. It could support failing refuges and help them to survive as independent, autonomous organisations run along feminist lines. It could ensure that Asian refuges do not advocate or pursue the practice of reconciliation. It could help enforce high-quality, comprehensive advice, support and practical help to women. It could ensure that good practice is replicated within the movement as a whole. At SBS we will continue to support autonomous Asian refuges which are struggling to survive. It is also important that the Asian women's movement holds to account housing associations and refuges that fail to provide a service sensitive to the needs of Asian women. A more cohesive refuge movement must also campaign around issues such as domestic violence, forced marriages, immigration and battered women who kill.

Notes

1. Women's Aid Federation of England, *Domestic Violence Statistical Factsheet No. 1*, Bristol 2001.
2. Betsy Stanko, 'The Day to Count: A Snapshot of the Impact of Domestic Violence in the UK', *Criminal Justice*, vol. 1, no. 2, 2000.

4

'It was written in her kismet':
forced marriage

Hannana Siddiqui

Forced marriage has touched the lives of many women at SBS, including workers and members of the management committee. Some have been forced into marriage, while others have found ways of escaping it, sometimes stepping out on their own, shocked by their parents' breach of trust and refusal to acknowledge their right to choose. Others still have overcome family pressures by making an agreement with a man to marry, and then divorcing quietly afterwards. Some use marriage to run away from the restrictions imposed by their parents, only to find their new husbands and in-laws just as oppressive. Many endure unhappy married lives, while others may eventually separate or divorce.

Pragna Patel, from a Hindu background, describes pressure from her family to marry a man in India at the age of 17. She says:

> I was taken to the village my mother came from and forced to see a boy who had been chosen for me. The next thing I knew I was engaged! My mother's mother and older sister put pressure on her and she in turn pressurised me. I knew no one. It was a traumatising experience. I remember weeping and weeping and weeping. I met the boy for 15 minutes. I didn't think I'd be with him for the rest of my life. I was taken to his home and his mother asked me what my decision was. I said I wanted time to think. When I got home I sat on a stool facing a semi-circle of woman. I said no. I wouldn't accept. My mother's older sister said I must. They kept up the pressure saying: 'what makes you so special?' I wept and

continued to say no but it was out of my control. I was so desperate that I confided in a couple of male cousins. They felt helpless. I
even went to see the priest in the village church. He was fat and
lying on a bed. In English I asked for his help. He said: 'My child,
have faith in God!'... After a year I won and I loved the victory.[1]

Since the beginning of 1999 we have experienced unprecedented
levels of public discussion about forced marriage: a subject which
was once of little interest to any group other than that of Asian
women is now hotly debated by civil servants, politicians, community leaders and the media alike. It was sparked off by the tragic
case of Rukshana Naz, a 19-year-old Asian woman, who was murdered in Derby in 1998. Her brother ritualistically strangled her
with a ligature while her mother held her down by her feet. Her
mother said, 'It was written in her kismet [fate]'. Her brother claimed
provocation, using a cultural defence to argue that the killing was
committed in the name of 'honour'. Rukshana was murdered for
'shaming her family' by refusing to stay in a marriage where the
man had been chosen for her. Instead, she had decided to return to
the man she loved and by whom she was pregnant at the time of
her death. Rukshana's brother and mother were convicted of her
murder in May 1999.

Some women are driven to self-harm and suicide. Asian women,
particularly those aged between 15 and 34, are two to three times
more likely to commit suicide than women in the general population.
Forced marriage is often quoted as a reason. One woman at SBS,
'Rifat', had been forced into marriage by her father and relatives.
She agreed because of fear and enormous emotional pressure – her
mother was dying of cancer and wanted to see her settled. Her
father, who had previously been violent to Rifat and her mother,
threatened to kill her. Her other relatives threatened to ostracise her
once her mother died if she refused to marry. In an interview Rifat
said:

Somehow I did not think she was going to die. On the way to the
hospital my aunt said my mother was very ill, and I better not say
anything about being unhappy because I would cause her to die. I
walked into the ward and she was in a really bad state, she was
like a skeleton. I hugged her and the first question she asked was

'are you happy?' I was crying like hell and the words wouldn't come out of my mouth, but I forced myself to say yes, I'm very happy. She said 'I know you are lying to me, I know you only said this to make me happy.' I hugged her, and spoke to her for about ten minutes. The next morning I came in and within an hour she died in my arms. I never got a chance to speak to her at all.[2]

After her mother died, Rifat's husband joined her from Pakistan:

That was the worst day of my life because I didn't want to see him and he physically repelled me. I couldn't bear to look at him, and they wanted me to spend the rest of my life with him. I hated him. I don't know where the hate came from, but after my mother died, I just hated him. We went to London and it was just me and him, sitting in a room silently. I tried to start conversations, but it didn't work. He was in his own little world. I got an Asian TV channel for him, and every day he would wake up at 10 am and watch TV and not make any effort to talk, or help himself in the kitchen, or do anything. I was out at work all day and when I got back I had to slave for him … day in, day out. I told him the doctor said there was something wrong with me and I wasn't allowed to have sex for a couple of months. I lied to him, and I lied to the family so they wouldn't force me to sleep with him. But I became depressed, a nervous wreck. I cried my heart out, but the family said I had to go along with it. It was my fate, it was my destiny.[3]

It was then that Rifat contemplated suicide by taking an overdose and using sharp knives on herself. A friend happened to telephone in time and persuaded her to leave her husband rather than kill herself. Some women, however, do not receive help in time.

A fine line

The central problem is drawing the dividing line between forced and arranged marriage. The fear is that by criticising the cultural practice of arranged marriage, racist assumptions are made about Asian communities. So commentators and politicians have been at pains to separate arranged marriage, as a respectable cultural practice, from forced marriage, which is abusive and unacceptable.

However, the line between an arranged marriage and a forced marriage is a fine one. A forced marriage, as opposed to an arranged marriage, is one where there is no free and valid consent given by one or both parties. Many women feel that, in practice, there is little difference between the two. The desire to please parents who exert emotional pressure is itself experienced as coercion.

Arranged marriage, like forced marriage, has existed for centuries in many cultures. Until fairly recently the British aristocracy practised arranged marriage, some of which were no doubt forced – a reality often forgotten by the media and others when discussing the issue.

Forced marriages involve an element of coercion, which includes physical and mental duress. Many agencies fail to recognise that forced marriage is a form of domestic violence and/or child abuse. It is also a gross violation of women's human rights. Although men can be affected, cases overwhelmingly involve young women and girls. Many older, first-generation women living in the UK were forced into marriage abroad in the Indian subcontinent when the concept of choice was virtually non-existent. They would not have conceived of refusing to marry and were expected to make their marriage work at all costs. The practice of arranged marriage has, of course, changed and there is now more choice both here and in the Indian subcontinent, and there are variations between different sections of the community. Cases have also been reported in other tight-knit and traditional societies, such as Middle Eastern, East Asian, Turkish, African, Chinese, Japanese and Jewish communities. Forced marriage cuts across class and caste boundaries, affecting rich and poor alike.

There are no comprehensive or official data on prevalence. Even where statistics on domestic violence or child abuse are collated, cases of forced marriage are rarely identified and categorised. The indications are that, like other forms of domestic abuse, the problem is common but hidden. SBS deals with about 300 cases and enquiries per year. The police in Bradford and the Foreign and Commonwealth Office also each receive about 300 cases a year. The media often use an estimated annual figure of 1,000 women. This could be the tip of the iceberg.

A crime of honour

Some government officials, politicians and others have attempted to present forced marriage as a gender-neutral issue. Forced marriage is primarily about the control of female sexuality and autonomy. Women's 'sexual purity' reflects on the honour of the family. Some women and girls are under pressure to have virginity tests by their families to check on their moral behaviour. One woman came to SBS after fleeing from her family in Pakistan, who threatened to kill her unless she submitted to a virginity test before they married her off. If she proved not to be a virgin, she was going to be beaten and sold to a tribe in the mountains.

Even where men are forced into marriage, social norms allow them to commit domestic violence and adultery, and neglect or abandon their wives, whereas women are placed under considerable pressure to reconcile themselves to abusive situations. Some women are married in this country, while others are taken abroad. Sometimes women are married by proxy. The prospect of dowry can also be a driving force behind such marriages. Women are forced to marry men much older than themselves and to enhance the status of the family. In this way, women are sold, bartered and bought like mere commodities.

The Home Office Working Group on Forced Marriage

The scandal of Rukshana Naz's death, and the case of Jack and Zena Briggs added pressure on the government to act. Jack Briggs, a white English man, and his wife Zena, an Asian woman, have been on the run and in hiding for over six years from Zena's family, who once threatened to kill them. Her family hired private detectives, bounty hunters and a hitman to track them down. Zena's family wanted her to marry a cousin in Pakistan, to whom she had been betrothed after her birth. In August 1999, the Home Office established a Working Group to examine and report on the issue of forced marriage. This followed a parliamentary debate in February 1999 led by Ann Cryer MP and a seminar co-convened by SBS and the Institute of Public Policy and Research (IPPR) in June 1999 where SBS called for a government inquiry into the matter.

The government had never before set up a Working Group to examine forced marriage or any issue involving black or minority women. Baroness Uddin and Lord Ahmed were appointed co-chairs. I was invited to join from SBS. As most of the members were from Muslim backgrounds, the government also invited Hindus and Sikhs. SBS was concerned that membership was being based around religious identities. I made it clear that SBS was a secular organisation and that people should be invited on the basis of their expertise rather than their religious group. My concerns were not taken on board. So, not surprisingly, from the start, the Working Group seemed to be divided into two camps: some members supported the position that we would be wrong to expose Asian communities 'warts and all' and that we must be alert to the sensitivities of the community. The SBS position, in contrast, was that we could not be afraid of exposing our 'warts' if we wanted to deal with the problem of forced marriage. Encouragingly, Mike O'Brien had already unequivocally stated that the need to respect minority cultures should not be used to deny minority women protection from forced marriage. He talked of a 'mature multiculturalism' and said memorably that 'Multi-cultural sensitivity is no excuse for moral blindness.'[4]

SBS has argued against cultural relativism for many years. The approach of the Working Group was less robust. It emphasised the need to educate the community and encourage intergenerational dialogue. SBS, however, insisted that the brief of the Working Group had to include a survey of current practice and issue guidance and recommendations for action by agencies and government departments.

A matter for the community

Some people on the Working Group were clearly selected because of their perceived influence within the community. The initial emphasis of the Working Group was to consult community leaders. Lord Ahmed, for instance, attended many large religious gatherings, particularly in the Midlands, addressing crowds and meetings of predominately Asian men.

The government's attitude was reflected in the initial debate led by Ann Cryer in the House of Commons in February 1999. She said:

My appeal is to the leaders of the Asian Muslim communities. I hope that they will encourage their people to put their daughters' happiness, welfare and human rights first. If they do, their communities will progress and prosper, in line with the Sikh and Hindu communities.[5]

Ann Cryer not only mistakenly assumes that Sikh and Hindu communities do not force women into marriage, but also calls on community leaders to lead the way for change. In this context, any public acknowledgement of the problem by community leaders was applauded uncritically. Nevertheless, some community leaders accused Ann Cryer of stirring up racial and religious hatred in her local area in Keighley and Bradford. Also, as a white woman, her right to raise these issues was questioned by some Asian women. SBS and a few women from Bradford supported her, but with reservations.

'Stone her to death'

Many community leaders deny the problem of forced marriage and/or are hostile to women refusing forced marriage and the women's organisations that represent them; instead they attack them as 'home wreckers' and lobby to get them shut down. Some in the community said that had Rukshana Naz been in Pakistan, she would have, and indeed should have, been stoned to death for leaving her husband and becoming pregnant by her boyfriend. Manzoor Moghal, chairman of the Leicester-based Federation of Muslim Organisations said, 'If a woman becomes pregnant like this, she can expect to be frozen out of the community. That goes for all religions from Asia.'[6]

Many community and religious leaders are themselves embroiled in the harassment of women, often with impunity. Indeed their very position of power protects them and others involved. Take the case of 'Nasreen' and 'Rashid'. Nasreen, from Bradford, and Rashid, who lived in Pakistan, had met and fallen in love when Nasreen was visiting relatives in Pakistan. In April 1998, Rashid came to the UK. The couple asked Nasreen's father for permission to marry. Nasreen was beaten by her father, brother and sister, and imprisoned within the home. Rashid was barred from the house. Nasreen finally escaped and went to London, where the couple married. They had a civil and religious Muslim ceremony. Rashid hoped Nasreen's family would now be more accepting of them as a married couple, and suggested they should return to Bradford for her family's blessing. A community leader in Bradford encouraged them and agreed to mediate. The couple returned to Bradford and were warmly greeted by Nasreen's family. Her father promised to hold a ceremony for the family and forced the couple to separate until then.

In September 1998, Rashid received a distressed telephone call from Nasreen, who said that she had to go to Pakistan to buy clothes for the ceremony on pain of death. Rashid rushed to Bradford, but was persuaded by Nasreen's brother to go to the house of a family friend, where Nasreen would join him. He was kept waiting for five hours, at the end of which Nasreen's father arrived and said that Nasreen had gone to Pakistan. Rashid managed to make a call to the police and tell them his wife had been abducted. He was told to go to the police station. However, Rashid was forcibly taken to another house and locked inside a room for the night. The next day he was taken to the house of a former Asian councillor and community leader, and beaten by a number of men. They wanted him to sign divorce papers. Rashid refused. None of the men has been prosecuted for the assault on Rashid, despite his statement to the police. Indeed, the police told SBS that they were concerned about the reaction of the community if they arrested and charged anyone in connection with the case.

Some have argued that the debate on forced marriage is an attack on their cultural and religious heritage or a form of racism and Islamaphobia. For example, Jahangir Mohammed said it was a 'subtle and cunning attack on the whole system of arranged marriage'. He added:

> This is a relatively small problem within the community, played up by the Home Office in collusion with secular and feminist groups for their own political purposes ... the Home Office is giving the issue high profile in the hope that every young Moslem woman that goes to Pakistan will doubt the motive of her parents and thus create disharmony in the family.[7]

Change within the community is not uniform or even deep-rooted. The Muslim Parliament has said that forced marriage is wrong and that sex within it is rape. The positive nature of this statement, however, has been compromised by their assertion that children born in a forced marriage are illegitimate, which only serves to punish children and their mothers. They have also complained that the government is going too far by focusing on a 'fire-fighting' approach to forced marriage rather than encouraging a grassroots change in attitudes.

Others have used the issue of forced marriage to strike bargains with government, in return for support for their own, more conservative demands. After one of their conferences in November 1999, the Union of Muslim Organisations of UK and Eire issued a press release, stating:

This conference declares that forced marriages are against the letter and spirit of the Shari'ah [Muslim family law] as marriage is described in the Holy Qur'an as a firm and solemn convenant between the bride and the bridegroom and hence free and voluntary consent between the two parties is essential for a valid Islamic marriage. Secondly, arranged marriages are to be recommended and love marriages without the consent of the parents are to be discouraged as it is has been proven statistically that arranged marriages are stable and more successful and ensure the proper upbringing of children as law-abiding and morally oriented citizens. Furthermore, the Conference believes that it is the responsibility of the Ulama and Muslim Organisations to correct the distorted image of Islam portrayed in the media and emphasise the contribution of the Shari'ah in raising the status of women to one of legal equality with men.

However, the conference also welcomed

the assurance given by the Home Office Minister, Mr Mike O'Brien, to a UMO Delegation on 4 November 1999 that efforts will be made to expedite action for the application of Muslim Family Law to the Muslim community in the United Kingdom.

The Muslim Family Law is unlikely to give Muslim women equal rights to child custody, divorce and other matters. In introducing this religious and customary personal law in the UK, the government would undermine the very human rights it purports to uphold.

Some submissions to the Working Group called for the training of religious leaders, particularly for poorly educated imams (Muslim priests) from abroad in the hope that educated, middle-class imams will not hold conservative views on marriage. Education or class, however, are no guarantors of human rights. They just help religious leaders to express their conservative views in a sophisticated way.

Members of the Hindu community were up in arms about the soap opera *Coronation Street*, which in 2001 had a storyline about a Hindu family torn apart by the daughter running away from home because her parents wanted her to marry a cousin abroad. Forced marriage is often justified in order to counter the corrupting influence of the West, even of racism and imperialism. The stated aim is to protect the interests of young people, to preserve religious and cultural heritage and a strong identity.

But what about the state?

The general thrust of the government's response to the issue of forced marriage lacks an important element: the state's responsibility to protect women. Whenever the government does consider the idea of state protection, it turns its attention to the immigration rules.

Prior to the general election in 1997, some women MPs had been concerned about immigration and had said that immigration controls were necessary to prevent forced marriage (see Chapter 7, 'Jumping through Hoops'). For example, men who used marriage to enter the country could be deported if the woman separated from him within the probationary one-year period as a result of domestic violence or desertion. SBS argued that the solution to forced marriage generally lay in empowering women to escape these abusive situations rather than maintaining racist immigration controls. The one-year rule placed undue pressure on young immigrant couples at an early stage in their marriage where one spouse is not settled and economically dependent. The same would not be acceptable to white or British couples, who, due to a number of pressures, tend on average to break up within two years of marriage. The one-year rule was also open to abuse by a settled spouse who wanted to exploit a non-settled spouse. The MPs did not agree. It was clear that there was trouble ahead.

Following abolition of the primary purpose rule after the election in 1997, Yasmin Alibhai-Brown criticised the government for not protecting women from forced marriage because, in her view, more women were being used by men to enter the country. In July 1998, the *Independent* published a series of articles suggesting that forced marriage was on the increase because of the rising number of men entering the UK. SBS wrote a letter to the paper disputing this: the rise in the number of applications was no surprise, as the primary purpose rule had been abolished and more men would naturally obtain visas. This did not necessarily mean that more women were being forced into marriage.

By the time of the SBS/IPPR seminar in 1999 the ground had shifted again. Yasmin Alibhai-Brown agreed that a return to the primary purpose rule was not the way forward, but still felt that immigration controls may help some women escape forced marriage. An immigration solicitor, however, claimed more women were complaining of forced marriage as a result of abolition. Mike O'Brien did not favour a return to primary purpose, recognising it as unfair. Instead, he wanted to know how to help women who sponsor men into the country to disclose information to immigration officials about being forced into marriage. This time SBS was reassured.

The media also took up the issue of immigration control, particularly the BBC television programme *Newsnight*. In 1999 *Newsnight* criticised the abolition of the primary purpose rule, arguing that more Asian women from Bradford were being taken abroad to be forced into marriage.[8] They centred the piece on Razia Sodagar, who had set up an Asian women's group, 'Our Voice', to deal with forced marriage. In fact, the group was not calling for a return to the primary purpose rule but favoured an extension to the one-year rule, a point that did not come across clearly in the programme. Razia felt that if men had to wait longer to obtain their permanent stay in the UK, they would think twice about using women to enter the country on the basis of marriage. Only Mike O'Brien was left in the studio at the end of the programme to defend the decision to abolish the primary purpose rule. In 2000, *Newsnight* showed another feature, based in Pakistan, of British Asian women being abducted there and forced into marriage in order to sponsor men into the UK, and repeated much of the previous argument on immigration controls.

The case for more immigration controls is not strong. Many marriages take place in the UK, while some women are abducted and taken abroad. Some may return and sponsor men into the UK, whilst others are left overseas indefinitely. There are many other reasons why couples marry abroad, including the need to maintain kinship and family ties or keep wealth within the family: circumventing the immigration rules is not the main or only reason. We would argue that the role of immigration rules as a solution to forced marriage has been blown out of proportion, and has diverted attention from the real issues.

Many agencies, including entry clearance officers, state that the real problem is not the rules, for they already have to check if the marriage is genuine, but the fact that women are too afraid to confront their families and openly oppose their marriage. They want their disclosure to be kept confidential. The Immigration and Nationality Department must disclose reasons for refusal of a visa on appeal. They are unable to maintain confidentiality, as they have to justify their reasons for refusal. The right to reasons for refusal is a fundamental human right. Essentially, immigration officers face the same problem as other professionals. What do you do when a woman discloses forced marriage, but does not want to confront her family in order to escape it? Women need advice, information, support and protection rather than more immigration controls in order to escape forced marriage. Some have suggested that all spouses and fiancés should be interviewed by entry clearance. This would simply place extra burdens on all couples in an attempt to reach the few cases of forced marriage. This could amount to a return to the primary purpose rule through the back door.

In the final analysis, the aim of the government is to keep black and migrant people out of Britain through the strict use of immigration law. If they were keen on protecting women, then liberalising the immigrations laws would be the answer. If there were no immigration rules to bypass, families would not have to force women into marriage in order to allow non-British men to settle in the UK.

Women speak up

In November 1999, SBS organised the first meeting between the Home Office Working Group, attended by the co-chairs, and survivors of forced marriage. Prior to this, the Working Group had not consulted women directly. The meeting was highly emotional, and it made an impact. The women made it clear that community leaders did not speak for them, and what they wanted was more services: housing, counselling, women's support services and help from agencies. The meeting highlighted differences of politics between SBS and the co-chairs, leading to some heated exchanges. When challenged about their preoccupation with consulting community leaders, Baroness Uddin said that they were all feminists, but nevertheless there was a need to consult community leaders.

Although some women's aid groups made written submissions about forced marriage to the Working Group, a number of conservative individuals and organisations also did so. Many of these were Muslim scholars, institutions and women's groups, or Asian family-counselling services. Although all submissions stated that forced marriage was wrong, suggested solutions varied. These differences often reflected a political battle being fought on the wider arena of women's rights between feminists and non-feminists, secularists and fundamentalists, and between those who wanted universal human rights and those who wanted cultural and religious rights. The latter wanted a more conciliatory approach, a dialogue with the community rather than heavy-handed intervention by the state. Racism, Islamaphobia and cultural diversity were used as justifications to water down recommendations and the whole approach of the government and the Working Group to the issue of forced marriage.

SBS itself made a submission to the Working Group. This was supported by thirty-five predominantly Asian and other black and minority women's refuges and resource centres. It also received support from white or mixed-race women's aid groups, including national bodies such as Women's Aid Federation of England and Scottish Women's Aid. It was important for SBS to be accountable to women's groups and victims, as it was in a unique position to represent their views on the Working Group. It also strengthened our hand in battles being fought within the Working Group.

'Mediation is murder!'

There was a strong and unexpected consensus among the women's groups. SBS argued that the state should mainstream the issue of forced marriage by incorporating it in its national strategy on violence against women and children, and that there should be national minimum standards of good practice within a human rights framework. This included challenging policies or practices which ignored the problem in order to respect cultural difference, and opposing the practice of mediation and reconciliation in situations of abuse, such as forced marriage. These issues are highlighted by the comments of 'Hina', who said to SBS:

> Social services and the police step in straight away where there is child abuse, but not where young Asian women and girls are under the same or greater risk because of forced marriage, like I was from the age of ten. They are afraid of interfering in the culture and being called racist. When they do get involved, mediation often comes first, safety second. The little control women have over their lives is then completely taken away from them. Women are treated as if they were guilty until proven innocent.

Mediation creates unnecessary dangers for women facing abuse. The practice is widespread within the community. Women are already under considerable pressure to reconcile with community leaders and elders being used as informal mediators. Women often lack power in mediation and feel intimidated into making agreements which do not protect their interests. SBS and other women's groups find that once women return home, agreements made by their families are usually breached, often after a 'honeymoon' period when women feel safe, following which they are subject to forced marriage and other abuses. Of course women have the right to choose, but the role of agencies is to provide alternatives. Their role is to advise and encourage women to break away from abusive situations through law enforcement and by providing welfare and legal services. Mediation compromises their position, often creating a conflict of interest, undermining their legal and moral duty to protect women from abuse. Some mediation services themselves refuse to act in cases of abuse. Even the marriage bureau of Birmingham's Central Mosque, which aims to rescue marriages on the point of breakdown, reports that in six years they have seen only five 'successful' reconciliations among more than 200 divorces.[9]

The dangers of mediation are highlighted by the case of Vandana

Patel, who in 1991 was stabbed to death by her husband in the supposed safety of Stoke Newington Police Station's Domestic Violence Unit in North London. He was convicted of her murder. The meeting had been organised by the police (see Chapter 8, 'The Tricky Blue Line). Yet the police continue with mediation and in one case, at least, have established a post where an officer is responsible for mediating between the Asian community and women escaping forced marriage. In what other circumstances involving crime would the police establish a post involving such mediation?

No agreement could be reached on the issue of mediation within the Home Office Working Group, despite protracted negotiations. Other members of the Working Group said women have a right to choose. And so the Working Group report endorsed the practice of mediation for women facing forced marriage. It was claimed in the report that the evidence to the Working Group indicated it should be offered by agencies. However, evidence against it outweighed arguments by a few who supported the practice. Many women's groups and all the local authorities canvassed opposed it on grounds of safety. The Home Office does not promote mediation for women experiencing domestic violence in the wider community, so why do so for Asian and other minority women? It seems that the reason for endorsing it has more to do with appeasing community leaders. Mediation is a less threatening option than women and girls leaving home and prosecuting or taking out injunctions against their families. The abuse itself is often left unchallenged and the woman chastened and held in check. It seems that 'mature multiculturalism' has still to come of age and break from the power politics of its parents. Representing SBS, I felt that I had no option but to resign from the Working Group, apparently an unprecedented move.

Following my resignation, SBS and other women's groups protested with a demonstration outside the Home Office. The resignation overshadowed the report as it received considerable media coverage. One of the slogans on the demonstration was 'mediation is murder', recalling the case of Vandana Patel. In a joint seminar organised by Interights (a legal international human rights group), the Centre for Islamic and Middle Eastern Law (CIMEL) at the School of Oriental and African Studies, and SBS held in July 2000, the Pakistani human rights lawyer Hina Jilani talked about the dangers of mediation. She talked from bitter experience. One of her clients, Samia Sarwar, was shot dead by a hired gunman in her office during a mediation meeting between Samia and her mother. The gunman had accompanied her mother. Samia Sarwar had left her husband after ten years of marital abuse and was seeking a divorce in order to marry her lover.

The Foreign Office offensive

The Foreign and Commonwealth Office (FCO) has been the first in government to take up the issue of forced marriage. In January 1997, the FCO published a leaflet on forced marriage, giving advice to women on what to do when travelling abroad. It states that the FCO has limited powers to assist British citizens who may be automatically entitled to dual nationality while they are visiting the country of their parents' origin. SBS condemned the use of dual nationality to deny assistance to British citizens, when the same was not the case for white hostages held abroad. In many cases, women surreptitiously contact the British Consulate, begging to be rescued because they are being held prisoner, sometimes under armed guard. Until recently, the standard response of the Consulate was that they were unable to go to them, but if the women came to them they would be able to assist. It is often left to concerned boyfriends, friends and other representatives, such as NGOs and lawyers, to locate and rescue women. In many cases, they lack resources and the power to force the police and the authorities to act because of the widespread problem of corruption and traditional views about women.

One of the more complex cases in which we enlisted the reluctant support of the FCO was that of Nasreen and Rashid. Nasreen was believed to be held by her uncle under armed guard in Pakistan and subject to beatings and rape by her uncle, and abuse from her father, brother and sister whenever they visited the country. Local people, including the police and officials, had ignored Nasreen's predicament because her uncle was a powerful local politician involved in criminal activity.

Rashid was unable to travel to Pakistan because of the threats against his life. He was in hiding in the UK and under pressure to pronounce an Islamic divorce. Rashid had contacted police and politicians in Pakistan, at all levels, including the then prime minister, Nawaz Sharif, begging for help. In December 1998, Rashid managed to send a petition for habeas corpus, which ordered the family to produce Nasreen before a Pakistani court. At first, the uncle disappeared with Nasreen. However, when officials tracked him down, Nasreen was produced in court where she claimed that she was not being held against her will and was due to return to the UK in two weeks. Rashid felt that Nasreen had been deceived into saying this with false promises of a return to the UK. He even wondered if her sister had been impersonating her, as she had done before. The case was dismissed. Soon afterwards the British High Commission received a letter purporting to be from Nasreen, stating she was safe and well. Neither the handwriting nor the signature was hers.

The FCO eventually agreed to contact the Minister for Women in Pakistan. However, the FCO could not guarantee what the Pakistani authorities would do once the case was handed over to them. They said they had little control because of the issue of dual nationality. There was considerable concern that any action could trigger a response from the family, who might panic and kill Nasreen rather than release her, when she could give vital evidence against them. Their honour too was at stake. In November 1999, the British High Commission in Pakistan received a telephone call from a woman who stated she was Nasreen, seeking the help of the consular services. She was told she should present herself at the High Commission. SBS argued that this amounted to fresh evidence. The lawyers in Pakistan, however, felt they could not take effective legal action unless Rashid went to Pakistan to give evidence. Apart from the danger to his life, Rashid had claimed asylum in the UK. SBS argued that the FCO should issue legal proceedings on behalf of Nasreen. They refused, stating that it was beyond their legal remit. Rashid had also been refused legal aid to initiate his own legal proceedings in the UK.

In the meantime, a military coup in Pakistan had replaced the previous government. Through a tortuous route, SBS made contact with Dr Attiya Inayatullah, a member of the National Security Council, who had a history of working on women's issues, and the chief executive, General Musharraf, who gave his personal approval for the government to act. SBS asked the British High Commission to make contact with Attiya Inayatullah's Office. The High Commission agreed. It seemed SBS was now aiding the FCO and the British High Commission to make new contacts with the Pakistani government!

At first the Pakistani government were keen. They were hoping to make an announcement against honour crimes on International Women's Day 2000 to gain international recognition as a forward-looking caretaker government. However, the government soon became nervous because the previous court judgment had dismissed Rashid's application. They said they could not use their powers to stage a rescue. Instead, despite SBS objections, they decided to take the matter to court. We were concerned that Nasreen might again be too frightened to speak up in court. SBS persuaded the British High Commission to attend the hearing and requested that they and the legal representatives take any available opportunity to speak privately with Nasreen to ascertain her true wishes. SBS also requested that Nasreen be provided with counselling. The Pakistani authorities told SBS that the lawyers in the case were very experienced and their plan was indeed to find a way of providing counselling for Nasreen before she gave a statement in court.

The case was heard in May 2000. Nasreen and her sister were produced in court to establish Nasreen's identity. Two men, believed to be her uncle and brother, also accompanied Nasreen. She was required to state her wishes in open court in the presence of her relatives. She said she wanted to remain and remarry in Pakistan. She denied she was being held against her will and said she was in the process of obtaining a divorce from Rashid. The judge granted a private interview with consular staff following this statement. There was a five-minute discussion and Nasreen repeated the same statement. The case was dismissed. The matter was also now closed for all the authorities concerned. On the basis of a five-minute interview, the consular official claimed that Nasreen's demeanour had been that of a confident woman. In our experience, many women need considerable time and reassurance to disclose abuse and to seek help. It is possible that the length of time (nearly two years) that Nasreen had been forcibly separated from her husband had led to brainwashing and resignation to her fate. She may have hoped that one day she would be allowed to return safely to the UK once she remarried according to her family's wishes. Many other women have used these survival strategies. Officials in the FCO commented that this case required 'too much work and too much fuss'. Yet our demands had been very simple: to establish if Nasreen was safe and if she wanted to return home. All cases deserve much work and much fuss if we are to offer opportunities to women to escape forced marriage.

The case of 'Gurmeet' highlights what can be achieved by good practice and the will to act. In 1999, Gurmeet, a Sikh woman, had been taken to India by her parents in order to marry. Her boyfriend contacted SBS and we talked to the FCO about a rescue. The British High Commission agreed to go in search of Gurmeet, who was eventually found on the day of her engagement. A woman official at the British High Commission, following some pressure from SBS, took the unusual step of taking direct action. Consular staff went to the village where Gurmeet was being held and worked with the police to create an opportunity to talk to her at a local police station. Although at first too frightened to admit the truth, Gurmeet eventually sought the help of the British High Commission, who arranged for her to return to the UK. This case was significant because it was the first in which the British Consulate had taken a proactive role. It sets a precedent for future cases. A lengthy private interview with a woman official and a safe and encouraging environment helped Gurmeet make a statement before a magistrate. Much of the response of the FCO has depended on the willingness of individual staff to act rather than adopt a consistent institutional approach. Some have argued that the British government was free to act in the case of Gurmeet because dual nationality does not apply to India. Yet this fact is no excuse for poor practice.

By early 2000, changes were afoot in the FCO. More staff have been deployed at the South Asia desk and senior officers have been appointed to institute reform. One senior official visited their posts in the Indian subcontinent and consulted lawyers and organisations. They have also 'gone out' into the community in the UK and, like the Home Office, consulted community leaders. When one official was asked by SBS why they did not see workers from the local black women's refuge after an FCO visit to Bradford, he said he did not know it existed. When asked if they intend to visit Southall or SBS, they said that they intended to meet some local Asian councillors in the area instead!

The Home Office Working Group report failed to call for a review on the law of dual nationality, despite the efforts of SBS and groups such as Interights. In August 2000, the Home Office and the FCO issued a Joint Action Plan. It concentrated on the role of the FCO and the need to help women taken abroad. This led to some positive change, including a dramatic u-turn on their policy on dual nationality. The FCO said that dual-national victims were entitled to the same protection from the British Consulate as mono-nationals if they normally resided in the UK. Each case involving a dual national was to be pursued in a more 'imaginative and creative' way by the British Consulate until and if challenged by the authorities of the other country. Other reforms included addressing internal guidance to consular staff and producing updated information leaflets for victims. In 2001, the FCO even employed Narina Anwar, a young Asian woman, who, with her two sisters, using their own initiative, had escaped forced marriage in Pakistan. While we welcomed these reforms, we remained concerned about the fact that there was little consultation with women's groups. We also continued to experience problems with case handling. For instance, when the British Consulate, for the first time, attempted to rescue a woman in Pakistan by going to the place where she was being held, they failed to explain to her why they had come and how they could assist her. Confused and frightened, the woman did not leave with the consular officials, but later persuaded her husband to let her return to the UK so that she could arrange to sponsor him. Once here, she fled the family home. As a result of this case, the FCO have refused to stage any more rescues in Pakistan. Some still argue that the FCO and consular services are reluctant to help because the issue of forced marriage is 'too sensitive'. Although some progress has been made on this front, it appears that good diplomatic and international relations are more important than saving Asian women's lives.

Our own backyard

SBS has come across many cases where professional agencies are either ignorant of the problem or do not even recognise it as abuse. Even now, with more awareness, many assume that the main problem is about women and girls being abducted and forced into marriage abroad. Despite the Working Group's recommendation that all departments should respond to the problem, most government departments, including those dealing with social services, education (except for a video aimed at school children produced by the FCO and Department of Education), health and social security have done little or nothing to tackle forced marriage. There appears to be some apprehension about doing so. For example, representatives of the Department of Education had expressed concerns that schools were being placed under greater pressure to investigate all cases of Asian girls taken on extended holidays abroad. They were concerned about criticism from parents, governing bodies and Asian communities for making racist assumptions. *The Times* added to these fears by starting an article, 'Teachers are to be encouraged to go directly to the police or social services if they suspect that one of their female pupils is being forced into marriage by their parents.'[10]

One of our main recommendations to the Working Group was that all departments issue best-practice guidance on forced marriage to service providers. Only the police and the FCO seem to be responding to this (the FCO has also recently been working on guidelines for social services, but has met with resistance or a lack of interest from the Department of Health). Furthermore, there is no significant new money available to deal with forced marriage, or to enable better funding of women's refuges and resource centres, and no proposed reforms to improve access to legal aid and housing. Although the Homelessness Act 2002 extended the definition of vulnerable people in priority need for rehousing to include those at risk of violence or facing threats of violence, we still experience immense problems housing single women escaping domestic violence and forced marriage.

The legal route

The Home Office Working Group recognised that the criminal law can be used to protect against forced marriage and that there were problems in obtaining legal aid in civil cases. However, some within the Working Group wanted the law to be seen as a last resort. SBS argued that women must be encouraged to use the legal system to demand protection, and that failures within the system had to be addressed as a matter of priority. Wider social change takes place partly through positive legal precedents by deterring perpetrators of crime and by the confidence they inspire in women.

The Working Group report did not specify a need for a new offence of forced marriage. SBS and other women's groups did not advocate it, mainly because they wanted a better enforcement of current law. However, feminist jurisprudence has recently argued for a need to recognise domestic violence as a specific offence. The Lord Chancellor's department was considering a new offence, or at least examining domestic violence as an aggravating factor in crimes against women, in the way that racial motivation is regarded as an aggravating factor in race crimes. In June 2003, the government's consultation document on domestic violence dropped these proposals. In this context, it made sense to some to argue for an offence of forced marriage. Forced marriage is already an offence in Norway, although no one has so far been prosecuted.

To SBS it seemed that a law to ban forced marriage could lead to racial harassment and discrimination in the UK, where the issue only affects minority communities. Abduction for the purposes of unlawful sexual intercourse is already a criminal offence. In July 2000, a Sexual Offences Review by the Home Office recommended that the current offence be replaced by a new offence of abduction with the intent to commit a serious sexual offence, specifically with forced marriage in mind:

> We are particularly concerned about the potential for girls to be taken in order to be forced into marriage or a sexual relationship abroad, and thought that the law ought to continue to offer a specific remedy. A forced marriage is not valid, and forced sex within that marriage would be likely to count as rape. Our new offence of abduction to commit a sexual offence should be available for use for those abductions where the intention is to take the victim abroad.

Only one case of abduction related to forced marriage seems to have been successfully prosecuted to date. In 1998, Sakina Khan and Mohammed Bashir pleaded guilty to and were convicted on charges of kidnapping and administering drugs to their daughter, Rehana Bashir, in order to force her to marry in Pakistan. Rehana regained consciousness at the airport and refused to board the flight.[11]

Women who have attempted to argue rape following a forced marriage have had difficulties in obtaining convictions. The Crown Prosecution Service has consulted us in order to improve its policy on the prosecution of cases involving forced marriage. In some cases, civil law remedies have to be considered when tackling forced marriage. While forced marriage is voidable, the operation of aspects of civil and family law and the availability of financial help for legal assistance need to be addressed.

Whilst wardship and family proceedings can be used to obtain help for a minor, obtaining civil orders to protect adults, particularly those held abroad, is extremely difficult. In the case of Nasreen, Rashid attempted to obtain a writ of habeas corpus in the UK. The case did not go ahead because legal aid was denied, despite appeals. The reason given by the Legal Services Commission official, perhaps inadvertently, was that they 'always refuse legal aid in such cases'.

Over the years SBS has pursued cases challenging the concept of duress under English matrimonial law in instances of forced marriage. Physical duress is more often accepted by the courts than mental or social pressures in petitions for nullity, although the Court of Appeal judgment in the case of *Hinari* v. *Hinari* (1984) stated that the test for duress is 'whether the mind of the applicant (the victim) has in fact been overborne, however that was caused'. Previously, many women preferred to withdraw or not initiate annulment proceedings because of pressure from family, concerns about the legitimacy of children, or because of the difficulties of giving evidence in court and dealing with a long contested case. Although many prefer the relatively easier route of divorce or judicial separation, younger women are now applying for annulment. In 2002, we obtained, so far as we know, the first annulment in England and Wales in a forced marriage case.

Inside and outside the Home Office

SBS has been criticised by some anti-racists for participating in the Working Group on the grounds that it will compromise its politics in working with the state. SBS feared that without active participation, our views would be marginalised and ignored. As with many government initiatives, community leaders and Islamists were quick to co-operate: not because they trusted the state, but because they hoped to control the level of governmental interference in their communities and their own power within them. My resignation from the Working Group marked a point of departure. It illustrated both our ability to influence the state, and to walk away on a point of principle that could not be compromised or watered down. It shows that it is possible to sit and talk around a table in the Home Office and to stand and demonstrate outside!

In July 2001, SBS published an interim report on forced marriage, to mark the first anniversary of the Home Office Working Group Report. It assessed the extent to which government and other agencies had attempted to tackle forced marriage and to hold them accountable to black and minority women. We stated the points we had made to the United Nations in June 2001 that, despite the initiatives within the police force and the Foreign and Commonwealth Office (FCO), the Home Office and other government departments had remained silent on the issue. In addition, there was little or no consultation, no extra resources, no consistent set of guidelines helping to set standards or reforms in legislation and other areas of social policy. Our report was to be used as a campaigning tool to invite more people to support our demands and add pressure on the government to institute reform. Government and police officials at the launch were unhappy about the report because of the way it exposed their failures. The Crown Prosecution Service gave a written response, denying that they had failed to deal with forced marriage but acknowledging that they were trying to improve! However, the Greater London Authority adopted our section on mediation for their strategy on domestic violence despite criticism from religious organisations.

More recently, we have noticed a shift – deaths that would once have been used to highlight forced marriage are now being redefined as honour killings. Forced marriage has become a political football, extensively kicked around by the likes of Home Secretary David Blunkett, and a shorthand for condemning minority communities and for setting out the standards to which immigrants must aspire if they wish to settle in the UK. Some Labour MPs have suggested that the race riots were caused by non-English-speaking, poor male immigrants entering the UK, having successfully coerced some woman into marriage – forgetting that most of the Asian men who rioted were born and brought up in Britain and speak fluent English! When we responded by writing to the press, only the *Telegraph* was prepared to publish the letter! The following is an extract:

> As a group of women with a 22-year history of fighting abuses against Asian women by the community and the British state, we are outraged by Blunkett's disingenuous use of forced marriage as an excuse to justify the government's approach to race relations and immigration in this country. David Blunkett has stated that Asian communities in this country need to adopt British 'norms of acceptability' pointing to forced marriage in these communities as alien to 'British' values. Does he include the right to detain suspected 'terrorists' without trial and other measures which erode civil liberties in his concept of civilised British values? Does he mean that it is our sense of 'Englishness' that inspired Asian women to fight abuses within our communities and not our sense of injustice, our commitment to human rights and our need to live free from violence?

Blunkett's use of women's rights to promote a racist agenda stands in sharp contrast to Mike O'Brien's attempts to develop a 'mature multiculturalism'. There is a clear and present danger of issues like forced marriage being hijacked by racists, which is why we insist on mainstreaming it in the debate on domestic violence. We find ourselves standing once again on that slippery intersection between race and gender, a no man's land, so to speak.

Notes

1. Julia Bard, 'Not so Dutiful Daughter', *Jewish Socialist Journal*, Spring 2000.
2. Gavin Bell, 'Indecent Proposal', *The Scotsman*, 8 April 2000.
3. Ibid.
4. House of Commons Adjournment Debate on Human Rights (Women), *Hansard*, 10 February 1999.
5. Ibid.
6. Bill Daniels, '"Shamed" Girl Killers Given Life', *Mirror*, 26 May 1999.
7. James Clark, 'Suffering in Silence', *Daily Mail*, 6 August 1999.
8. *Newsnight*, BBC2, 12 July 1999.
9. Angelique Chrisafis, 'Lifting the Veil', *Guardian*, 14 August 2001.
10. Alexandra Frean, 'Forced Marriages "Not Legitimate"', *The Times*, 4 March 2000.
11. *R. v. Khan and Bashir* [1999], 1 Cr. App. R. (S) 329.

5

Silent witnesses:

domestic violence and black children

Meena Patel

> I dedicate this article to the children with whom we have worked
> and the children who have died as a result of violence and abuse — in
> particular to Victoria Climbié, who died tragically at the hands of her
> great aunt and her great aunt's boyfriend.

Very sparse nationwide statistics are available for the number of children affected by domestic violence. The Women's Aid Federation says that 28,500 children stayed in refuges in England in 1997/98. Some 70 per cent of children staying with mothers in refuges have also been abused by their fathers.[1] Yet, very little attention has been paid to the impact of domestic violence on children.[2] The majority of women who suffer emotional, physical, sexual assaults from their partners have children. Many of these children have witnessed the abuse, which results in emotional and behavioural problems. They often struggle to express their feelings of shame, guilt, fear and confusion. Children feel responsible for the violence: an 11-year-old boy said: 'I was scared of my dad. When he hit my mother I was scared that he would hit me and that is why I did not get involved to stop him.' Professionals, such as teachers, are often unable to recognise or deal with children who have problems. Where black children are concerned, racism is an additional factor: violence and abuse within the home can be compounded by racism and bullying in school.

This chapter is based on my experience over the years of working with women and children, both boys and girls, up to the age of 16, many of whom we have known from a young age. I explore the specific experiences of black children both inside and outside the home. I consider not just the problems of children who have left violent fathers but also the small minority of cases of girls whom we have helped to leave home because they experienced violence from their mothers. There is a need for more systematic work with children. Although we ourselves have not had the resources to work directly with children (apart from teenage girls), by assisting women to leave a violent situation we have indirectly assisted their children. In 1994 we set up a pilot project for children between the ages of 6 and 10 who had either witnessed or been subjected to violence. The project was set up as an art therapy group during the summer, where regular work could be done over the six-week period. The aim was to create an environment for children to express themselves and acquire social skills and confidence. As a result of the success of the pilot project we continued to offer this service over the summer period for the next three years. Due to lack of resources this project then had to be dropped, although research[3] on local facilities had highlighted our project as an important one because women felt safe enough to bring their children to our centre.

For many children, as for their mothers, domestic violence gives rise to the most traumatic period in their lives. They face deep uncertainty as to where they will be going and what the future holds for them. These children have witnessed their mother being assaulted and sexually and emotionally abused, with long-term psychological effects. In these situations the children are often forced to take sides, when they may love both their parents, to avoid further violence to their mother or to other children in the home. For many it is about pleasing their fathers. In some cases the boys act out what their fathers do and subject younger children in the family to violence.

All children have to cope with the process of uprooting that takes place when a woman leaves a violent spouse. They may not want to leave the comfort of their homes. They have to change schools and perhaps locality, a traumatic experience for most children at the best of times, but particularly difficult during a family crisis. It means leaving friends, family networks and support structures behind. It often leads to poverty and a change in status, as the mother may not be in employment. In the transitional phase, a woman and her children may find a refuge space. Although the refuge workers are committed and refuge facilities are improving all the time, it is often not pleasant to share cooking and living space with other similarly stressed families. For many children, having to go into a refuge is embarrassing and they worry about how others will treat them.

Worse for black children

It is likely, although the evidence is anecdotal as no research has been conducted in this area, that Asian children have prolonged exposure to violence because the cultural pressures for an Asian woman to stay within her marriage are greater than in society at large. As children of Asian parents, they will have to face racism and isolation. If their mother's right to stay in this country is dependent on their father, the children will worry about the prospect of deportation to an unfamiliar country. Many Asian fathers threaten to, and some actually do, abduct their children to their country of origin.

Children of asylum seekers face further stigma. Both the media and the state have whipped up a frenzy of feeling against bogus refugees so that the white community blames the refugees for soaking up resources. Where families are unable to afford school uniforms, the children are easy to recognise as refugees, get bullied at school and are unable to participate in the same way as their peer group. Those children who are placed in classes with younger children feel they cannot continue at school for fear of being ridiculed, whilst others placed with their peer group feel they cannot cope as their language skills are not the same (see Chapter 7, 'Jumping through Hoops').

Asian notions of 'family' can have a debilitating impact on children. The concept of izzat or family honour, which compromises the actions of all women, can enhance the feeling of shame for Asian children. It is reported that the rate of divorce and separation is lower in Asian communities; thus the sense of shame for a child in a lone-parent family is likely to be greater. If a woman leaves a violent marriage, she is likely to be ostracised by the rest of the family and community, which can lead to a greater sense of isolation for the children. Once the woman has lost her *izzat* as a result of her actions, she worries about who would marry her daughter(s). One mother said: 'I thought my husband would change, and as my daughter began getting older I thought that if I left then no one would marry my daughter. The community would point their finger at me and because of this my daughter would not find a suitable husband.'

Girls suffer different kinds of pressure from boys within a lone-parent Asian family. Despite the mother's experiences, she may want the girl to have an arranged marriage, to uphold the honour of the family, to be a good daughter, wife and mother. Boys are expected to take on the role of the man of the house and will often take on a disciplinary role vis-à-vis their sisters and even become violent towards their mothers. I have seen young boys who are allowed to have a say in how the home is run and to control their mother's behaviour, appearance and dress. A woman's decision to stay in or leave a violent marriage is often influenced by the impact it will have on the children. She may stay in a violent relationship for the sake of the children. It is also true that women will finally leave a violent marriage when the evidence of damage being caused to the children as a result is incontrovertible – when children become scared, do not achieve well in school, have low concentration levels, experience bed-wetting, and engage in violent outbursts towards the mother or other younger siblings, or when they are at direct risk of abuse themselves. One mother said that, 'I left because the children were getting damaged. My 5-year-old son would hide behind the doors, did not know how to behave toward his father, always tried to please him. The older son became scared of him.'

The vast majority of the women who come to us for assistance are unemployed, and are unaware of their rights. They have to learn to negotiate welfare benefits, learn the language, and acquire training skills and confidence to make their way in a society where the cultural norms may be unfamiliar to them. Where the mother faces language difficulties, the children may have to take on the role of interpreter with regard to state agencies such as social services, the council, the GP and sometimes at the police station, particularly when initial information needs to be passed on. This is a great responsibility for the children. If interviews with the authorities do not go well, children may feel that they did not represent their mother's point of view well enough. They also hear about the traumatic experiences that the mother has been subjected to. It is embarrassing for many women to talk about their lives. They are unlikely to talk about any sexual abuse they may have suffered if they have to communicate through their children.

Acknowledging the existence of sexual abuse of children by uncles, fathers or other members of the family is still very much a taboo in black families. Children may also feel that the family may break up as a result and it is therefore better not to say anything. Perpetrators are often not blamed and the abuse continues. In one case I helped a woman obtain court orders to evict her violent husband from the matrimonial home. She was reconciled with her husband a few months later for the sake of the children. About a year later, her son (8 years old) told her that his father was doing strange things to him at night and that he did not like it. He told his mother that he would not speak to anybody but me and was adamant I stay with him through the social services interview. The woman instigated divorce proceedings. Over the years the boy expressed his anger towards his father by lashing out at his younger sister. Counselling was provided by social services but he felt let down because the counsellor left after six weeks. 'What is the point if they all leave?' he demanded.

Service responses

Social services are more likely to intervene in a domestic violence case if children are involved, as it is their statutory responsibility to look after the interests of children. However, our experience has shown that Asian women and children seeking help from social services are often turned away on the assumption that Asian communities have their own mechanisms – the extended family and community and religious leaders – to resolve problems. Social services fear that they may be perceived as being racist if they intervene in Asian family life. This kind of response denies children their right to live free from violence. Our work has shown that on average it takes at least ten years for a woman to leave a violent situation. They will have tried the extended family, as well as community leaders and religious leaders, to resolve their problems before they come to us. White professionals find that black children's problems are too complex and tend to interpret their response as a rebellion against an oppressive culture and religion, or as a desire to become western-ised. Women also feel that the statutory sector would not under-stand their culture. Studies have shown that women are afraid of informing social services in case their children are removed. This is true for many of the women that we see. In one particular case a woman had been told by the police that if she did not do some-thing about the violence her children would be removed. It is vital that statutory bodies project a positive image that they are there to assist and not to remove children. However, in other cases, where a woman has left a violent partner, the police have been reluctant in removing the children and have informed husbands that they have the right to have contact with their children. Local authorities need to be involved to ensure that appropriate services are made available in every area.

Mothers who have managed to access refuges with their children have in some cases been able to get support and counselling for their children in order to deal with their immediate problems. However, this is a short-term response. The psychological effects on children need to be dealt with over a long period of time. Many children have never spoken about the abuse and violence that they had witnessed or been subjected to. Thangam Debbonaire believes that there is a chronic need for funds for outreach and aftercare work with children escaping domestic violence, especially those who have never been in a refuge or those who have left.[4]

Are children being heard?

Many children are fearful of reporting violence to the authorities for fear of not being believed and being returned to their homes. Children between the ages of 14 and 17 who manage to seek assist-ance are often reconciled with their families. With the younger children the question is often about the degree of violence they have faced and whether the mother will protect herself and her children by obtaining an ouster–exclusion order to remove the perpetrator from the home. There is a distinct difference in the way social services deal with children who are running away from abusive parents as opposed to children who are running away from domestic violence with their mothers. They are more likely to attempt reconciliation in the belief that the youngsters are being merely rebellious and that it is possible to resolve the 'culture clash'. Young black people also fear the repercussions of informing on their parents. A young Somali woman aged 16 said:

> The violence started when I was at high school, I had no one to turn to. I talked to my friends but could not talk to teachers. I did not think that they would do anything and if I told them they would talk to my parents. I was scared of this. I did call social services but they put the phone down on me and I have heard that they don't really do anything for Somalian people.

This is typical of the view of statutory bodies in our experience. The non-interventionist approach towards black families by statutory bodies is illustrated by the following case in which social services failed four young Asian girls seeking protection. They felt that they were not being heard and that the system had failed them.

Shazia, aged 22, and her three teenage sisters lived with their mother. Their father spent most of his time out of the country. All four had been subjected to violence and abuse from their mother over a number of years. Their mother placed restrictions on them: they were not allowed to go out or to have friends. If they did not return home on time from school they were subjected to physical abuse. Shazia approached social services for help because her mother had attempted to strangle her younger sister and she was scared of what might happen to them if the violence continued. She was afraid that her mother would kill her sister one day. Social services had informed her that they would need to write to their mother to set up a meeting with her. Shazia pleaded with them not to write or contact her mother, as things at home would get worse for them.

Shazia approached our organisation for assistance. She described how scared she was and stated that she needed to protect her sisters. She was afraid that one of her sisters would end up dead. We went back to social services to ask them to take the children into care whilst they investigated the case. They again refused to assist us. Instead they informed us that they had already written to the mother. When Shazia heard this she started shaking with fear and crying. She said that she had to go back home and see if her sisters were safe. At this stage we involved a solicitor, who prepared papers for us to be in court the next day to have the younger sisters removed. We were not sure whether the mother had received the letter from social services that day, so we devised a plan. I was to drop her near her home and she would wave to me from the window once she got in if things had gone wrong. That is exactly what happened and Shazia ran out of the house in a state. Her sisters had been beaten for reporting the mother to social services.

At this stage the only course of action was to contact the police and involve the Child Protection Team (CPT). The CPT asked for my help to remove the other sisters from the home. When we went to get them, we found that the CPT, not the social workers, were involved in the removal. The young girls were quaking with fear. They begged me to get them out of the house. The two younger girls had bruising around the body. I found out later that an anonymous report had been made before to social services about the abuse but no action had been taken.

Social services called several case conferences, from which they tried to exclude us. Under the Children Act, social services are expected to work together with voluntary or private agencies and education, health and housing workers to provide the best possible service for children in need. We think they tried to exclude us because they were worried that we would monitor what they did and that we would encourage the girls to press for their rights. But Shazia had insisted that I should be present, since I was the only one who had listened to her. At most case conferences, we find that we are the only organisation with relevant case histories on the family and the issues involved. Indeed, many of the cases are under investigation at our instigation. At these case conferences, the girls were told that they had to attend the mosque, as this was part of their culture and tradition. Shazia opposed this and said that they never went to the mosque and that, in fact, women do not go to the mosque. The authorities also tried to enforce mediation. It was unsuccessful because the eldest girl was adamant that she and her sisters did not want to return. Her own strength and the support she received from me enabled her to resist pressure from the authorities where others might have failed. They failed to listen to the girls, who were saying that they did not want to see their mother at that time. In this case the police worked jointly with us in taking statements and involved us at all levels. The girls did not want to pursue any charges as they still loved their mother.

This case also raises the issue of women as perpetrators of violence. Not enough attention has been paid to this area, partly because it is a very small minority of women who are violent and partly because feminists are wary of state attempts to deflect attention from the gendered nature of violence – it is predominantly men who are violent towards women in patriarchal societies. On the basis of my experience, I would say that women who are violent to their children are likely to get harsher treatment then men from the authorities because they are seen to deviate from their traditional role as carers. Some single women who are struggling to bring up children on their own often snap rather than respond rationally because they are unable to cope. Single women might end up being violent to their children because they feel that they do not have enough sanctions at their disposal to control unruly children in the absence of a father figure. The children themselves may be responding to loss by displaying disruptive behaviour patterns. It is reactive parenting at moments of stress. At times like this, social services and other agencies such as schools can step in, to identify problems and offer further support – as they did in the case of a young mother by providing longer nursery hours for pre-school children so that the mother could go to college – or provide expert guidance to the mother on dealing with the child's behaviour. Asian women may feel a greater need to bring up children, especially girls, within traditional cultural norms as a way of gaining respectability in the community.

It is very important to monitor the practices of state agencies as they have a tendency to try to reconcile families inappropriately. Recently a local school approached us to help a pupil of theirs, who, along with her sisters and brother, was being subjected to violence. Our immediate priority was to protect them. We managed to place the three girls, who all attended the same school, in a refuge. However, we were not able to rescue the younger brother because he was at home. The oldest was able to apply for a residency order to protect her two younger sisters. When we informed social services that the youngest brother had been subjected to violence, their response was that they were satisfied that the boy was safe and that the bruises that he had sustained were as a result of a fall, and that therefore no further action was required. The social worker even quoted the right to family life enshrined in the Human Rights Act in defence of her decision! Whilst at the refuge the girls were seen by social workers, who arranged for the girls to be reconciled with their family. All three girls went back home. A few weeks later we were contacted by the youngest girl (15), who stated that her sisters were getting married and that social services had not given her the opportunity to express her feelings about returning home; nor were they involved in monitoring the situation at home. This young girl is now self-harming and will not go to social services, as they failed her.

These cases show how statutory bodies often fail young children. The law requires social services to make an assessment where a child is in need and investigate allegations of child abuse. While we are not advocating the kind of overzealous removal of children by social services which has got them a bad press, we are saying that where children are being subjected to violence and abuse, like Shazia, they should be placed in care whilst investigations are carried out. Placing children on an at-risk register is another way of monitoring a situation. Where Asian children are attempting to escape forced marriages, social services often will not intervene as this is considered a cultural practice. Social services often say there is a lack of resources, that frontline staff are under immense pressure, and therefore children are slipping through the net. Whilst the issue of resources needs to be addressed urgently by the government, it cannot be used as an excuse for differential standards for children of different racial and cultural backgrounds.

Child protection?

Both the issue of funding and differential standards of care were central to the tragic case of Victoria Climbié, for whom Southall Black Sisters together with the Family Foundation group held a vigil and public meeting in December 2002. Victoria Climbié was an 8-year-old girl from West Africa who was sent to the UK by her parents to be looked after by her great aunt in the hope of a better life. Instead she was subjected to months of horrific torture and neglect by her great aunt and her aunt's boyfriend. They beat her on a daily basis with all manner of instruments and starved her. They tied her in a bin bag and made her sleep in a cold bath tub in her own urine and excrement. Eventually, in February 2000, Victoria died of hypothermia. Her great aunt and her boyfriend were tried and convicted for her murder.

Victoria's tragic death prompted the setting up of a major inquiry headed by Lord Laming into the circumstances of her death and the shocking mistakes made by a number of local authorities, the police, health services and even a children's charity, all of whom had had contact with Victoria but failed to protect her. The inquiry delivered some of the most scathing criticisms of the failures of the multi-agency approach to child protection to be seen in the UK. At the heart of this criticism were the arrogance of those in the most senior positions in the welfare system, their failure to accept responsibility for Victoria's death, and the complete breakdown of the multi-agency approach to child protection. The report made many recommendations, particularly aimed at improving accountability, but it did not in our view, give any emphasis to the lack of funding or to the need to ensure that child protection is not left at the bottom of the political agenda.

SBS felt compelled to make a submission to the Laming inquiry to raise the question of multiculturalism and its implications for the protection of children from minority communities. In our view, it was no accident that the failure to protect Victoria arose in part from the many misguided notions of her cultural background held by the professionals who had contact with her. Her social workers had made sweeping cultural assumptions about Victoria's relationship with her aunt. For instance, Victoria's bizarre behaviour of standing to attention at the side of her hospital bed whenever her aunt visited her was taken to be a sign of 'respect for her elders' rather than a sign of fear!

SBS's involvement in the Victoria Climbié campaign had a two-fold aim: to provide support to the few individuals who were trying to campaign around the case and to highlight yet again the problematic aspects of multiculturalism that had played such a significant part in the state's failure to protect Victoria but that were in danger of being overlooked.

Fear of abduction

A substantial part of our work with children has involved pre-emptive work around abduction and/or enabling women to recover children who have been abducted. Separation from violent partners does not necessarily guarantee safety for women or their children. Fathers use family members, or in northern England bounty hunters, who actively track down women based on information provided by the taxi networks. Bounty hunters also use friends and family contacts within the DSS to trace women's current whereabouts through their National Insurance numbers. More recently private detectives have been used to track down women and children. Violent men often threaten to abduct children as a way of getting back at their wives for daring to leave, for going against their culture and tradition, and as a means of getting women to return home. In some situations children have been abducted and taken abroad. The abduction of children can have a psychological and emotional impact on the child for the rest of his/her life. Children are often manipulated to hate the absent parent. Many women are constantly afraid that their children will be abducted during contact or tracked down and, in some cases, taken out of the country.

Saira was referred to us by the homeless persons unit of Ealing Council. Saira had managed to escape a violent husband who was wealthy and influential, but had been forced to leave her three sons behind. She was frightened that her husband would take the children out of the country and she would never see them again. The same day that Saira came to us we attempted to remove the children whilst they were at school. We managed to remove the oldest two, but by the time we arrived at the youngest child's school we were informed that the father had taken him. We obtained a court order for the child to be allowed to live with his mother. However, the father had gone into hiding, making it impossible to enforce the order. Saira was sure that an impenetrable wall of silence had been built by her husband with the assistance of the community. Family members informed Saira that her son had been sighted in Pakistan and later in America. Saira is desperate to find her son and continues to search for him, even though they have been separated for ten years.

Those children who are taken abroad, particularly to the Asian subcontinent, are very rarely reunited with their mothers. Many fathers have family and homes abroad. Children can easily be hidden away because the community will collude in that process both here and abroad. Some may have dual nationality, which allows the British state to shrug off responsibility to find them and return them home. The Hague Convention provides for the return of children who have been wrongfully abducted from the country where they are habitually resident. However, not all countries are signatories to the Convention, and even where they are it may take time before children are returned. The judicial system in other countries may be corrupt or extremely slow. In addition, court orders obtained in the UK for the return of children who are abducted to the Indian subcontinent are not enforceable in those countries.

Children are exposed to the danger of being abducted at the time of contact with their fathers. Since the Children Act 1989 came into force, the courts have interpreted the Act's emphasis on the welfare of children to mean continued contact with their fathers. Often a history of violence towards the mother will not be enough for a judge to ban contact or order supervised contact, unless the mother can procure expert reports or psychological evidence about the trauma caused to the child. Women's fears of abduction are often not taken seriously.

In some cases where we have helped women fleeing domestic violence in their country of origin and coming to the UK with their children, and where the father has lodged an application, the British courts have forced the return of the children to the father or ordered the issue of custody to be decided by the overseas court. In these cases, the courts have resisted arguments about risks posed to women and their children if they are returned to a country where they would be subject to domestic violence or child abuse. In Islamic states, many women also complain of sexual discrimination, where they would not have equal access to custody rights, and may even be punished by the state for transgressing social mores. These issues are not being adequately addressed by groups like Reunite, who have championed the cause of women whose children have been abducted and taken overseas. Reunite has been reluctant to criticise the British courts.

The legal pitfalls

One of the major concerns for women when leaving a violent relationship is the issue of residence and contact with their children. The Children Act emphasises the importance of families in children's lives and states that both parents have equal right to contact and residency. In April 1999, *Dispatches*, the Channel 4 documentary slot, highlighted the failure of the judicial system to take domestic violence into account when deciding whether or not a child should continue to see a non-custodial parent after separation even if it causes untold terror for the child.

We advise women to take their children with them, otherwise residency orders are hard to obtain. In some cases where women are forced to flee a violent situation, they have to leave without their children. For them it is an uphill struggle to be reunited with their children, as the law will often not remove children from a settled environment even though they may have witnessed the abuse and/or been subjected to violence. On one occasion, a woman in such a situation rang up, desperate to talk to somebody. She believed that the 'legal system let her down'. Her husband was in the matrimonial home with the children and she was forced to pay child maintenance. She often had no money to pay her rent. She cried, 'How can I live? Maybe I would have been better off in the home. He pursues me even though we are divorced. Why are men able to escape the system and women trapped within it?' She felt that it would have been better to keep silent than to speak up.

The other hurdle for women is contact. More and more men seek contact orders for their children. Contact orders give the absent parent further power to harass, bully and endanger the lives of the mother and children. In child services, contact is widely believed to be in the interest of the child but we have found that it is often used by the father to make life difficult for the woman. We have found that increasingly men use arguments such as: the children will be better off with them rather than living in poverty in a lone-parent household; the children will suffer a loss of cultural identity because the woman will place herself outside the community once she divorces her husband; the extended family will not be able to contribute to their upbringing; the girls will not be able to have an arranged marriage if they live with their mother as she will be seen as a fallen woman by the community because she has left her husband. As argued elsewhere, the pre-eminence of multicultural-ism in state policy makes the courts particularly sympathetic to such arguments and may order contact and even custody. Our experience has shown us that when women fear for their lives and those of their children, these fears are well founded. We believe that only the individual woman knows how far her husband would go to track her and her children down.

In some cases, where there may be concerns about the father's behaviour and the possibly adverse impact of contact, supervised access may be offered. This often takes place in a contact centre with trained staff to ensure that the absent parent does not use contact to harass the woman or children. However, these centres are few and far between. The waiting time is long and the sessions are short, often only a couple of hours long, and are offered on a short-term basis. Many contact centres are still in churches or are informal arrangements. As a result of lobbying by women's groups, the gov-ernment has now committed itself to improving and increasing proper contact centres.

It is the duty of the Children and Family Court Advisory and Support Services (CAFCASS) to ascertain the feelings of children with regard to contact. However, children are often confused about their feelings. Many children may want to have contact with their father even if they or their mother have been subjected to violence from him. On the other hand, they may feel that they are betraying their mother if they say they want to see their father. In other cases, children who express a wish for no contact with their father may be ignored. The number of CAFCASS officers who believe that women get manipulated by those 'women's libbers' who run refuges into denying contact to the fathers or believe that a mother has influ-enced the child adversely is shockingly high.

Over the years we have seen many women and children die as a result of not being believed by the system. In 2000, Shazia Rathore and her two children Saba and Zeeshan were stabbed to death by her ex-husband. He had gone to the house to pick up the children on a weekend custody visit.[5] In January 1996, Imtiaz Begum, her son and three daughters were killed by her husband after she collected her son from a contact visit. He is now serving five life sentences for murder. Those women who refuse contact are threatened with or imprisoned for breaching contact orders. They are seen as hostile or malicious in their behaviour. Despite horrific cases like these, the Lord Chancellor's department, in their consultation paper *Making Contact Work* (2001), implies that mothers who oppose contact are 'irrational'. Indeed, in February 2002, the government announced a raft of measures to penalise parents who failed to comply with contact orders, including fines, community service, attending parenting classes and being forced to undergo psychiatric help. Both the report and the government's announcement failed to understand why women oppose contact and risks associated with domestic violence.

However, there have been positive test cases where violent fathers were denied direct contact because of the damaging effects of domestic violence on children. In addition, the government has introduced Good Practice Guidelines, which allow courts to make a finding of fact where domestic violence has been alleged in contact hearings, and thus deny contact or order supervised contact. As we know, many women will not have witnesses when subjected to violence and may not contact the police or other bodies for fear of repercussions. Asian women may not speak the language and sometimes are unaware of the system, and the issue of shame and honour may deter them from seeking help. Young children may not speak about the violence for all the reasons listed above. Indeed, a survey by the Women's Aid Federation of England (WAFE) shows that, despite some improvements, contact orders are still being granted in cases of domestic violence and child abuse. Rights of Women challenges the assumption that it is always in the best interests of the child to have contact with the father.[6] Their view is that the law should be amended to include a general presumption against contact in circumstances of domestic violence. This is already the case in New Zealand where there is a legislative presumption against residence or unsupervised access being granted to violent partners. WAFE is also calling for similar changes.

The way we care for our children has become the litmus test of a humane society. The success of the anti-smacking campaign shows how far we have travelled down the road where even casual violence towards children is no longer acceptable. This is the prevailing ethos within which we conduct debates about the welfare of children and the development of social policy to deliver the best services. Of course lack of resources means that many children, like Victoria Climbié, slip through the net and experience terrible torture at the hands of their 'carers' and die appalling deaths. Apart from the question of resources, race and sex discrimination in society means that black children continue to get a raw deal from the state and that girls are more likely to be sexually and physically abused. Asian girls in particular face a clampdown on their individual aspirations as they are expected to be the vehicles of traditional cultural values to future generations.

Notes

1. *Domestic Violence Statistical Factsheet No. 3*, WAFE, August 1999.
2. *Domestic Violence Statistical Factsheet No. 1*, WAFE, August 2001.
3. *Community Solutions: A Study of Community Capacity in Southall*, Southall Regeneration Partnership and Ealing Regeneration and Housing, London 1998.
4. Thangam Debbonaire, 'Work with Children in Women's Aid Refuges and After', in Audrey Mullender and Rebecca Morely, eds, *Children Living with Domestic Violence: Putting Men's Abuse of Women on the Child Care Agenda*, Whiting & Birch, London 1996.
5. Helen Carter, 'Jury Hears Boy's 999 Murder Call'. *Guardian*, 24 October 2000.
6. Article 12 of the UN Convention on the Rights of the Child came into force in September 1990.

6

Sad, mad or angry?

Mental illness and domestic violence

Hannana Siddiqui and Meena Patel

Many of the women we see at the centre have mental health problems which have arisen directly as a result of the abuse they have suffered. A small percentage of women may have a pre-existing psychiatric disorder, which may or may not have been aggravated by their problems and can blur the already tenuous distinctions between the two areas. Over the years we have learnt to recognise those women who may require medical treatment because of their psychiatric condition and to refer them to the relevant experts. However, we have found that the majority of women's experience of mental illness and depression is caused by environmental factors and requires social welfare intervention to overcome it. Too often, such women have been subjected to the medical model of treatment without serious attention being paid to the circumstances in which they live. A woman who attempts suicide may be diagnosed as suffering from depression and prescribed drugs when what she may really need is assistance to escape from the oppression which makes her suicidal in the first place. The connection between abuse and depression is not understood, and women can be treated as if they are 'mad' even if all they do is leave a violent situation or rebel against oppressive practices. An assertive woman who refuses to conform to the stereo-type of a passive and obedient wife, sister, daughter and daughter-in-law can be regarded as mentally ill or deliberately labelled as such to delegitimise her claim to freedom and equality. Within the

Asian community, where mental illness is still a taboo, women can find themselves in a catch-22 position: if they rebel, they may set in motion even greater oppression, such as a forced marriage to an unsuitable person as a way of controlling their 'madness'.

This chapter looks at the range of mental health problems that we have encountered over the years and the strategies that we have used to deal with them, the interventions we have made to change state policy so that it is more sensitive to the needs of Asian women, and the way in which the state and the community collude in pathologising women when it is convenient to do so. However, we have continuing dilemmas on when and if to section women, their consequent loss of civil liberties, certain treatments like electro-convulsive therapy (ECT) that could cause lasting damage, and overdependency on drugs. There is also a pressing need for research on Asian women and their mental health needs. We do not even know how many Asian women are languishing in hospitals, many of whom we suspect may be there as a result of misdiagnosis.

An early case (1987), that of 15-year-old twins 'Parminder' and 'Ravinder', represented a steep learning curve for us in distinguishing between the social and medical aspects of psychiatric illness. They complained of violence from their father. They were neglected and abused by their stepmother, who denied them food and clothing. Parminder was made to look after and cook for three younger stepbrothers and stepsisters. Their mother had left home when the sisters were born. Their father had threatened her with a knife. There had since been no contact with their mother. The sisters were also afraid that they would be taken to India to be married when they reached the age of 16. We took our normal course of action and planned for them to leave home when they turned 16. For a few months, we helped the sisters take their personal belongings out of the house. They did this little by little so that their father and step-mother would not become suspicious. We also contacted a housing association. They were willing to offer them a flat once they left home. One of the workers at SBS became their legal guardian. It seemed the perfect solution. The sisters eventually left home and moved into their own flat.

At first the sisters did well. They both went to college and did their GCSEs. Ravinder in particular obtained good results. Parminder, however, became increasingly hyperactive and began to refuse to come near Southall, although it was safe for her to do so. She said there were 'too many Asians' in the area and she had grown to hate them. Ravinder informed us that at home Parminder had become obsessed with cleanliness and talked about wanting to be pure. She was talking to herself. One evening, we received a call from the hospital. The nurse told us that Parminder had been sectioned. She had been babysitting for a friend and had threatened to throw the baby out of the window. We were shocked. Why would Parminder do such a thing? We had noticed that she was behaving strangely, but had not recognised the signs of mental illness.

Parminder's breakdown revealed a hidden story. Psychiatric treatment uncovered a long history of sexual abuse from her father. However, not even the experts at the Tavistock Clinic felt that they could make a connection between the abuse and the mental illness. In their view, Parminder had paranoid schizophrenia which may or may not have been triggered by the abuse. Her claim for criminal injuries compensation was rejected because the Tavistock could not provide a report establishing the link. It was too traumatic for her to appeal against this decision.

Ravinder, too, was horrified. She had not been aware of the sexual abuse and said it had not happened to her. She refused to believe her sister's story. Gradually, however, Parminder recovered from her acute state; for many years she went in and out of hospital care. When not in hospital, she was housed in a hostel with high support needs, where she received considerable assistance, particularly from her caseworker. Although the untimely death of her caseworker destabilised Parminder for a while, she was eventually able to make a recovery, having acknowledged her illness.

Parminder left the hostel and moved into housing association accommodation with her partner, whom she had met in hospital where he too was receiving treatment for a mental illness. We were extremely worried when we heard that Parminder was pregnant. She gave birth to a son and the couple married. Parminder learnt to manage her condition successfully under the care of the hospital. It may be that the responsibility of having to care for a young baby helped to stabilise her condition. It certainly changed our attitudes towards the reproductive rights of those with psychiatric problems.

We continue to maintain contact with them; Meena Patel, who has become a close friend, has been unofficially adopted as 'aunty' to their son.

During Parminder's breakdown, Ravinder had remained in their flat. She increasingly isolated herself and refused any assistance from us. She, too, began to show signs of mental illness, which she refused to acknowledge. She resisted any medical help. Her illness, however, is not as extreme as that of Parminder and has not been properly diagnosed. It is ironic that we saw Ravinder as a success story. However, her inability to come to terms with her illness – the first step towards improvement – has left her in a situation worse than Parminder. To us it is clear that she suffers from paranoia. She talks to herself, is extremely judgemental of others and unreasonably argumentative. She is barely able to function on a day-to-day basis. She has lost her job and has refused to pay rent or other bills for essentials. She also refuses to claim benefits or seek help to deal with her debts. As a result, Ravinder has been evicted from the flat and now lives in a hostel for the homeless. Ravinder continues to search for a family and, in her desperation, has even considered reconciliation with her father. Her stepmother, however, does not want her and her father has also become mentally ill.

This was a complex case where the lines between mental illness and psychiatric disorder were so blurred that even the experts could not disentangle them. We did not have the resources to undertake intensive outreach work and maintain a constant check on the sisters. Although we were right in helping the sisters to escape abuse, we wondered whether it would have been better to place them in a more supportive environment when they left home, rather than in a flat on their own. It became clear to us that both sisters had been too young to cope on their own and needed a more gradual adjustment to the outside world. However, despite our inexperience, with the help of health professionals such as psychiatrists, hostel workers and the charity Mind (in Hammersmith and Fulham), we were able to turn the situation around, particularly for Parminder. Her condition has now stabilised with effective monitoring by professionals, enabling her to live a happy and fulfilling life. We know that drugs and sectioning may be the only option in some instances – for example, when a patient is a risk to themselves or others, as was the case with Parminder. The intervention of the mental health services was crucial in this case in coping with a crisis situation and providing long-term support.

Women in prison

Some cases of untreatable mental illness show up the deficiencies of both the social and medical models. In the case of Roopinder, a young Asian woman who was convicted of the murder of her ten-week-old baby in 1992, she was found to be suffering from a personality disorder which was untreatable. On appeal in 1995 we succeeded in reducing her murder conviction to manslaughter, although taking instructions from women like Roopinder, when they are in a volatile state of mind, is extremely difficult. She had to be helped to accept ownership of her decisions. We faced similar problems in the case of Porn Enticknap, a Thai woman who, in 1994, was charged with the murder of her husband. She believed her husband and his family were using black magic to kill her and her child. There was a history of abuse from her husband, who brought her into the UK as a 'mail order bride', forcing her to work long hours as a machinist at home. She felt exploited and belittled by his abusive comments. Porn was diagnosed as suffering from mental illness, which caused considerable problems in obtaining instructions from her. She was suffering from delusions in prison and could not give a coherent account of what had happened. However, her manslaughter plea on the grounds of diminished responsibility was accepted by the Crown Prosecution Service and a hospital order was issued.

Although a hospital order was appropriate in the cases of Roopinder and Porn, we worry that women may be wrongly sentenced to special secure hospitals with prison-like conditions for indefinite periods, rather than receive hospital treatment or appropriate care in the community. In Roopinder's case we had great difficulties in finding appropriately supported accommodation for her needs. Neither end of the spectrum was suitable: secure units for the severely mentally ill patients or low-support hostels. Our dilemma was resolved when she agreed to attend hospital regularly for limited treatment and supervision, medication and group therapy.

The prison environment does little to help women recover from depression or mental illness. Indeed it can exacerbate their condition, as illustrated by the high number of women who are dependent on drugs, commit suicide or self-harm in prison. In order to maintain a docile population, prisons routinely prescribe anti-depressants, creating overdependency which is hard to break even when women are released from prison, as witnessed in the case of Emma Humphries. Emma was released in 1995 following a successful appeal against her conviction after serving a ten-year sentence for the murder of her violent partner. She died in 1998 after accidentally taking an overdose of the prescription drugs to which she had become accustomed in prison.

'The actions of my husband and family'

The underlying social causes of depression and mental breakdown amongst black women relate to problems such as domestic violence; forced marriage; demands for dowry; restrictions on lifestyle, such as limitation on movement, dress and friendships; and denial of education and career opportunities. Other contributing factors can be racism, immigration/asylum issues, poverty and homelessness.

Research has shown that Asian women are two to three times more likely than women in the general population to commit suicide. Studies have also shown that the rate of attempted and contemplated suicide is high, including one from our local hospital in Ealing.[1] Our experience clearly reflects these findings. Most women who come to SBS have contemplated suicide, many have attempted it at least once, and a few, tragically, have committed suicide. Many self-harm in other ways through self-mutilation and eating disorders. Most suffer from depression, ranging from mild to severe clinical depression, including conditions such as post-traumatic stress disorder[2] and battered women's syndrome.

The fact that Asian women are more likely to kill or harm themselves does not mean Asian communities are more oppressive than white society. However, Asian and other women from minority communities have greater obstacles to overcome both inside and outside the community when escaping abuse. These obstacles are the result of a double discrimination, racial and sexual, against black and minority women.

Why do Asian women feel they have no option but to kill themselves? Some suicides are a sign of despair, where there is no will to live, but how many were unintended – self-harm gone wrong? The goals for women who self-harm are different to those who want to kill themselves. However, self-harm increases the likelihood of committing suicide. Many attempted suicides and other self-harming practices are a cry for help and a desire for a better life, rather than death. Often these are coping or survival strategies used by women to release tension, escape pressures, protest and/or exercise some control over their lives. Imrana Afzal, who had escaped a forced marriage in Pakistan, explains why she self-harmed:

> I slit my wrist as a protest. I slit my wrist on 14 August which is the day of Independence for both India and Pakistan after the British Raj, as a protest to illustrate that is what you actually are expecting me to do. To say I am made of flesh and I am made of blood, and I do bleed and this is hurting me. And you say you want my happiness, but this is not conducive to my happiness at all.[3]

Women harm themselves externally and internally in different ways to gain attention, to atone for guilt, to cleanse and obtain relief. Although there is insufficient research into why women use particular methods, it may be the case that some Asian women use fire to show their good character to the world, based on popular notions of the test of fire to prove female sexual purity in Hinduism. Our experience shows that hanging, pills and household substances such as bleach are the favoured methods in the UK. Fire is more widely used in the Asian community than in the wider community, perhaps reflecting subcontinental practices. Some methods may be used due to their accessibility: for example, kerosene is more widely available in the Indian subcontinent, while pills are more readily accessible in the UK. Suicide and self-harm may be used to restore honour or, in some cases, to bring shame and dishonour. For instance, one woman asked SBS, 'If I wrote a suicide note naming my husband and his family, would that dishonour them?'

Suicide or homicide?

In 1984, Krishna Sharma hanged herself after years of domestic violence. The coroner pronounced a verdict of suicide. We felt that she had been driven to kill herself as a result of her husband's abuse. We often ask ourselves if the death of an Asian woman was indeed a suicide or a homicide. But the evidence is difficult to find, especially if the woman's family and community close ranks and/or the criminal justice system fails to investigate the matter fully.

Nazia and her daughter Sana were killed in a house fire in a locked bedroom in Bradford in March 1999. Moments before her death, Nazia had made a call to the emergency services and said 'my husband burned me, please help me'. On an earlier occasion, Nazia had informed the police that she was due to leave her husband. She alleged domestic violence.

Nazia's husband was charged with murder, although the case was initially dismissed by the magistrate's court due to insufficient evidence. The Crown Prosecution Service applied to reopen the case. In July 2000, the case was dismissed for the same reasons by Sheffield Crown Court and a verdict of not guilty entered. The judge ruled that the crucial tape-recorded message where Nazia accused her husband was inadmissible. The judge had looked into the possibility of 'concoction' of this statement by the deceased and excluded the tape on the basis of witness statements which alleged that Nazia had threatened to burn down the house and destroy her husband's furniture. Some believed it was suicide or a faked suicide; others claimed revenge was the motive, or that Nazia accidentally killed herself and her daughter when she had lit the fire. However, one of these later witnesses subsequently married Nazia's husband! The history of abuse remained unexamined. We felt the jury should have been asked to assess the evidence and give a verdict.

Suicide seemed an unlikely explanation because Nazia had made a positive decision to leave her husband and had already made all the arrangements. SBS took up the case. Hannana Siddiqui worked with a journalist, Eve Ann Prentice, from The Times, to investigate the matter. We also enlisted the help of local contacts in the area. All the witnesses that we managed to speak to were too afraid to be identified. Nazia's friends were afraid of reprisals or fearful of causing problems with their own family and the wider community. Nazia was married to a cousin, and her family were too closely connected with her husband's family to raise questions.

The police stated that they were surprised by the court's decision, but felt there was little more they could do. Eve Prentice found that the coroner had the power to reconvene the inquest, which had opened prior to the criminal case. We had a problem in finding anyone close to Nazia to request an inquest. The Times raised the case in order to encourage people to come forward. SBS had written to the coroner requesting an inquest and that SBS be recognised as an interested third party in the case as well as experts who could provide evidence to assist the courts in examining background cultural and social issues. An inquest was now the only way left to provide proper public scrutiny of two violent and unnatural deaths.

In late 2001, the West Yorkshire coroner consulted Nazia's family, including the husband, who did not want an inquest. Subsequently, the coroner decided not to resume the adjourned inquest. He also refused to recognise SBS as an interested party. We applied for a judicial review of his decision and began a campaign calling for justice for Nazia Bi and her daughter Sana. This was the first time a non-governmental organisation had challenged a coroner's decision not to recognise it as an interested party in a domestic violence case. Third-party intervention can also help to improve the state's response to domestic violence, suicide, murder and honour killings of Asian and minority women (see also Chapter 11, 'Shifting Terrains').

Driven to kill

In cases of women who kill violent partners, we have attempted to show that mental health is directly affected by a set of social circumstances involving domestic violence, which can make women act out of anger and fear and not necessarily as a result of a psychiatric disorder. However, although we have presented expert reports to explain this, the courts are more open to medical experts, thus pathologising women's response to domestic violence.

Whilst the murder of women by men may be considered less worthy of a hearing, women who are driven to kill a violent man often receive considerable attention and investigation from the criminal justice system. Women are often prosecuted and convicted of murder, rather than the lesser offence of manslaughter, despite a history of domestic violence from the deceased. In comparison, men are more likely to be successful in having their plea of man-slaughter accepted by the Crown Prosecution Service (see 'Shifting Terrains') and the courts on the grounds of diminished responsi-bility and provocation, despite a history of violence against the deceased.

It is assumed women are mad or bad rather than angry or acting in self-defence in committing what is, for women, the relatively unusual act of killing. Where a plea of manslaughter is successful, diminished responsibility is the most common defence for women. This individualises the problem by giving the woman a specific psychiatric history. Society, including the courts, prefers to delink social pressures from the act of killing: accepting that domestic violence provoked a woman to kill represents a direct challenge to patriarchy. However, even when a woman pleads diminished respon-sibility, our experience suggests that she will have to produce twice the medical evidence of that of a man. Zoora Shah had to produce a number of psychiatric reports to show the Court of Appeal that she was severely depressed when she killed an abusive man. Neverthe-less, her appeal was dismissed because she had previously lied about the killing. It seems that even medical evidence counts for little for battered women, who are not seen as deserving of justice.

Where women have refused to use psychiatric evidence they have been heavily penalised. For example, Sara Thornton initially refused to use any psychiatric evidence in her appeal against her conviction for the murder of her alcoholic and abusive husband. She wanted to use the sole defence of provocation; however, that appeal was dis-missed. It was only when she added diminished responsibility to her defence that her conviction for murder was overturned. Kiranjit, for her part, argued both provocation and diminished responsibility, and was ultimately successful with the latter defence.

'And the community says I must stay with him'

Mental illness is a taboo within Asian and many other communities. Anyone acting outside the norm can be labelled mentally ill. There is often a stigma, leading to ostracism, and a wariness and fear of the mentally ill, thinking it may be 'catching'. They are treated as if they are less intelligent, isolated and ridiculed like the 'village fool'. Their families feel confused, burdened, and want to hide them from the outside world or quickly get rid of them through forced marriage, hospitalisation or by abandoning them abroad. The most extreme version of this belief is the view that mental illness is a form of possession by demons and evil spirits.

In this context, women suffering from mental health problems receive little support or sympathy. The community also does little to protect women from abuse. Indeed, the active involvement of elders and community leaders adds to pressures on women to return to violent situations at home. A woman's non-conformist behaviour affects the marriage prospect of her sisters, and the woman may find herself married off to the lowest bidder or to a man with an undisclosed history of mental illness. In one case, a young Asian woman's family took her to Bangladesh to give her electric shock treatment for 'mental illness' after she refused to marry. We managed to prevent this by using contacts in Bangladesh to help her return to the UK before she received the treatment or was forced into marriage.

Even where medical help is sought it may be inappropriate. The family may take the woman to the family GP, many of whom are Asian. The GP may feel a loyalty to the family and be sympathetic to their beliefs. Breach of confidentiality by Asian family GPs has been known to occur quite regularly. The GP may put her on drugs and even section her. He may simply ignore or medicalise the problem. A woman may go to an unofficial 'witchdoctor', who will use black magic to heal her, or to the priest, who will drive out the evil spirit through prayer, and sometimes even a beating. In 1992, a father and a Muslim priest were involved in torturing a 20-year-old Asian woman, Kousar Bashir, to death during a ritual exorcism. The woman's father was convicted of murder after acting on the instructions of the priest, who was found guilty of causing grievous bodily harm. The woman endured eight days of brutal beatings to rid her of an evil spirit called 'John Wayne'. She was starved of food and sleep, and hot chilli powder was pushed down her throat. She was also savagely beaten, kicked and stamped upon. Members of her family were told that she did not feel any pain when the beatings were taking place.

These responses are not confined to Asian communities. Some African-Caribbean women also talk about turning to witchcraft or to the Christian Church. Sometimes Asian women have converted to Christianity, feeling their own religion is oppressive and/or that they have been rejected by their own community. In one case, an Asian woman who had converted to Christianity was persuaded by her church to drop both her divorce petition and her case for child custody against her husband on the grounds that it was against her religion. She talked about evil spirits ruling her life and how she must 'behave herself' in order to escape them.

The professional approach

In the 1980s, Dr Miriam Stoppard asserted in a radio interview that Western models of medical intervention may not be appropriate for Asian women because there were internal mechanisms in the Asian community, such as the extended family network, to deal with them. The need to respect different cultures has been used by professional agencies and policymakers to promote the non-interventionist approach in minority communities. Domestic violence and other oppressive practices against women are not addressed because it is assumed that outside interference would amount to intolerance or racism.

While non-intervention is a common approach, we find that where there is a response, it often involves medicalisation or mediation, rather than social welfare intervention. Failure to intervene, inconsistent responses, inadequate housing, counselling and community care services, racial discrimination or misdiagnosis of the problem and its causes remain major causes for concern.

Many professionals, including doctors, social workers, police officers and the courts, in effect collude with violent and abusive family and community members by accepting their interpretation of the situation. Women within these communities are thus silenced and their needs remain unmet.

'Nina', a young Asian woman, had experienced domestic violence from her husband and his extended family. As a result, she took an overdose and was treated in, but not admitted to, hospital. She had only attempted self-harm on one occasion and had no diagnosed mental illness. Upon separation, her husband applied for a residence order for their child. In support of his application, his mother said:

> I fully support my son's application for residence and believe it would be the [child's] best interest to reside with the applicant as opposed to the respondent. I am concerned that [sic] the respondent's history of self-harm and believe that it is likely to happen again given the present circumstances. The respondent has been ringing us regularly since the court proceedings started. I do not think she is sure of what she is doing and I fear that she may become mentally unstable again. In the past she has tried to commit suicide and as a result was admitted to hospital. There is another occasion when she cut her finger and again was rushed to hospital. The respondent does this to get attention and to emotionally blackmail the applicant into doing what she wants.

The court did not make a ruling on the case as the woman was persuaded to reconcile with her husband, although, at a later stage, the couple separated again. Violent partners and family members often allege 'mental illness' to undermine women's right to justice.

In some instances, professionals view the problem as that of a 'culture clash' between women and their families – Westernisation has led to Asian women demanding rights and more freedom. In these cases, mediation is often considered an option by professional agencies, particularly if the family is exerting pressure on them. This can simply add to the stress that the woman is already facing.

Most people complaining of depression are quickly prescribed anti-depressants and sleeping pills by their GP. Some are referred to psychiatric help and a few to counselling and psychotherapy. Most women at SBS who have sought help for depression have been prescribed drugs; very few receive any other help. Asylum seekers and those with an insecure immigration status cannot even access adequate medical help as many GPs refuse to register them. Black women are overrepresented in mental health wards and units, particularly African-Caribbean women, although there is a substantial number of Asian women in areas such as Southall. Some of this is due to racial stereotyping, some of it to the fact that women have stepped outside the acceptable norms of behaviour.

Racism, too, plays its part in driving black and minority women to depression, and in how agencies respond to their needs. Refugee women or those with immigration problems, for example, become depressed because of fear of deportation and uncertainty about their and their children's future. This situation is compounded by a history of abuse, and fears about gender persecution or abuse once they return to the country of their origin.

Many women can recover or cope with depression and mental illness if they are provided with appropriate help. This means dealing with their social welfare, legal and housing needs. At times, they may also need medical help, but this must be correctly assessed, if possible at an early stage. Sometimes women are unable to make decisions without counselling or psychiatric help, whilst others may want this intervention once they have resolved some of their practical problems. For example, they may have to leave an abusive situation, obtain court orders or find safe housing. Professional agencies tend to separate mental health issues from social welfare intervention. Some cases are referred to SBS and other agencies for welfare assistance, but this is less common than women being diverted into medical services. We often find that we have to act as advocates on behalf of women to make other professionals aware of their social welfare needs and the underlying social causes of their depression, such as domestic violence.

Lack of resources also makes it difficult to assist women. Many agencies do not have proper interpretation facilities, and even fewer have specialist workers. There are long waiting lists and a dearth of black female counsellors, psychiatrists and psychologists; those who do exist may not offer free services under the NHS or may lack an understanding of domestic violence and other forms of abuse. In our experience, psychiatrists have shown a lack of understanding of how the race and gender axis impacts on the mental health of black women. They may also hold conservative views about women. Non-directive counselling services may also fail to consider the need to give advice and make appropriate referrals. In casework we tend to provide more directive counselling and offer advice and practical assistance. Recently we have established a formal counselling service with a qualified therapist. This combined approach, offering both formal counselling and social welfare assistance, has been very effective in alleviating mental health problems.

Other agencies also have a major role in supporting women to escape abuse and overcome mental illness. However, these agencies have little understanding of the issues or lack a willingness to improve services, leading to a loss of rights and protection. Parminder gave a statement to the police about the physical and sexual abuse she experienced from her father. The Crown Prosecution Service, however, did not prosecute because of her mental state. In other cases, professionals have been unable to spot depression or illness because of stereotypical views of Asian women. For example, if an Asian woman is passive, with other family members speaking for her, it is assumed that this is the norm and depression may not be detected. Sometimes women present their mental health and social problems in other ways, for example by complaining of frequent aches and pains. Alternatively, African and Caribbean women are perceived as loud and aggressive. Such behaviour is itself seen to be abnormal and a sign of mental illness. And if they fail to state their problem, then it is assumed they do not have one!

While women's aid, rape crisis and in particular black women's groups may offer some of the best services, they are underfunded and scarce. Unfortunately, few women's refuges and hostels can accept women with mental health problems due to their high support needs. Local authority housing departments and social services also may refuse to accept women as vulnerable if depression or mental illness is not medically diagnosed, which may be difficult to obtain in borderline cases or where women refuse to acknowledge their illness. Even where women are accepted, they may be placed in isolated bed-and-breakfast or hostel accommodation. Placement with hostels or services which specifically meet the needs of the mentally ill are few and far between and have long waiting lists. In these placements, women are often separated from their children. There is a need to develop more specialist safe emergency and long-term housing to meet the high support needs of mentally ill black women and their children.

The failure of community care services means that abused black women are driven back into abusive situations, which leads to a deterioration in their mental health. Indeed, it is assumed that the extended family and the community will look after their own, where the burden is shifted to husbands, other women in the family and even children.

Intensive specialist work is essential in enabling women to escape abuse and rebuild their lives by making informed decisions, giving instructions and maintaining a consistent course of action. We often find that agencies refuse to recognise our role as vital advocates, experts and counsellors. Effective action is illustrated by cases where there has been close cooperation and equal partnership between agencies. It is the one area of service delivery where the multi-agency approach is not only beneficial but necessary.

Going to the courts

Twenty years ago, we challenged the community by protesting outside the homes of perpetrators of violence and exposing them. In Krishna Sharma's case (see Timeline) we stood outside the coroner's court; we now go inside the courts to demand justice. In the case of Kuldip Kaur, who committed suicide by dousing herself with petrol in the early 1990s, we gave evidence to the coroner, who was hostile to the introduction of the gender/domestic violence equation into the case. He thought that our report was inadequate because it did not address the question of how men were affected by domestic violence!

Coroner's courts are obliged by law to hold inquests where deaths have occurred in circumstances in which there are questions as to how the deceased has died. The inquest procedure takes on greater significance precisely because there is no other legal forum of investigation into such suicides. The motto of the Coroners Officers Association is 'advocates for the dead to safeguard the living'. A central plank of our work around suicides has been to persuade coroners to make recommendations to public authorities to take action to prevent similar fatalities. In other words, we have attempted to hold them to their motto.

In November 1995, Nighet Gilani, a 55-year-old Asian woman, was killed by a train when she walked onto a railway track in Northolt, West London. Just prior to her death, she had fled to a refuge to escape domestic violence from her husband. She was later reconciled with him and returned home, but less than a month later she was dead.

Nighet Gilani did not have anyone to speak for her. Her family were in India. We worked hard to track down her friends to encourage them to give evidence about the abuse she suffered. But neither of the two women we found felt comfortable about going public. So we decided to speak for Nighet by making third-party representations. A newly appointed West London coroner, Alison Thompson, was willing for us to provide expert and background evidence to the case, but refused to acknowledge us as an interested party. We were called to give evidence at the end of the hearing. We argued that the coroner could make a finding showing that Nighet's suicide had been caused by her husband's violence. We explained how Asian women are more likely than white women to kill themselves, and that the court should recognise Nighet's suicide as another example where domestic violence was the cause. We suggested that the coroner ask the Home Office or the Department of Health to establish an interdepartmental group to investigate the link between domestic violence and suicide and self-harm amongst Asian women, and institute reform to address the problem. The coroner said that while she could not make such a recommendation in this case, she would bear it in mind for the future. This recognition in itself represented a victory. We had ensured that not only the interests of Nighet but also those of other Asian women in her situation had been voiced.

Why can't he be more like Quincy?

We presented expert evidence in the case of Assa Devi Padan at the Coroner's court at the request of her children, two adult daughters in their early twenties and a 14-year-old son attempting to understand her death. Assa had hanged herself in June 2000. Assa's daughters told us that their mother had been subjected to repeated abuse from her husband in their 23-year marriage, particularly when he had been drinking. The children too had suffered violence. Assa and her husband had exchanged legal letters about divorce, none of which had been followed through. In 2000, Assa's husband went to India. Again he threatened to divorce her, but this time he had also arranged to marry a young woman in India. He accused Assa of being unfaithful and denied being the father of their son. Assa told her daughters how her husband had subjected her to rape for many years, and how he had affairs with a number of women, and had visited prostitutes.

Assa was worried about her husband's pending remarriage. She came under pressure from her family to save her marriage. Assa was also worried about the allegations of adultery, which would ruin their family honour and,' in particular, affect the marriage prospects of her young daughters. Assa went to India with her son and brother in order to save the marriage. Her brother and son returned to the UK while Assa stayed behind. Her son asserted that while they were in India his father had attempted to throw his mother in front of an oncoming train. Their mother had complained of a severe beating from him. The children and other relatives had seen the injuries afterwards and taken photographs. She returned to the UK with her husband, who later claimed he only came back temporarily in order to escort his wife. On the day of her death, Assa's husband had once again left her and flown to India.

The children accepted that their mother may have committed suicide, but they felt that their father had actively assisted her or driven her to such a desperate act. At the inquest, opened in October 2000 and resumed in September 2001, counsel prepared a legal argument using the Human Rights Act 1998 (see Chapter 11, 'Shifting Terrains').

SBS gave written and oral evidence in court arguing that the history of domestic violence had driven Assa to suicide. The pressure to save her marriage and the dishonour that accompanied a divorce and allegations of adultery were also used by the husband as part of his pattern of abusive behaviour. We suggested the coroner make a recommendation to government and other bodies to address the problem. Indeed, in this case it was felt that police had failed to follow up the case after attending an incident of domestic violence. The GP had noticed that Assa Devi was depressed due to a marital problem and had referred her to a counsellor, to whom she had given more details about the abuse. We argued that the GP should have followed through this referral and obtained reports from the counsellor.

Although the coroner recognised that there had been some domestic violence in the past, he did not mention the violence just prior to Assa's death despite an admission by the husband, via his counsel, that there were recent injuries. However, the coroner expressed his sympathy for a depressed man, who in the early years of his marriage may have turned to violence and alcohol as a result of bankruptcy. Indeed, when questioning Hannana Siddiqui, who gave the expert evidence, he said women may nag or provoke men to violence – an assertion strongly repudiated by us. The coroner also questioned whether the concept of honour was specific to Asian or other minority groups. Hannana argued that notions of family honour prevalent amongst the British aristocracy and the upper middle classes was very much a thing of the past, and did not now prevent white women from escaping domestic violence; that it carried a specific cultural meaning for women in certain minority communities, particularly in terms of pressures to make the marriage work at all costs.

Despite our concerted efforts, the coroner did not recognise domestic violence as a contributory factor in Assa Devi's death; nor did he acknowledge the cultural dimension to the case when he argued that Prince Edward VIII had to abdicate the throne because he brought dishonour on the monarchy by marrying a divorcee! He argued that Assa Devi committed suicide as a result of depression brought on by the prospect of divorce, and did not take into account the social problem of domestic violence. The coroner in this case lamented the fact that, due to rules governing the remit of an inquest, he could not fully explore the reasons for Assa's death; he had looked into the 'how' rather than the 'why'. Instead, he invited SBS to make a submission to a Home Office Coroners' Review, which was reviewing rules governing inquests and coroner's courts. Coroners' powers are in dire need of reform: confusingly they have no legal authority to sentence, reprimand or even apportion blame, but at the same time they have other powers that go beyond that of a magistrate or judge in that they can summon witnesses and carry out whatever forensic investigations on a corpse they deem fit.[4] Although the issue of domestic violence as one cause of suicide in Asian women was aired in public – a moral and political victory – Assa's daughters were disappointed that the coroner did not recognise the history of domestic violence as a contributory factor to their mother's death. One of her daughters, Kulvinder (who now works for SBS), said afterwards:

> I went to the Inquest with a hope of getting answers to my questions and getting justice for my mother. Instead, I was outraged by the coroner's remarks and evident sympathy for my brutal father. The coroner demonstrated his ignorance of the issues relating to my mother's life and subsequently her death. The coroner's attitude ultimately led to my loss of faith in the system.

The coroners we have come across in our work are predominantly white, middle-class men with prehistoric views. It is a pity they lack the more imaginative investigative style of the American television coroner Quincy, who pushes boundaries in pursuit of justice and protection for the underdog!

Growing momentum

Studies carried out by researchers in the medical field, such as Veena Soni Raleigh, Dinesh Bhugra and Dr John Merrill, tended to centre on statistical information rather than examining the causes of suicide among Asian women. Although we had addressed the issue in the media and at some medical conferences, one of the earliest events was hosted by the Confederation of Indian Organisations and Aveleon Associates in 1994. SBS provided the keynote speech making the connection between domestic violence and abusive behaviour and the high rate of suicide and self-harm amongst Asian women. Many people, however, were nervous about the event, fearing a backlash from the community – so the event was kept restricted to women's groups and sympathetic professionals.

In 1995 mounting pressure led to the establishment of an advisory group on Asian women and suicide, chaired by the Conservative peer Baroness Flather, within the NHS Ethnic Health Unit in the Department of Health. SBS was represented, and we ensured other Asian women's groups were also invited to join – including both Brent Asian Women's Refuge and Newham Asian Women's Project. Civil servants and academics, including Veena Raleigh and Dinesh Bugra, were also invited. The central tension within the group was the extent to which the high rates of suicide were caused by women's psychiatric condition – the view held by some of the civil servants and academics – or their social circumstances, which was proposed by the women's groups, who were supported by Veena Raleigh. We called for a reduction of suicide rates amongst Asian women by 15 per cent by the year 2000, the national target set for all suicides by the Department of Health. (Now the target is 20 per cent by the year 2010.) We argued that this could be achieved by improving service provision to tackle the problem. Despite these discussions, little came out of the advisory group. The Conservative administration was reluctant to provide more resources, and the issue was considered too 'sensitive' to raise in wider public policy.

However, by 1999 the Department of Health (DoH) was forced to acknowledge the problem in its white paper *Saving Lives: Our Healthier Nation*, which quoted Raleigh's research on suicide rates amongst Asian women. Since then, the government's response has been inconsistent, with some local health authorities supporting voluntary-sector or internal health service projects. In the last few years, Asian women's groups in particular have led the way in developing projects, often supported by their local health authority, providing services for victims and/or publications on Asian women's suicide and self-harm. These projects include Zindagi (part of Newham Asian Women's Project), the Asian Women's Resource Centre in Brent, Karma Nirvana in Derby, and 42nd Street/Asian Women's Mental Health Coalition and the Manchester Mental Health Authority. The DoH has also funded the production of a video by the North Birmingham Mental Health NHS Trust.

The DoH, however, has not undertaken to tackle the problem in any comprehensive way by making more resources available or in addressing policy issues across the board. SBS has called for an inter-departmental group within government to address the issue of domestic violence and black women's mental health. However, although the report by the Home Office Working Group on Forced Marriage in June 2000, at our insistence, acknowledged the link between forced marriage and the high rate of suicide and self-harm amongst Asian women, little or no work has been done by most government departments in addressing this issue, even though one of the new priority areas for the Home Office is to tackle domestic violence through better intervention by the health service. Recently, the DoH carried out a consultation on women's mental health; although it made the link between domestic violence and mental ill health, it had little to say about the needs of black and minority women.

The responsibility does not only rest with health professionals, but also with many others, including social workers, teachers, advice workers, police officers, lawyers and the courts. Coroners' courts need to broaden their remit, eradicate their conservatism and use their powers to examine causes of death amongst Asian women, thus recommending changes in social policy and practice. In 1996, one brave coroner, James Turnbull, commented on BBC television that stress on Asian women in Bradford led to a small number of 'encouraged' suicides following pressure from families. He said:

> It might be unfair to suggest that there have been cases of un-provable murder, but I strongly suspect that there have been cases of provable encouragement to suicide, which is nearly the same thing.[5]

Since these comments coroners have generally remained silent on the issue. However, we are aiming to educate coroners on a case-by-case basis, sometimes supported by publicity and campaigning. We are also raising the issues on a national level by making submissions to government and the Coroners' Review.. In 2002, an inquest into the death of an Asian woman, Noreen Akhtar, found she had hanged herself after going ahead with a marriage arranged by her family. In her suicide note she said, 'I wanted to keep you all happy. I also wanted my own happiness – I couldn't have both.' A consultant psychiatrist who had been treating Noreen told the inquest she was depressed because she did not identify with traditional Islamic values regarding women and came under pressure from her family to accept an arranged marriage. Whittaker – the coroner in the Nazia Bi case – said that the tradition of arranged marriage sometimes meant women were caught between two worlds. He said:

> I don't seek to minimise it. I hope that members of the Asian community will recognise this as a real problem. It needs address-ing, and if there is any integration and marrying of the cultures, a way forward ought to be looked for with great seriousness.[6]

Besides an obvious reluctance to acknowledge forced marriage in an attempt to be culturally sensitive, Whittaker calls on the Asian community to address the problem by adopting more Western values. He ignores the fact that many within the community, such as women's groups, have been challenging these practices, and misses the opportunity to acknowledge the role and responsibilities of the state in tackling the problem of forced marriage.

For over twenty-one years we have not had the resources to undertake consistent work on the issue of domestic violence and mental health. In 2001, SBS eventually received substantial funding. The Diana Princess of Wales Memorial Fund agreed to support a three-year project examining the issue of domestic violence and mental health problems amongst black women. The project aims to bring together our knowledge and that of other professionals: looking at good models of intervention, seeking to deal with social welfare issues as well as medical concern in order to influence good practice and social policy, and lobbying for more government action. It also aims to challenge community and social attitudes and practices concerning domestic violence and Asian female suicide, self-harm and mental breakdown. It seems that finally we can bring some sort of justice for women like Krishna Sharma, Kuldip Kaur, Nighet Gilani, Assa Devi Padan, Nazia Bi and her daughter Sana.

Notes

1. Veena Soni Raleigh, 'Suicide Patterns and Trends in People of Indian Sub-Continent and Caribbean Origin in England and Wales', *Ethnicity and Health*, vol. 1, no. 1, 1996; D. Bhugra et al., 'Attempted Suicide in West London, 1. Rates across Ethnic Communities', and 'Attempted Suicide in West London, ll. Inter-group Comparisons', *Psychological Medicine*, vol. 29, 1999; J. Merrill et al., 'Asian Suicides', *British Journal of Psychiatry*, vol. 156, 1990, and 'Ethnic Differences in Self-poisoning; A Comparison of Asian and White Groups', *British Journal of Psychiatry*, vol. 148, 1986.

2. An anxiety disorder caused by major personal stress after a serious or frightening event.

3. *The Richard and Judy Show*, Channel 4, 26 April 2002.

4. Christopher Middleton, 'Court in a Time Warp', *Guardian*, Society supplement, 17 July 2002.

5. Martin Wainwright '"High Suicide Risk" for Asian Women', *Guardian*, 27 April 1996.

6. Clare Lomax, 'Tragic Wife Hanged Herself in Her Home', *Telegraph and Argus*, 4 May 2002.

7

Jumping through hoops:
immigration and domestic violence

Poonam Joshi

There cannot be a single black or Asian family in the UK that has not been affected negatively by immigration laws. Through the history of my own family and friends I have seen how immigration laws have shaped the lives of black people. My parents were invited to work in the UK in the 1960s at a time when there was a labour shortage. My parents were fortunate that they had both of their children with them. Many of their fellow migrants discovered that, whilst they were welcome as workers, their families were not. I remember stories of family friends who were unable to bring their children to join them, as the immigration authorities did not believe the children were genuinely theirs. The practice of keeping families apart was just one of the ways in which the state controlled the lives of immigrants. In the late 1970s a distant relative of the family came from India to marry in the UK. At Heathrow airport she was subjected to the infamous virginity test. Several months later her marriage broke down due to domestic violence, and she came to live with us for several years. I was only a child but over the years it became clear to me that she felt that she had been abused twice over: first by the state and then by her husband. What was also clear was that this was 'something that should not be spoken about'. And so, and I am sure not for the first time, a veil was drawn over the particular way women suffer the brunt of immigration laws, and how their own communities are complicit with the state in failing them.

The purpose of this chapter is to discuss how black women in particular are not only affected by racist immigration laws but also, due to their gender, denied the protection and concessions accorded to black men. SBS has been unique in making the voices of these women heard. This chapter will focus on our campaigns in this area and the changes secured as a result.

The wider picture

Immigration law is at the cutting edge of black communities' experience of racism at the hands of the state. Any claim by government or media that the two issues are not connected can only appear hollow and unjustifiable. The media have concentrated on abuses by asylum seekers rather than abuses against them. In 2001, when Conservative MP John Townend spoke of his fears that the British were becoming a 'mongrel nation' as a result of increasing numbers of asylum seekers, the connection between the two issues became crystal clear. Witness also the mental acrobatics that Jack Straw had to perform when he tried to defend his race law in a letter to the *Guardian*:

> Hugo Young's dismissal of the Race Relations (amendment) Act 2000, the most radical change to race equality legislation in a generation, as 'a law of national and ethnic and racial discrimination' is bizarre. The act outlaws race discrimination in public functions not covered by the original Race Relations Act 1976, and places a positive duty on listed public authorities to promote racial equality actively.
>
> We had a drafting problem with the act, however, in that immigration control by the United Kingdom (and every country in the world) *does discriminate by nationality*.[1]

Immigration laws are by nature racist, created to prevent certain categories of foreigners from coming into the country. In the last two decades successive governments have sought to reduce the duties they have to immigrants and asylum seekers, steadily reducing the money, housing and services available to them. Governments pretend that immigration laws affect all foreigners fairly, but we who have been touched by these laws know that they do not. Both Conservative and Labour governments have sought to justify draconian immigration law as the basis for good race relations. The reality is that racists are unable to distinguish between a black asylum seeker and a black British citizen who was born in the UK. A racist is not likely to check the stamp on someone's passport before going on the rampage.

In fact some sections of our communities feel their position in this country to be so tenuous that they will be the first to criticise and attack asylum seekers. I have had a few conversations with entrepreneurial Asians who were unable to acknowledge that the worst 'crime' bogus asylum seekers can commit is to seek a better life as economic migrants, exactly as their own parents and grandparents did. Such is the public hysteria about the financial cost to the country that little attempt is made to look at the financial gain, and not just in terms of improved economic productivity. Often economic migrants are those whose livelihoods have been destroyed by the activities of British multinational investments abroad, which themselves bring huge financial benefit to British society.

In November 2002 the Blair government enacted the Nationality, Immigration and Asylum Act 2002. This introduced a host of draconian measures, including ending asylum support to asylum seekers who did not claim asylum on arrival in the UK, introducing a list of safe countries from which asylum claims will be presumed to be unfounded,[2] and whose nationals will no longer have right of appeal in the UK, and the establishment of accommodation centres for asylum seekers and their families in isolated locations.

The events of 11 September 2001 have led to an increased hostility towards asylum seekers, with the label of 'terrorist' being added to that of 'bogus'. The Anti-Terrorism, Crime and Security Act was rushed through Parliament in 2001. It allows foreign nationals suspected of being involved in international terrorism to be interned without trial. It could be used to deny entry to people who may be fleeing their country because their 'legitimate' political activities in that country may have been branded 'terrorist'. In other words, most asylum seekers are, by definition, dissidents; an authoritarian state may seek to quell opposition by treating them as terrorists.

The political climate surrounding asylum has been explosively recharged by the discovery that some of the alleged Islamist terrorists operating in the UK, including one former Taliban fighter, are asylum seekers. The shadow Home Secretary, Oliver Letwin, has been demanding that the UK derogate from the European Convention on Human Rights. Following the arrest of the alleged terrorists in Manchester and London, the Conservative Party launched a demand for a tough asylum policy. In response Mr Blair, speaking to the BBC, listed the measures that had come into force under the Nationality, Immigration and Asylum Act 2002, but added: 'if the measures don't work, then we will have to consider further measures, including looking at the obligations we have under the convention on human rights.'[3] Already one of these measures, to end financial support to asylum seekers who do not claim immediately, has been challenged and held by the High Court to be in breach of the Human Rights Act 1998. The National Coalition of Anti Deportation Campaigns has estimated that since 8 January 2003, when the measure came into force, 7,000 asylum seekers, or 60 per cent of applicants, had been refused support.[4] On 21 October 2002, in a written answer to a parliamentary question, then Immigration Minister Beverley Hughes admitted that 65 per cent of people receiving positive decisions had made in-country claims. In 1996, the Social Security Advisory Committee (SSAC), the main UK advisory body on Social Security, held that there are many valid reasons why people do not make their asylum claims immediately on arrival, including lack of knowledge of the process, language difficulties and fear of officialdom. In many of our cases, women make in-country applications for asylum after their marriages break down. They, too, would be excluded. This reality has been overlooked in the government's decision to place spin and populism before compliance with basic human rights.

Despite the fact that asylum and immigration are 'hot' issues, SBS has had difficulties in generating press interest in the campaigns of its clients. The media are generally interested in stories that might show up asylum seekers as an undifferentiated mass of 'scroungers' or 'terrorists', not in how immigration rules can trap women in violent marriages. The vast majority of women who come to SBS are first- or second-generation migrants, predominantly from South Asia.

More than half of our clients have come from abroad to the UK to join their husbands. Others entered the UK with husbands who came here to claim asylum. The majority of these women seek help from SBS because they are in violent marriages or have fled violence. The right of these women to stay in the UK is invariably dependent upon them remaining in violent marriages.

Closing all the doors:
the legal framework of discrimination

Since the 1960s, successive governments have imposed increasing restrictions on the migration of black people to the UK. The 1970s saw the introduction of legislation that prevented black people entering as workers, impacting on both men and women. By the late 1970s primary immigration, particularly from the black Commonwealth countries, had been greatly reduced. In the early 1980s the Conservative government introduced a set of rules to prevent people from abroad being able to enter the UK and stay here permanently through marriage. The key changes were the introduction of the primary purpose rule, the one-year rule (OYR), and the no-recourse-to-public-funds requirement.

The primary purpose rule (PPR) required applicants to prove that the main purpose of marriage was not settlement in the UK. Entry Clearance Officers (ECOs) judged whether a marriage was genuine or not based on their perception of South Asian culture and customs. For example, ECOs believed that in a genuine marriage the bride moves in with her husband and in-laws. The former Home Secretary, William Whitelaw, defended this interpretation of the PPR, stating that 'the abode of a husband in a marriage should normally be viewed as the natural place of residence of the family.'[5] On this basis many Asian men who applied to join their wives in the UK were refused entry on the basis that a man would not move to join his wife unless his main reason for moving was to migrate to the UK.

The one-year rule introduced the requirement that people coming to the UK to join their spouse must remain in the marriage for at least one year before they can apply to stay permanently. The application for leave to remain must be supported by both parties. A person from abroad who does not apply at the end of the probationary period automatically becomes an overstayer, liable to being removed from the UK even if the marriage is continuing. A person whose marriage breaks down for whatever reason before obtaining settlement is equally vulnerable to removal.

Finally, the no-recourse-to-public-funds requirement dictated that persons coming to the UK must be financially supported by their spouses or must support themselves by working. They are not entitled to welfare benefits, council housing or to use publicly funded facilities such as refuges unless they are able to pay rent.

Campaigning against the one-year rule

The main focus of our campaigning work has been against the one-year rule. The OYR made no concession to those whose genuine marriage had subsequently broken down, particularly due to violence from the UK-based spouse. Women whose marriage broke down due to domestic violence had only two options in order to avoid deportation: to apply for refugee status on the grounds of gender persecution; or to apply for leave to remain on compassionate grounds. These cases were rarely successful even where women had remained in marriages for a number of years and had children, unless a coordinated and long-term public campaign was fought on an individual basis.

The first SBS campaign to raise issues around both immigration rules and gender persecution was that in support of Rabia Janjua in 1989. Rabia Janjua was a Pakistani national who had been raped and as a result was guilty of the Islamic crime of *zina* under Shariah (Islamic) law. The offence of *zina* is committed if a person has either premarital or extramarital sex. The penalties for *zina* are flogging, stoning or the death penalty for both the parties involved. As a victim of rape, Rabia would not be found guilty of *zina* if she could prove that she had been raped. Unfortunately for Rabia, in order to clear her name she would have to produce four male witnesses in her support. In view of these harsh laws, Rabia felt that she had no option but to marry her rapist in order to 'legitimise' the relationship. In spite of the marriage, Rabia and her husband were both charged by the state with *zina*, and Rabia's husband arranged for both of them to come to the UK in the mid-1980s.

In the UK Rabia continued to be subjected to the violence that she had experienced from her husband in Pakistan. She obtained an injunction to evict her husband from their home. However, she was unable to keep up with the mortgage payments and was eventually forced to move to a bed and breakfast with her two young sons. Rabia's husband informed the police that she was an illegal entrant. Rabia was taken by immigration officers to a detention centre. Rabia's youngest son, who was only eleven days old, was left behind at the B&B although immigration officers later denied knowledge of this. The immigration authorities had intended to send Rabia back to Pakistan on a flight the same day. Rabia was already an SBS client. We arranged for journalists to call the detention centre until Rabia was released.

Rabia's immigration status was particularly complicated. Rabia did not know whether her husband had taken any steps to regularise her status in the UK. SBS found experienced immigration lawyers for Rabia and were central to the process of formulating the legal arguments. SBS argued that due to the zina laws Rabia would be at risk of prosecution by the state if she returned to Pakistan and that the state would fail to protect her. Whilst both men and women could be charged with zina, in practice the zina laws affected women more harshly. Any woman found guilty of zina would be permanently ostracised by society and would be vulnerable to exploitation and harm and possibly subjected to public flogging and stoning to death – as was our fear in Rabia's case. SBS also worked closely with human rights lawyers in Pakistan in order to gather evidence on the criminal charges against Rabia and the sentence that she would face. SBS embarked upon a media campaign to highlight Rabia's plight. The campaign highlighted how racist immigration laws in the UK and patriarchal and misogynistic religious laws in Pakistan had operated to trap women in Rabia's position. Prior to Rabia's case being heard at court, the Independent published an interview with her. Shortly after the publication of the interview the Home Office granted Rabia leave to remain in the UK on compassionate grounds. The entire campaign lasted three or four months; we were astonished at the speed with which the Home Office caved into the pressure from the media campaign. It was clear that without assistance from SBS and the media campaign Rabia would have been returned to Pakistan.

Throughout the 1990s SBS continued to support women in their individual campaigns for leave to remain in the UK. By the late 1990s SBS's campaign against the one-year rule was gathering momentum but no concrete changes had been effected. One of the last pre-concession campaigns that SBS ran was that in support of Chandrakala Gautam, a Rajput Hindu from India, in 1998. However, SBS did not have the resources to campaign for all our clients and there were very few organisations who had the experience or resources to assist women with immigration and domestic violence problems. As a result the obvious starting point in our immigration work was to campaign for the abolition of the one-year rule, using the slogan 'A stark choice: domestic violence or deportation?'

In 1992, Labour MP Barbara Roche invited SBS to make submissions to the Home Affairs Select Committee investigating domestic violence. SBS made written and oral submissions on immigration and wider problems relating to black women's experiences of domestic violence. SBS was one of only four organisations, including Victim Support and the Women's Aid Federation, invited to make oral submissions on how women were affected by domestic violence. We knew that neither the state nor any of the organisations purporting to speak on behalf of women would address the particular difficulties faced by women with immigration problems trying to flee violence. Although SBS was given only five minutes to talk about immigration, the impact was sufficient for Labour members to make a commitment to tackle the problem of violence and immigration when a Labour government was elected. SBS continued to lobby Labour in opposition in the hope that a Labour government would be more sympathetic to changes to the OYR. In 1997 as part of its pre-election manifesto the Labour Party had stated its commitment to eradicating domestic violence. However, no mention was made of tackling the problems of women with immigration problems suffering domestic violence. SBS continued to oppose the OYR through leafleting, talks around the country and individual campaigns. We also considered alternative options to the abolition of the OYR with the assistance of immigration lawyers in preparation for making detailed submissions to the Home Office.

The primary purpose rule was abolished shortly after the formation of a Labour government in May 1997 in order to appease an increasingly influential and affluent Asian community. At the time of its abolition, Home Secretary Jack Straw said that the PPR was being ended because 'it is arbitrary, unfair and ineffective and has penalised genuine cases, divided families and unnecessarily increased the administrative burden of the immigration system.'[6] The abolition of the PPR was expected to bring immediate benefits to more than 1,000 couples who were barred from the UK on the basis of the rule in 1996 alone.

We carried out our own research on the number of women who were affected by the OYR in the eighteen months between January 1994 and July 1995. We found that 512 women who had escaped from domestic violence were threatened with deportation. The Home Office refused to abolish the OYR even though the numbers of people affected would have been much lower than those affected by the PPR. Why did the Home Office choose to abolish the PPR rather than the OYR? A clue to their decision lies in the way the PPR dispro-portionately affected black men trying to enter the UK. In 1984, 46 per cent of husbands and male fiancés from the Indian subcontinent were refused entry to the UK, 88 per cent on primary-purpose grounds. However, the majority of people liable to deportation due to the breakdown of their marriage within the probationary one year are women. Black communities consistently campaigned against the PPR and its role in keeping families apart. While the male-led minority communities campaigned to abolish the PPR in support of the institution of marriage, few people within the black communi-ties were prepared to acknowledge, let alone campaign on behalf of, the victims of marital breakdown: the women who had first suffered violence and now risked deportation. The PPR undermined the institution of marriage (particularly arranged marriage) and the con-tinuation of a patriarchal diasporic community. Conversely the abo-lition of the OYR would primarily benefit women who sought to escape violent marriages.

The 1997 election was the first in which black communities carried key votes in marginal seats. The political parties consulted the self-appointed 'community leaders' on what their communities wanted. Unsurprisingly the abolition of the PPR was on the community leaders' wish list, and was duly delivered by the newly elected Labour government within months of its election. The government appeased opponents of abolition by arguing that the continued operation of OYR and the no-recourse-to-public-funds rule would weed out the bogus marriages. But as Home Office statistics for 1994 show, 370 women were refused under the one-year rule out of a total of 14,920 women who were granted settlement after marriage. Even if all 370 were refused because the marriage was not genuine, it is simply too small a figure to justify the continuance of the OYR.

Upon abolition of the PPR, SBS immediately made submissions to the new Secretary of State for Immigration, Mike O'Brien, demanding the abolition of the one-year rule. The Home Office made it clear that they would not consider abolishing the OYR, having removed the PPR. However, the Home Office agreed to enter into a consultative process on the issue of OYR and domestic violence. SBS put forward a range of options including the abolition of the OYR, a change to the OYR itself and the introduction of concessions to those affected by it. It became apparent early on that the Home Office would only be prepared to consent to a concession. SBS then concentrated on three areas of concern: first, what proof women would have to provide that domestic violence had taken place; second, pressurising the Home Office to remove the no-recourse-to-public-funds rule so that women would not face financial destitution if they left their homes; and, third, arguing that women who had been in violent marriages for several years and who had effectively become overstayers should be included in the concession.

We knew that the USA and a number of European countries required proof of domestic violence either by way of criminal convictions or civil injunctions, unlike Australia, where women could provide reports from a range of professionals including doctors, social workers and community workers as proof of violence. SBS explained that it was extremely difficult for women to obtain injunctions and criminal convictions, for reasons that are discussed in greater detail below. SBS argued that the statement of the woman along with two other types of proof from professionals such as doctors, social workers and community workers should be sufficient evidence of domestic violence. SBS also attempted to influence the Department of Social Security regarding the no-recourse-to-public-funds rule, but to no avail. Finally, in relation to overstayers, SBS argued that the Home Office had declared a similar amnesty in respect of domestic workers and that the numbers involved were so few that concessions to OYR would not be received hysterically by the right-wing media.

In 1998, 109 Members of Parliament signed an Early Day Motion organised by SBS expressing concern and urging the government to protect black women and their children who were trapped in violent situations due to their insecure immigration status. The government finally announced the concession to OYR for victims of domestic violence in June 1999.

One step forward...

The concession allowed a woman to live in the UK permanently if her marriage had broken down within the probationary first year due to domestic violence. She had to prove that violence took place by way of a criminal conviction, criminal caution or injunction.

...two steps back

Whilst SBS welcomed the introduction of the concession, it was clear that there were serious shortcomings. SBS monitored the operation of the concession, and in October 2001 we submitted the findings of our survey to the Home Office Minister, Beverley Hughes MP.[7] As the concession largely failed to assist those it was introduced to protect, our recommendations to the Home Office remained the same as those made prior to its introduction.

Many of the agencies that responded to our survey found that the standard of proof that women were required to meet under the concession was too high, too rigidly applied and generally unreasonable. The concession failed to acknowledge the often interlinked reasons why women were unable to obtain the types of evidence required. The factors that prevented women from seeking help whilst still experiencing violence included the fear of further violence, the fear of being deported, and the lack of public funds to enable them to live in safety. Women feared for their lives especially if they involved the police. They lacked both knowledge of police powers and access to advocates to represent their needs, and they also feared that the community would isolate them. In many cases women were imprisoned by their abusers and had no way, even if they knew how, of seeking help. Finally the concession failed to protect women who sought help more than twelve months after they had entered the UK and had become overstayers. These women had to apply for leave to remain outside of the concession even though they were clearly victims of violence.

The domestic violence rule – one step forward again?

In November 2002 the government announced that it intended to incorporate the domestic violence concession into the Immigration Rules and widen the type of evidence that was acceptable in proving the conditions of the concession. The minister, Beverley Hughes, stated that the government had introduced these changes as a result of its review and the representations received.[8]

The domestic violence rule has two advantages over the concession. First, incorporation into the rules means that a domestic violence application will now attract a right of appeal. Second, the Home Office will now accept more than one form of evidence from the following: criminal conviction, criminal caution, injunction, an undertaking given within court proceedings, a medical report from a hospital doctor or a letter from a GP confirming the applicant has injuries consistent with being the victim of domestic violence, a police report confirming attendance at the home of the applicant as a result of a domestic violence incident, a letter from a social services department confirming its involvement in connection with domestic violence, and a letter of support or report from a women's refuge. Although we welcome the fact that a more reasonable standard of proof is now required (it marks another victory for the campaign), we remain concerned about a number of continuing limitations.

Proving the violence

We are concerned about the failure to recognise that some victims may have difficulty in obtaining supporting evidence of domestic violence other than their own testimony. We demand that other types of reliable evidence should also be accepted, such as witness evidence, and where there is a finding of domestic violence in cases other than criminal or civil court injunction hearings – for example, in immigration appeals and in child contact hearings. We believe that evidence from a broader group of professionals should be accepted, such as advice workers, and other experts. Where only one type of evidence is available, the Home Office should accept it as sufficient to prove domestic violence. Whilst the Home Office has broadened the range of types of evidence required, it has not acknowledged the difficulties inherent in obtaining each type of evidence for a woman fleeing violence.

Criminal law

Many agencies reported that women faced considerable difficulties in reporting violence, let alone obtaining the convictions and cautions required. Even after they had escaped their abusers many women were reluctant to press criminal charges against their husbands or in-laws due to cultural pressure from their family or community, hopes of a reunion, or because they did not feel able to give evidence in trial. The threat of being deported was also an important factor in women's reluctance to report domestic violence to the police. In many cases women are aware of police maltreatment of women in their countries of origin, and this view is often reinforced by their abusers, whose intention it is to isolate them.

The inherent problem with the Rule is its requirement for criminal convictions and cautions, which is at odds with the low priority that the criminal justice system gives to domestic violence. The police are often reluctant to treat the matter as a criminal one. Cases quoted in the survey showed that the police prefer to divert women away from the criminal justice system and, at best, encourage them to apply for civil protection even if the women are willing to pursue criminal proceedings. The police and CPS are often reluctant to pursue an investigation due to difficulties in obtaining corroborative evidence. Domestic violence invariably takes place behind closed doors, and the only witnesses to the violence tend to be the husband's family. Only women with injuries are likely to be taken seriously and those who are subjected to mental abuse, however horrific, will be told to seek relief through the family courts.

It is curious that the Home Office has stated that a criminal caution can be used as proof, given that it is unlikely that cautions would be given in domestic violence matters. A caution is a formal warning given by the police. In order for the police to offer a caution the abuser must admit the alleged offence. It is unlikely that an abuser will admit to being violent. Cautions tend to be used in minor criminal matters, for example theft or possession of cannabis, where the suspect has no previous convictions. It is standard practice that the police do not offer cautions where allegations of violence are made.

Too little, too late: civil injunctions

The purpose of the law relating to injunctions is to provide protection against future violence, not to punish the perpetrator for past violence or to prove that violence took place in the past. Civil courts are unable to provide women much by way of protection or proof for the purpose of the domestic violence rule.

Women who leave their marriages within the probationary period are the least likely to have any ties with their husbands and in-laws through children or joint finances, and will often have the greatest difficulty in obtaining an injunction. In these cases the abuser often has no incentive to continue harassing the woman and more often than not the woman leaves the abuser not through choice but because the abuser has driven the woman out of the matrimonial home.

A common problem that weakens an application is when a woman has waited for several weeks since the last incident of violence before making an application. A woman might wait because she does not know how to get legal advice or that she is even entitled to it. For most women the priority is to find accommodation and then find a lawyer. In some cases women have not been eligible for emergency legal aid, and by the time legal aid is granted there has been too great a delay since the last incident of violence to obtain an injunction. Many women move in with relatives who pressurise them to return to their husbands or not take any action against them. Women who are thrown out of their homes often find that their husband will not try to contact them and there are no further threats made. Other women move to addresses that are not known to their husband. The view of the court is that in all these cases women are no longer at risk of harm or have successfully protected themselves from future harm and do not need the protection of a court order. The group of women most likely to be able to obtain an injunction – women in long-term marriages with children or joint finances – which will place them at further risk from the abuser, are excluded by the domestic violence rule, as they are inevitably overstayers.

A key improvement under the Rule is the inclusion of undertakings as an acceptable form of evidence. As we argued in our submission to the Home Office, the requirement for injunctions as evidence under the concession was contrary to the ethos of the family courts, which is to encourage parties to resolve matters amicably and to reduce costs. Although many women may succeed in obtaining an *ex parte* injunction, women are frequently encouraged by the courts and sometimes their own representatives to accept an undertaking from their abuser that he will not harass or harm them. An undertaking does not prove that violence has taken place. After the concession was introduced, family lawyers were known to argue that women applicants were seeking injunctions to support their immigration applications, not because they were scared. In these circumstances a lawyer for the abusive husband could then argue that his or her client was willing to offer an undertaking which would protect the woman, with the implication that a refusal to accept the undertaking exposed the woman's real reason for applying for the injunction.

Suneeta's story

Suneeta's case was dealt with under the Concession before the Rule was introduced. However, it highlights the difficulties of proving violence for the purposes of the Concession and the Rule. Suneeta came from India to the UK following her arranged marriage to Ashok. Ashok raped Suneeta on her wedding night. She was too ashamed to tell her family. Suneeta did not believe she had any choice but to agree to her husband's wishes. After Suneeta joined Ashok in the UK, Ashok anally raped Suneeta every night. Suneeta was sure that her in-laws knew what was happening, as they would have heard her crying. However, Suneeta's in-laws were themselves extremely hostile to Suneeta and often threatened to throw her out of the house. Due to the sexual abuse, Suneeta developed an infection. Ashok would not allow Suneeta to go to the doctor by herself; either he or his mother went with her.

Ashok then decided to send Suneeta back to India. Suneeta's family begged Ashok not to throw her out of his home. Suneeta's aunt, who lived nearby, took Suneeta into her home hoping that Ashok would change his mind. Even after Suneeta told her aunt about the abuse, her aunt told her that she had to go back to her husband. Suneeta's aunt contacted the police but pressurised Suneeta to focus mainly on recovering her wedding jewellery rather than reporting the rape. Six weeks after Suneeta left her in-laws' home Ashok called her and threatened to kill her if she did not return to India. Suneeta fled to stay with other relatives near London, who took her to SBS for advice.

Suneeta could only have obtained an emergency injunction if she could prove that she was at risk of significant harm. Although Suneeta had received a threat to kill her, the gravest violence had taken place several weeks earlier. Suneeta had moved far away from Ashok and didn't think that he would harm her as she was now with her uncles. On this basis Suneeta did not get emergency legal aid. An ordinary application for legal aid can take two weeks to process. It can take up to a further four weeks to get a hearing date after legal aid has been granted. By the time Suneeta got to court, seven weeks had passed since the threat, and three months since she had been thrown out by Ashok.

At the hearing Ashok offered to give an undertaking. Ashok's lawyer argued that Suneeta had made up the allegations of violence to help her immigration application. Ashok's lawyers threatened to report Suneeta to the Legal Aid Board for 'misusing' public funds by applying for an injunction for immigration purposes. Ashok's lawyer also asked why Suneeta's family begged Ashok to take her back if the violence had really taken place. The judge told Suneeta that, should she not accept the undertaking, he would not be able to hear her case for another two months. He also said that if she did not agree to the undertaking, he would draw the same conclusions as Ashok's lawyers. The judge could not understand why a family would force a woman to go back to a man who had raped and abused her. Suneeta's only other remedy would have been for criminal charges to be brought against her husband for her rape. The police only took Suneeta's statement after her solicitor had called them several times, but they decided not to take the investigation any further as Suneeta had no medical evidence to support her case. In any event it was doubtful that Suneeta had the emotional strength to cope with the proceedings. At that time Suneeta had been with her family for two months and was still suffering from a sexual infection, as she had not been to see a GP.

After the injunction proceedings had concluded, Suneeta's relatives said that they did not have the time to bring Suneeta into Central London and transferred her immigration case to a local firm of solicitors. As Suneeta had no recourse to public funds, she was very much dependent on her relatives and was forced to follow their advice. Under the terms of the Concession Suneeta had no suitable evidence with which to support her case. Under the Rule, Suneeta was required to produce two forms of evidence, and her husband's undertaking would still not be enough.

The cost of leaving

The domestic violence rule has not addressed the issue of access to public funds, an issue that many agencies in our survey found deeply problematic. Many women would not report or leave domestic violence and risk further reprisals against themselves or their children unless they knew they could find safe accommodation and support themselves. Access to public funds is a precondition to making the domestic violence rule effective in protecting women with immigration problems. Women entering under the one-year rule have the right to work and many will find employment once they have had the opportunity to find housing and the appropriate support. However, soon after fleeing the matrimonial home most women will either be dependent on family and friends or effectively homeless and destitute unless they are able to obtain a refuge space. Women with children should be accommodated by the local authority, which has a duty to house the children. Yet a woman without dependants will find that no duties are owed to her. Refuges that are financed through public funds find themselves bearing the brunt of supporting such women without receiving any payment.

The one-year rule also limits the choices women have as to where they live. One SBS client, an Asian woman who was unable to speak English, wanted to remain in the Southall area. However, the only refuge space available was on the Isle of Wight. Some agencies were able to access limited funds by invoking the Children Act or the National Assistance Act, but others complained of difficulties in getting local authorities to help even under such legislation – some local authorities have threatened to take children into care or offer the air fare for women and children to return to their country of origin! SBS has tried to pressurise and engage the government to provide benefits and housing to women fleeing violence.

At a meeting in 2001 between the government and black women's refuges/resource centres, part of the Supporting People initiative, women's groups recommended that the immediate situation should be alleviated by a central government fund to enable abused women with no recourse to public funds to gain access to housing and living costs pending the outcome of immigration applications, including appeals. It was felt that in the long run wider changes in the welfare benefit system were needed. Women should be entitled to council housing and social security benefits, particularly income support and housing benefit, which can be reclaimed from the sponsor (provided there is no risk of reprisal or further violence).

The government has for many years been resistant to the idea of granting benefits, mainly because they fear opening the floodgates to other groups of migrants demanding concessions. However, part of its policy seems to be based on ignorance. When SBS raised the matter informally with the Home Secretary, David Blunkett, in 2002, he seemed to be under the impression that women with no access to public funds can flee to a refuge to escape domestic violence! The Home Office is now looking at 'options' to solve this problem with the Department of Works and Pensions, which we have also been lobbying – along with Women's Aid Federation of England, which, as a result of pressure from us, is now actively supporting the campaign. Some MPs, such as Margaret Moran, have been supportive, and groups such as Imkaan and Hackney Women's Aid are beginning to lobby on this issue.

Overstayers

One group, excluded by the Rule, is women who remain in violent marriages for many years because their husbands refuse to help them to apply to remain in the UK. Women also become overstayers because essential documents are often withheld by the abuser so that the women have no knowledge of their immigration status or of the time limits after which they become overstayers. Delays in obtaining help and information may also make a woman an overstayer. The longer a woman remains in a violent relationship, the more likely she is to have children. An abuser will often threaten the woman that she will be separated from the children if she reports the violence. But even if she obtains an injunction after she leaves a marriage, her application for leave to remain may be refused because it does not relate to a period when the parties were still together.

In the absence of amendments to the Rule many women will have to resort to other remedies to apply for leave to remain outside its terms. Under the Concession, women with alternative proof of violence (e.g. a GP's report, letters from social workers or refuges) have in exceptional cases succeeded, but there are many women who cannot obtain even these types of evidence. Our survey has shown that many women were being rejected for settlement or were withdrawing their applications. White women do not have to meet such high standards of proof before they can access refuges, alternative accommodation and support. In non-immigration cases local authorities will simply accept the woman's account of violence before accommodating her. In contrast, minority women are subjected to stringent tests of their credibility.

Two steps back again...

To counterbalance the 'concessions' introduced under the one-year rule, the government has taken the retrogressive step of extending the probationary period to two years. Obviously, the Labour Party is keen not to be seen as soft on immigration. It will simply prolong the time women are entrapped in violent relationships, thus making them more vulnerable to escalating violence and increasing the risk of homicide and suicide. The extension of the probationary period

has been justified by the need to clamp down on bogus marriages
and is being proposed in the wake of the debate on forced marriage
and the need for Asian communities to integrate and adopt British
norms by stopping arranged marriage with spouses living abroad.
This will amount to the reintroduction of the primary-purpose rule
through the back door!

Gender persecution and asylum

Many of SBS's clients fear isolation, ostracism and even persecution
if they are returned to their country of origin due to their status as
divorced or separated women. If these women then turn to the
police or courts for protection, they may at best be told that the
courts or police do not get involved in domestic matters, and at
worst be vulnerable to abuse and even in some cases prosecution by
the authorities. Some of these clients are women who have been
unable to utilise the domestic violence rule because of its limitations, whilst others are women who came to the UK in some other
capacity (as a dependant of an asylum seeker, visitor, student, etc.).

SBS has sought to secure the protection available under international human rights legislation for these women. However, the
international legislation relating to refugees marginalizes and de-
politicises the persecution women face in a domestic context and
has been resistant to recognising these women as refugees. Although
SBS has not been at the forefront of changing asylum law, we have
certainly contributed to the wider debates that have led to a growing recognition of the particular forms of harm that women face
and their right to receive international protection. The international
human rights regime has proved reluctant to intrude into the 'private sphere of the home'. Violence within the home is still considered 'different, less severe, and less deserving of international
condemnation and sanction than officially sanctioned violence'.[9] This
is the battle that SBS faces both in the UK and internationally.

What is a refugee?

Women and children make up 80 per cent of the world's estimated
27 million refugees and displaced people, but the overwhelming

majority of asylum seekers are men. The main international instrument governing the treatment of refugees, the 1951 United Nations Convention on the Status of Refugees, defines a refugee in part as someone who,

> Owing to well-founded fear of being persecuted for reasons of race, religion, nationality, membership of a particular social group or political opinion, is outside the country of origin of [her] nationality and is unable or, owing to such fear, is unwilling to avail [herself] of the protection of that country.[10]

In order to qualify as a refugee an asylum applicant must show that the ill treatment they have received or are likely to receive amounts to persecution – that is, the sustained or systematic violation of basic human rights leading to serious harm. If persecution is established it must be shown that it was for one of the Convention grounds. Unlike race, religion or nationality, membership of a particular social group or political opinion, gender is not explicitly recognised as a Convention ground. This may not present itself as a problem for the many women who flee persecution on the same basis as their male counterparts, although even here a gender dimension to the experience is often ignored by the law.

Limitations of the Convention

The Convention has traditionally excluded women who fear persecution due to noncompliance with the religious or cultural norms of their society: for example, because they are resisting genital mutilation, a forced marriage, male violence or the imposition of a dress code. Since gender is not a Convention ground, women fearing gender-related persecution have had to fit their claims into one of the recognised Convention grounds. The most commonly used ground is that of persecution suffered by a particular social group, but case law has dictated that gender is too wide a category and has required that the attributes of a particular social group should be recognisable and discrete.

Furthermore, protests, whether acts of subversion or transgression in defying customary or even state laws, are seen to be personal rather than political forms of dissent. The Convention also requires that the state is in some way connected to the persecution, either by sanctioning it or failing to protect the women from the persecution. Furthermore, certain forms of ill-treatment, such as domestic violence, have traditionally been considered a form of harm carried out by private individuals. Historically little recognition has been given to the institutionalised nature of violence against women. Those attempting to flee violence are frequently subjected to community and state hostility that amounts to the state sanctioning of male violence. Whilst some countries have interpreted the UN Convention on Human Rights liberally to cover persecution by non-state agents, the UK's Jack Straw had called upon the EU to unify in interpreting the Convention as restrictively as possible to acknowledge only persecution by the state.

However, it is the type of cases that SBS deals with that present a particularly difficult problem of categorisation under the Convention. Most of these concern women who are at risk of sexual or domestic violence because of their status as divorced or separated women. SBS argues that it is the risk of persecution that unites these women in a recognisable group. However the courts have taken a different view and held that in the absence of any other unifying characteristics a common fear of persecution is not sufficient for the formation of a group.

Shah and Islam

In 1999 in the case of Shah and Islam the House of Lords recognised gender related persecution for the first time. It has been hailed as one of the most enlightened decisions made to date. Both Mrs Shah and Mrs Islam were Pakistani nationals who had claimed asylum in the UK. They were both married and had been exposed to false allegations of adultery and violence by their husbands in Pakistan, and claimed asylum on the grounds that they would be prosecuted under Shariah law on their return because of those allegations and further persecuted by their male relatives. SBS supported Mrs Islam and provided expert advice on the position of women in Pakistan to the legal team.

The case proceeded as far as the House of Lords, where it was held that the women were refugees within the meaning of the

Convention, as they feared persecution arising out of their membership of a particular social group in a country where there was not
only a lack of state protection but also institutionalised persecution.
The Lords held that

> a particular social group' consisted of a group of persons who
> share 'a common, immutable characteristic that was either beyond
> the power of an individual to change or was so fundamental to the
> individual's identity or conscience that it ought not to be required
> to be changed ... there need be no element of cohesiveness, co-
> operation or interdependence.

In other words, gender was an unchangeable characteristic that was
beyond the power of an individual to change. Therefore, as discrimination against women – including the violation of fundamental rights and freedoms – was prevalent in Pakistan, women were
considered to constitute 'a particular social group' within the terms
of the 1951 Convention. The majority of the Lords also rejected the
view that women in Pakistan who transgress social and religious
norms are not persecuted because the violence takes place in the
private sphere of the family. Thus the concept of persecution was
extended to include non-governmental agents, provided the state
failed to protect the women against the actions of the individuals.
However, the Lords made it clear that they did not find that women
were a social group per se, and that future cases would have to be
decided on their individual facts.

So why were the Lords prepared to make such a decision, contrary to the political imperative to interpret refugee and immigration
laws as restrictively as possible? It should be remembered that this
decision did not occur in a political vacuum. Rather, it has come
about as a result of the concerted demands of women worldwide to
reconceptualise women's rights as human rights. The last decade in
the UK has seen intense campaigning by women, black and white,
against male violence. This has forced the government to reform
certain legislation, and scrutinise the response of key state agencies
in such areas as homicide laws, rape, female genital mutilation and
more recently forced marriages. Whilst not all these issues have been
related to immigration and asylum questions, the wider climate
created – that of zero tolerance of violence against women – has

helped to shape enlightened thinking and practice with some consequence on immigration law and policy. The Refugee Women's Legal Group (RWLG), formed in 1996, is now established as an important legal force in the development and dissemination of a gender perspective to asylum laws in the UK and Europe. The group comprises specialist immigration practitioners and representatives from refugee and women's organisations. After extensive consultation with over 3,000 individuals, refugee and women's groups, immigration solicitors and advisers, the RWLG formulated gender guidelines similar to those adopted in Canada, the USA and Australia, to improve the assessment procedures for refugee women in asylum claims in the UK. Following the launch of the guidelines RWLG was invited to meet the Home Office to discuss the issues raised in the guidelines. The Home Office published its own gender guidelines in December 2000. These, however, dealt with the need to be sensitive in understanding how persecution can be gender-specific (e.g. rape, female genital mutilation), rather then recognising gender-related persecution.

Onwards from Shah and Islam

Whilst SBS welcomed the decision in Shah and Islam, the reality is that it remains vulnerable to restrictive judicial interpretations, or to reversal by politicians unless effective political campaigning continues. The official state response to Shah and Islam was to find ways of reversing the judgment. In October 1999, Home Secretary Jack Straw criticised the Law Lords in the case of Shah and Islam for being 'over liberal'. He said there was 'no way it can be realistically argued that that was in contemplation when the 1951 convention was put in place.'[11]

From a gendered perspective the law does not go far enough in reflecting the reality of women refugees' experiences of persecution. As commentators have pointed out, 'the judgment has failed to address the fundamentally political nature of women's experiences which, when properly interpreted, cover a wide range of ways in which women challenge established social and institutional norms.'[12] On this basis it could be argued that all forms of resistance against gender oppression should be regarded as political acts of protest.

The reality is that women's experiences ought to be closely examined because there is often considerable overlap between the 'social group' and 'political opinion' grounds contained in the Convention.

Where women have claimed asylum, SBS has found that the Home Office is reluctant to acknowledge the concept of gender persecution as set out in the case of *Shah and Islam* and has chosen to grant women exceptional leave to remain (ELR). Women understandably are reluctant to challenge the grant of ELR and proceed with their claim for refugee status. However, in spite of these problems SBS continues to support clients to apply for asylum on the basis of gender persecution. Since *Shah and Islam* the Tribunal has upheld a number of gender-based claims, including that of an Iranian woman, Miriam Fatemeh, who feared prosecution because of adultery after leaving her violent husband; a Pakistani woman, Robina Altaf, whose illegitimate children would be seen as evidence of sexual immorality; a single Pakistani woman without male protection at risk from the Mohajirs; and a Ukrainian woman, Dzhygun, forced into prostitution. On the other hand a Latvian woman, Mortuleva, subjected to violence by her ex-husband, was not recognised as being part of a particular social group because of the system in place in Latvia to help women fleeing violence.

Sadly not all the judiciary has been prepared to acknowledge the rights of female refugees. SBS supported the case of an Indian woman who had claimed asylum after her arrival in the UK on a visit to her in-laws. She claimed that her husband had been abusive towards her and her children in India, and that while she was in the UK her in-laws subjected her to abuse. She fled with the help of a male family friend, thus laying her open to false claims of adultery and threats from her in-laws and husband. She reported her in-laws for harassment and the police referred her to SBS, who helped her find an immigration solicitor. Our client had two young children who were her dependants on her asylum claim. The basis of our client's claim was that her husband would subject her to emotional and physical abuse if she were returned to India, and that the courts and police would fail to provide her with protection, particularly in light of the false adultery claims against her. Shortly after she had claimed asylum our client's husband started wardship proceedings from Delhi, in the High Court in London, applying for the children to be returned to India, and for matters of custody to be decided in Delhi. The High Court cast doubts on our client's credibility and ordered that the children be returned to India. Our client's solicitors appealed to the Court of Appeal on the basis that the family courts did not have power to override Section 15 of the Immigration and Asylum Act 1999, which dictated that an asylum seeker (or their dependants) could not be removed from the UK, pending the outcome of the asylum proceedings. Our client and her children had already been granted exceptional leave to remain, but were still appealing against the refusal of refugee status. The Court of Appeal held that Section 15 only bound the executive (i.e. the Home Office) and not the judiciary, in this case the wardship courts. Our client's application for leave to appeal to the House of Lords was refused and the children, both under the age of 6, were returned to their father's care. Our client remained in the UK, too fearful to return to India.

In February 2003 our client was granted refugee status. The adjudicator held that the case of *Shah and Islam* could be applied to Indian cases, making it an important decision for our client. The adjudicator was fully aware of the wardship proceedings but found our client to be more credible. Had the High Court or the Court of Appeal deferred making a decision until the outcome of the asylum proceedings, surely they could not have overridden the refugee status of the mother and children and returned the children in breach of their human rights. Our client is considering an appeal to the European Court of Human Rights. However, whilst a successful appeal would overturn this appalling decision, it will not reunite our client with her children or rectify this miscarriage of justice. Authorities in Australia, Canada and the United States have generally shown more sensitivity to cases involving gender persecution. However, there remain grave shortcomings internationally and in the UK regarding the priority given to women's human rights across the judiciary.

Conclusion

Both EU and British asylum policy remain unethical and opportunistic. As journalist Gary Younge comments,

> It is not foreigners per se our government loathes; it is poor people. Asylum seekers with their tales of torture, rape and solitary confinement, can get to the end of queue and wait for their vouchers. Britain wants professionals with IT skills, teaching qualifications and nursing certificates.[13]

While the West applauds the free movement of capital, it abhors the free movement of labour. According to the Home Office the number of work-permit holders has risen by more than a third since Labour came to power. The sharpest increase has been from Africa. Reports in the press indicate that 20,000 nurses from the Philippines, various African countries and India entered Britain in 2000 to rescue the hard-pressed NHS. Further quotas are being planned to meet specific skills shortages in the economy. At present there over 100,000 vacancies in the London area alone for unskilled workers, which the government admits can only be filled by economic migration. Demographic predictions suggest that the proportion of productive young people will not be able to sustain the welfare needs of an ageing population through their taxes. The UN Population Division estimated that the EU would need to take in 1.4 million migrants a year to keep the ratio of the working to non-working population constant at the 1995 level from now until 2050. At the same time asylum seekers, many of whom are willing and able to work, are not being allowed to work and are being denied even basic humanitarian support by government.

We need to look no further than the government's immigration policies to understand how class, race and gender bias operates under New Labour. We condemn their immigration laws as racist and do not campaign for concessions for women at the expense of men. We were not willing to argue for the retention of the primary-purpose rule in order to further our campaign for the abolition of the one-year rule. We will continue in our campaign to give black women a voice, but our struggle for autonomy cannot be built on the oppression of others.

Notes

1. Jack Straw, letter to the *Guardian*, 26 April 2001; stress added.
2. These are the countries due to join the enlarged European Union in 2004:

Cyprus, the Czech Republic, Estonia, Hungary, Latvia, Lithuania, Malta, Poland, Slovakia and Slovenia.

3. Patrick Wintour, Derogation from the ECHR, *Guardian*, 27 January 2003.

4. On 19 February 2003, Justice Collins, on Section 55 of Nationality, Immigration and Asylum Act 2002, said that there were quite clearly breaches of Articles 3, 6 and 8 of the Human Rights Act and that this has quite clearly influenced NASS to take the action to suspend issuing negative decisions; National Coalition of Anti Deportation Campaigns, Press Release, 20 February 2003. Figures for numbers of applicants refused support are extrapolated from Home Office statistics for January and February 2002 by NADC.

5. Jacqueline Bhabha and Frances Klug, 'Till the Law Us Do Part: Background Report on Immigration Rules', *Guardian*, 22 July 1985.

6. www.bbc.co.uk/politics97/news/06/0605/straw.shtml.

7. The survey was conducted in two parts covering two periods of time. The first survey covered the period 16 June 1999 to 30 April 2000. The second survey covered the period 1 May 2000 to 15 June 2001. In the first phase over 2000 postal questionnaires were sent to all relevant agencies, in particular solicitor's firms, immigration barristers, law centres, advice centres, women's groups and refuges from around the country. Of the 200 agencies that responded in the first phase 89 had cases involving immigration and domestic violence. In the second survey questionnaires were sent to these 89 agencies, of whom 66 responded. Of the 66, 41 had cases involving immigration and domestic violence. The agencies represented a very wide cross section of immigration and domestic violence practitioners.

8. *Hansard*, Column 6WS, 26 November 2002.

9. Heaven Crawley, *Refugees and Gender: Law and Process*, Jordan Publishing, Bristol 2001.

10. Art. 1A(2) Convention Relating to the Status of Refugees, 1951.

11. Alan Travis, 'Asylum Rules Eased for Women', *Guardian*, 5 December 2000.

12. Alison Stanley and Catriona Jarvis, *Legal Action*, July 1999.

13. Gary Younge, 'Penalising the Poor' *Guardian*, 19 March 2001.

8

The tricky blue line:
black women and policing

Pragna Patel

Since the present Labour government came to power, we have seen some major developments on policing, ranging from a raft of legislation designed to get 'tough on crime and the causes of crime', through to the inquiry into the Stephen Lawrence case and a wave of anti-terrorist measures in the wake of 11 September. Not all the initiatives are welcome since some have grave implications for the question of civil liberties. But the case of Stephen Lawrence stands out because it represents a seminal moment in the history of policing and police racism. Indeed it is now impossible to discuss policing and race relations without understanding the impact of the Stephen Lawrence case.

The case concerned the racist murder of a black (African-Caribbean) teenager in 1993 and the failure of the police to investigate the killing as a racist one. Police indifference, incompetence, corruption and racism meant that the white assailants of Stephen Lawrence, many of whom were known to the police, escaped a proper criminal investigation or trial altogether. The Lawrence family, with the help of lawyers and supporters, mounted an extraordinary campaign to demand justice and to force the British state to recognise what black people have known for the last three or four decades – the existence of institutional racism and the lack of police accountability. Their campaign gave rise to a high-profile public inquiry, chaired by Sir William Macpherson, on the police handling of the case and on police investigation of racial violence generally. The Macpherson report, published in February 1999, made a series of wide-ranging recommendations, and generated a public debate not seen since the Scarman report into the Brixton riots in the 1980s.

In our view, however, the terms of the inquiry did not go far enough, and the ensuing report betrayed the complete absence of an understanding of the experiences of black women who come into conflict or contact with the police and the prosecutorial system. Drawing on insights gained in twenty-four years of casework, this piece will look at developments in policing race and domestic violence to show how the issue of policing and black community relations is also a gendered issue and therefore more complex than it at first appears.

Recent developments and opportunities

The Race Relations Amendment Act 2000, which places a positive duty on every public authority – including the police – to initiate measures designed to promote racial equality, was overdue. It is no longer satisfactory simply to have a negative duty not to discriminate – positive measures must be in place to demonstrate that public bodies are achieving racial equality. So far so good. However, it will be interesting to see whether the failure of police to investigate domestic violence within minority communities, for instance, will fall within the scope of the Race Relations Amendment Act.

In a separate but not entirely unrelated area, a series of decisions by the European Court of Human Rights and the recent enactment of the Human Rights Act have paved the way for people to seek redress from the police where they have failed to carry out investigations with due diligence. Public bodies, including the police and social services, no longer enjoy complete immunity from legal actions in negligence. These legislative developments provide us with the language and extra tools with which to hold the police accountable.

The Macpherson inquiry spearheaded a series of initiatives around the country designed to improve police response to racial violence. SBS regards the plethora of police initiatives on racial violence and racism with some degree of scepticism. One immediate impact on our work has been an increasing number of requests by the police to address police conferences on the issues of race, domestic violence and forced marriages. Within SBS, these requests have led to animated debates as to how far we can or should work with the police given that the 'new thinking' has yet to translate on the ground in any satisfactory way. Nevertheless the level of engagement sought from us by the police and the Home Office on this and other issues is new. During the years of Tory rule, we grew skilled in the art of oppositional politics. There was no other space in which to engage with the state. But under New Labour a few doors have opened up providing an opportunity, however limited, to enter into a dialogue and influence the various state institutions.

The dilemma for SBS has centred on the question of how far we can engage with the police without compromising our autonomy. We are aware that change occurs by maintaining pressure from the outside as well as influencing from within, but the question of how far we can go without being co-opted is vital, as we discovered in our experiences with the Home Office Working Group on forced marriage (see Chapter 4, 'It Was Written in Her Kismet'). These questions are very pertinent when viewed in the context of our routine casework. With a few exceptions, our cases reveal a profound unwillingness amongst local rank-and-file officers to accept the charge that the police are institutionally racist and sexist, or that they need drastically to transform their operational culture of complacency and arrogance. Yet the problem for us is that without some kind of engagement, however ineffective, we close off even the remote possibility of influencing police policy in the post-Stephen Lawrence climate. There are no easy answers.

Racism and the police

Our experiences do not sit very comfortably within the boundaries of orthodox debates on racism and the police. Anti-racist commentators have noted that institutional racism is predicated upon the need to subordinate those in our society who are considered to be 'different' by virtue of their racial or ethnic background. It is argued that any effective anti-racist strategies must first unmask and then challenge precisely how such power comes to be expressed or practised. However, I would go further and suggest that any analysis of institutionalised racism will be incomplete unless it takes account of the experiences of black women. How institutionalised racism can and does intersect with patriarchal power to the detriment of both black women and racial equality demands urgent attention. Our experiences show us that when women who are victims of domestic violence make demands of the state for protection, they are likely to confront the racism of the state in the form of indifference and even hostility. But we find another more insidious process at work in keeping women powerless – multiculturalism (see Chapter 1, 'Some Recurring Themes'). Driven by the cases of women whose experiences of domestic violence are 'under-policed', often as a result of multicultural – 'culturally sensitive' – approaches, SBS has attempted to develop the debate beyond the narrow confines permitted by the Stephen Lawrence debate. Policing needs to be assessed not merely in terms of its impact on vague notions of the 'black community,' but also in terms of its impact on the most vulnerable sections of that community. To achieve this, we need to take a closer look at police initiatives on domestic violence within the context of overall developments in policing in the 1980s and 1990s. This includes the policing of black communities, and especially the consensus that has built up around multi-agency policing – which has, by and large, been hailed as a 'success', an indication that police practice on domestic violence has improved.

The cases highlighted below, many of which have arisen after the Macpherson report, show how the police have failed to implement some key recommendations – in particular those pertaining to advocacy. Instead the emphasis continues to be on 'partnership' approaches to policing domestic violence through multi-agency forums. One reason, we suspect, for our continuing difficulties with the local police is the fact that we refuse to be fully committed to local multi-agency forums in the absence of any far-reaching changes affecting police accountability.

In 1998 the Crime and Disorder Act was introduced, placing the 'partnership' approach to the policing of a range of social issues on a statutory footing. The local authority, police, police authorities and others now have an obligation to cooperate with each other and the wider community in order to cut crime in their locality. Underpinning these initiatives, however, is a discernable shift in the ideological thinking of Labour-controlled local authorities. The 'new labour re-alism' has translated into attempts at a consensus-building approach to social issues, in contrast to the approaches modelled on the old style GLC radicalism which emphasised the need for local democ-racy and accountability through mechanisms of independent moni-toring projects and the politics of municipal socialism.

We notice with increasing concern that the very terminology of the multi-agency approach reflects the shifts towards the 'new real-ism' or the new corporatism within local authority and police gov-ernance.[1] For instance the growing acceptance of the police as a 'service' provider rather than a 'force' which more accurately con-notes police monopoly of coercive powers, shows the inherent ten-dencies of the multi-agency approach to deny issues of structural power and inequality.

It is becoming more and more difficult for us to avoid being sucked into local multi-agency projects. For example, Ealing Council, which funds our core costs, have recently made our grant con-ditional upon our involvement in local multi-agency forums. Also about two years ago, a local council/police partnership on crime prevention was set up as a result of the Crime and Disorder Act. However, in order to obtain grants from the borough's regeneration funds for deprived areas such as Southall and Acton, it was neces-sary for voluntary groups to show that they would address issues like domestic violence in partnership with the council and Police Community Safety Unit, and other groups. SBS decided not to apply for such funding because we felt that a considerable amount of our resources would be wasted trying to agree definitions of domestic violence, let alone get to the stage where we could agree on a corporate policy which addressed the question of statutory and police accountability.

Paternalism, conspiracy or pragmatism?

The concept of multi-agency policing was first propounded in the early 1980s as the solution to the crisis of inner cities, by bringing about greater interdependency and consensus between state and other agencies through the sharing of aims and objectives.[2] But the concept was not without its critics. Some argued that such a multi-agency model, labelled 'paternalistic', posits a 'managerial' solution which fails to recognise the organic aspects of communities and the power differences between the state and communities. Others reject the concept altogether, stating that multi-agency policing is essentially an attempt to revert to a 'mythical' age of 'community policing' by consent, where the police enjoyed the support of the public. Such critics state that initiatives such as police-led multi-agency projects serve a very useful function in the control and surveillance aspects of policing youth and blacks in particular, albeit in a less obviously oppressive manner. This 'soft' policing strategy, they argue, complements 'hard' and militarised methods of policing.[3] This perspective has been labelled, somewhat unfairly in our view, 'conspiratorial', amounting to a 'police take-over', a means by which the police co-opt other agencies, and even the entire community, to pursue police-defined goals.

Whilst we do not subscribe to a grand conspiratorial analysis of policing, our own experiences and those of others, notably in black communities, do bear out some of these observations. Where the police are involved in multi-agency work, the underlying effect has been a widening of the net of social control, co-option of state and voluntary agencies and, most importantly, the breakdown of political resistance, thereby excluding radical voices within our communities. The need to seek legitimation for the coercive functions of the police remains a vital objective, particularly as the crisis of policing continues unabated, with revelations of police corruption, miscarriages of justice, deaths in custody and other police malpractice. It is difficult to disentangle the coercive and emergent 'welfare' or 'soft' functions of policing, but it is wrong to assume that those functions are always distinct.

The 'welfare' functions of policing exemplified by the multi-agency approach to domestic violence were also developed partly out of a need to respond to mounting criticism about police handling of child abuse, domestic violence and rape. The question, therefore, as to which aspect of policing – 'soft' or 'hard' – is emphasised often depends on which section of the community is being policed. The contradictory pull between policing by consent and policing by coercion is well typified in the confusion that existed as to whether the 'welfare' functions epitomised by Domestic Violence Units

(DVUs),[4] now replaced by Community Safety Units (CSUs) consti-tuted 'real' police work. Within rank-and-file police culture, the response to domestic violence does not correspond with the multi-agency rhetoric; DVUs and now CSUs are viewed by many officers as a distraction from the enforcement of law and order on the streets.

Policing of black communities: what's it got to do with domestic violence?

The history of policing in black communities is especially crucial to absorb if feminists are to avoid falling into the trap of uncritically accepting the police as legitimate agents of protection or as equal partners in combating domestic violence. The development of the multi-agency approach to the policing of black communities, and its extension to the policing of domestic violence, are perhaps not as unconnected as they first appear.

Community/multi-agency policing was first put into practice by Sir Kenneth Newman, Commissioner for London in the late 1970s and early 1980s in the wake of confrontations between black youths and police in Brixton, Southall, Tottenham and other inner cities around the country. This approach was also recommended by Lord Scarman in his inquiry into the Brixton disorders in 1981.[5] The main aim was to achieve consent for police operations amongst sections of black communities: youths who have been and continue to be targets for 'over-policing'.

At the same time in relation to racial violence – an area which historically has been 'under-policed' – the police were not able to claim 'success' in the way that they do with regard to domestic violence. Until the Stephen Lawrence case, there was a significant silence about multi-agency initiatives on racial violence.

Multi-agency forums have not led to increased confidence in the police, largely because they have not succeeded in addressing the issue of police abuse of power. Also, these forums are often pre-sided over by 'leaders of the community' who are not accountable to the communities they claim to represent. Witness, for example, the increasing alienation felt by African-Caribbean and South Asian youth manifested in the waves of confrontation with the police in

Brixton and Bradford (1995), Birmingham (1996), and more recently Bradford and Oldham (2001).

Research reveals that multi-agency forums can actually exacerbate pre-existing tensions between black people and the police because they fail to consult, disclose or even give advance warnings about their coercive operations. In our experience this is also true of the community consultative forum in Ealing, which is largely a rubber-stamping exercise for police operations. Despite a lack of confidence in the multi-agency approach in some quarters, it was extended to other areas of policing and was used by the police to draw sections of the community into its fold.

Whether it is more than just a coincidence that the first DVUs, set up in the 1980s, were in areas with high black populations is an interesting question. The fact is that Tottenham and Brixton were indeed the first areas in London to see the development of DVUs, which were often responsible for initiating multi-agency forums on domestic violence.

Multi-agency policing and domestic violence

The 1986 Metropolitan Police Internal Working Party Report was the first police endorsement of the multi-agency approach to domestic violence. Although, like most police reviews, it was never made public, leaked copies of the report showed that its two central recommendations were the adoption of pro-arrest policies – encouraging the police to treat domestic violence as a crime by arresting perpetrators – and multi-agency initiatives in local areas. The development of DVUs was therefore consistent with Scarman's recommendation on policing by consent. It is not just a coincidence that all DVUs and multi-agency domestic violence projects have been led by or have involved community liaison officers.

Our own casework, however, has shown that multi-agency forums have not led to women gaining greater access to the criminal justice system. A cursory glance at the work of DVUs throughout London showed how the need for effective criminal justice responses became subsumed under the need for liaison with local agencies via multi-agency forums, which in turn displaced responsibility for police accountability in dealing with domestic violence onto civil society and even individuals themselves. Whilst recognising the ongoing debate on the merits or otherwise of mandatory arrest policies (see below), the problem with the multi-agency approach is that the criminal justice system as a legitimate option of redress for women has been seriously undermined.

Two female officers at the Tottenham Police Station DVU stated that their multi-agency forum was set up 'to educate the police and the public that domestic violence is a serious problem and not just a police problem ... to get everyone together to discuss ideas, pool resources and find out what each group does and can offer women'. For the non-police agencies the rationale for participating was to let all organisations share information and 'build up trust for the police'.[6] In the early days, the two female officers were also critical of the 1987 Force Order, which fell short of recommending the disciplining of rank-and-file officers who failed in their response to domestic violence. But their call for such measures of accountability went unheard by the Metropolitan Police. Instead, Metropolitan Police directives placed emphasis on consensus building with groups which had hitherto remained hostile to the police. This underlying imperative was revealed by the community liaison officer in charge of the Brixton DVU in 1988.

> From a community liaison point of view, if you look at it totally cynically, it has been absolutely marvellous. It has brought and drawn us together with organisations in the community, particularly women and feminist groups. They have always been anti-us and it has broken down all sorts of barriers.... A female officer has been invited to be on the management committee of the local women's aid, which is unheard of.[7]

At the same time, the officer felt that the DVU was able to perform an intelligence-gathering function. Women were drawn into their confidence and the information gained was used to carry out a number of drug raids in the locality. Not surprisingly, many black women are particularly reluctant to involve the police for fear of enhancing the criminalisation of black men. This dilemma is not easily resolved and is the focus of ongoing debate between black feminists and anti-racist activists within black communities.

The debate, however, is one that ought to transcend the 'minority issue' ghetto within which it is so often perceived to be by the wider feminist movement, as it raises profound questions about the framework of relations that ought to be developed by feminists with the police. Feminists have argued that multi-agency policing works at an informal level where it is easier to demand accountability. However, in our experience it is precisely this informality that is dangerous, since it can lead to breaches of confidentiality, complacency and unacceptable working practices for which there is no redress. This is not the kind of accountability that we want, particularly when the police use multi-agency forums to sort out 'difficulties' with representatives, rather than encourage women to pursue the complaints system because they wish to avoid taking disciplinary measures against their own officers.

Another problem is that any attempt to voice criticism of police in such forums has met with a resolute denial that there are problems between the police and women's groups. Our experience at a multi-agency forum in Haringey which we were asked to address, revealed that critical voices in such forums are likely to succumb to acts of self-censorship for the sake of unity. Furthermore it becomes difficult to disengage from an entity to which one belongs and for which one is expected to shoulder equal responsibility. In other parts of the country, some forces have emphasised pro-arrest policies to improve the criminal justice system's handling of domestic violence, whilst many have merely established multi-agency forums. Often the police feel that setting up a multi-agency forum is all that is necessary to show that there is a 'shift' in their thinking and practice. Whilst some police divisions may be better in recording domestic violence, it is only one component of a better police response. It cannot be the only one. Also, in practice, these programmes can amount to a patronising conceptualisation of women's citizenship, since women are discouraged from making an informed choice about utilising criminal law to pursue justice.

The need for improving state response and the adequate provision of resources have not received the same level of attention in these forums as raising awareness and training in handling domestic violence. We remain highly sceptical of the training 'solution', having witnessed the spectacular failure of racial awareness training, which was particularly fashionable in the 1980s. These are not matters of individual prejudice. Structures and practices perpetuate an 'operational culture' that cannot be dislodged by awareness training on its own. A change in attitudes will require a more sweeping transformation in policing and prosecutorial institutions, involving mechanisms for independent monitoring and a willingness to investigate complaints. In the absence of such radical reforms, training offers at best the possibility of returning 'changed' individual officers to unchanged and often unchallengeable sexist and racist environments.

The death of Vandana Patel

The death of Vandana Patel, so tragically killed within the supposed safety of the DVU at Stoke Newington Police Station in 1991, and the failure by the police to institute a public inquiry into the matter, should have alerted all of us to the difficulty of working with the police in multi-agency forums. It precipitated an internal Metropolitan Police review into all procedures on domestic violence, but no apology to her family was forthcoming. Despite so-called increased awareness and training amongst senior ranking officers, attempts were made to legitimise the view that 'allowing parties to talk through their difficulties is a legitimate option'.

SBS and other Asian women's groups protested against her death and the practice of mediation amongst the police. We called for an independent inquiry. In a letter to the *Guardian* we wrote:

> The murder of Vandana Patel and the purported justification of their actions betray the reality of police thinking of domestic violence. If the police are to treat domestic violence as a criminal offence, as they should, then their overriding duty is to provide protection to the woman who faces it. It is not, then, for the police to adopt the role of mediators [with] the objective of reconciliation between the parties. There is no criminal offence where the police would seek to reconcile the perpetrator and the victim of crime, or allow them to 'talk through their difficulties' as a 'legitimate option'. There is clear conflict between the stated aim of the police to treat domestic violence as a crime and their practice which is often akin to 'marriage guidance'. It leads us to conclude that the police have yet to move away from the per-

ception of domestic violence as outside the scope of 'real' police work. The mentality of the door-step police officer, advising couples to 'patch up their differences', has found its way into the domestic violence units and has come to be institutionalised.

A series of seminars which followed as part of the internal police review, billed as an attempt to 'consult' and work in 'equal partnership' with all agencies interested in domestic violence, was organised throughout London. Despite the rhetoric of 'equal partnership', the final report was not available to the participating groups, including SBS, or to the public at large, for comment. When challenged, the officer at Scotland Yard responsible for the report simply said: 'That is the way it is.' We are called upon merely to sanction police policies and their predetermined agendas. If this is the case at the highest levels, how much more likely is the deficiency of the multi-agency model at the local level?

There is a growing acceptance of the multi-agency approach by many women's aid groups. Indeed the partnership between the police and women's aid in some areas is such that the police are even involved in running local women's projects on domestic violence. Criticism of the police is therefore muted. There is a general consensus that the police have 'solved the problem' through DVUs and other multi-agency initiatives which encourage the use of civil remedies. A WPC in Wembley DVU saw this as an achievement: 'In my experience, we have had far more success in helping women with civil remedies, helping women getting injunctions with powers of arrest.'

There has been considerable debate, among feminists in particular, as to what type of police intervention we should be demanding in domestic violence cases. Some argue that the police's priority should always be to uphold the criminal law and so arrest perpetrators, irrespective of a woman's wishes – in short, to adopt a mandatory arrest and even prosecution policy. Others argue that the police should adopt a 'softer' approach and recognise that for valid reasons, such as women's fear of further violence and the desire to retain control over their decisions, the police should be aware of the other options available to women and direct them to appropriate agencies. Our casework shows that the police fail at both approaches. More often than not they fail to give women appropriate advice and assistance to pursue other safe options, or to help those women who wish to utilise the criminal justice system. Furthermore, women's ignorance of the law and lack of confidence is exploited by the police, who try and prevent women from gaining access to the criminal justice system. This is especially true of the experiences of Asian and other minority women. Our stance is that women should have information about the whole range of options and be assisted in making a decision that they feel comfortable with. The fact that police officers are first and foremost law enforcers should not preclude them from dealing with cases with sensitivity and professionalism.

At present, almost all CSUs and their variants, such as anti-victimisation units, deal with a number of crimes including domestic violence, racial violence, juvenile crimes, homophobic crimes and so on. The problem, however, is that the varied focus of the unit means that there is inevitably an informal prioritisation of issues, usually due to lack of resources. Domestic violence is accorded low priority because of the continuing perception that it is a 'waste' of police time. Our experience of CSUs continues to reinforce many of the criticisms levelled at the DVUs. SBS has experienced great difficulty in getting hold of officers at CSUs – since most of the time an answer machine is all that is available. It can often take up to several days before a message is answered. Even when CSU officers do respond, the same attitudes that result in the 'under-policing' of domestic violence prevail.

Local experiences of multi-agency policing

The first attempt by Southall Police to set up a multi-agency forum was in February 1987. SBS attended two meetings, along with other invited groups such as the local victim support groups, probation services, psychiatric nurses and social workers. The terms of reference were set by the police. Their stated aim was to build up a profile of 'problem families' whose behaviour was seen to characterise domestic violence. To this end all agencies were asked to pass on their case files on domestic violence to the police. No indication was given as to how information contained in the files would be utilised. It became obvious that we were being asked to take on the task of 'social control' over such families, and our involvement within the group became untenable.[8]

In 1988, Southall Police asked the consultative group in Ealing to coordinate the domestic violence working panel known as the 'The Violence in the Home Committee'. The panel applied to the then Racial Equality Unit at Ealing Council for a grant. Its remit was widely drawn, to include children who suffer violence in the home as well as the 'occasional battered husband', because, as one member of the committee saw it, 'some men are married to wives bigger than them'. Such a display of ignorance about the gendered nature of domestic violence, its causes and consequences has been one of the reasons for our continuous reluctance to be involved in such forums.

A DVU was also set up at Ealing Police Station. When SBS met the two WPCs based there, they reinforced our view that, although well-meaning, their main aim was to supply women with the information necessary to seek protection through a range of agencies other than the criminal justice system itself. The multi-agency aspect of their work never really took off, partly because we refused to formalise our relationship. We preferred instead to liaise on a case-by-case basis, allowing ourselves maximum autonomy to raise difficult questions and to challenge police failures by way of the complaints system.

In one case in 1993, a young Asian woman badly beaten by her father, with injuries warranting examination by a police doctor, was told by a detective constable that she should take out a private summons against her father from her local magistrates' court, which would be 'just as effective as criminal proceedings'. Our client went to the magistrates' court, only to be advised by a concerned clerk that she would be at a considerable disadvantage if she was not legally represented. She was urged to return to the police station to demand action. She was then simply shunted about from one police station to another despite the fact that there was a DVU at one of the stations to which she was referred. It was only after much intensive pressure by SBS that she was able to force the police to take action. Her father was eventually charged and convicted of actual bodily harm. Later, with the help of SBS, she filed a complaint about the initial police response. As appears to be the norm, she came under intense pressure from the police to drop the complaint and to resolve the matter informally.

In another case, also in 1993, the husband of an Asian woman subjected her to violence and threatened to have her locked up in a mental institution. The police were called by the woman's daughter, but to her astonishment the police actually assaulted and arrested her. She spoke no English, but instead of providing an interpreter, the police spoke to her husband, and then forcibly dragged her off without her shoes to the police station after threatening to handcuff her. At the police station, she was searched and locked in a cell without explanation. Some hours later she was released without assistance. She did not make a formal complaint to the police for fear of reprisals. This is not an isolated case.

The practice of Ealing DVU, like many others, gave the appearance that the police had 'shifted', but in fact the criminal justice system remained untouched, feeding into the myth that women are 'reluctant' to press charges. In fact such under-policing was seen as an 'enlightened' approach by an officer in West London, who, when challenged by SBS on behalf of a local woman for failure to arrest a perpetrator, retorted that the police's aim was to operate a 'positive intervention policy' not a 'positive arrest policy'. This attitude ties in neatly with the national view on crime prevention that shifts responsibility from the state to the local community and the family itself.

In 2000, we found ourselves compelled to join the local multi-agency forum on domestic violence, which was defunct for a while but then given a new lease of life by Ealing Council. In the past, when necessary, we used to approach and work with the council directly, for example to develop a comprehensive local authority housing policy. When necessary we would set up a working group involving the housing department and other voluntary groups working around women and homelessness. Such methods of working were successful because they involved participants who shared similar perspectives and critiques, and were focused on the task in hand. However, by the year 2000 Ealing Council closed off all such avenues of influencing local policy on domestic violence, especially in relation to social services provision and homelessness. We were therefore forced to participate in the local multi-agency forum on domestic violence. It was set up to upgrade services on domestic violence in the borough by training professionals and thereby improving their response, enabling better inter-agency working and encouraging institutions to implement policies. However, it did not have a structure; nor did it have concrete aims and objectives. Hence it worked inefficiently. There is a large membership but only a small segment that is proactive. Getting agreement in a forum which represents such a wide range of organisations as community groups, the local authority, probation services, the police and victim support has meant that most recommendations have to be watered down. The police were at one time leading the forum, but Ealing Women's Aid now chairs it. Participation depends on the good will of the individuals who attend and does not lead to wider change in the institutions they represent. It is merely a talking shop. Currently SBS is working with the forum in trying to get the borough of Ealing to develop and implement a corporate policy on domestic violence so that all its departments respond with consistency.

In order to tackle the problems the forum faced, it was decided at a review meeting to set up an executive committee that would oversee and expedite the work of the forum. The committee consisted of the police, the council, Victim Support, SBS and Ealing Women's Aid. In the first meeting we tried to agree the terms of reference for the domestic violence forum, beginning with a definition of domestic violence. This included the statement that domestic violence involved 'usually a man, over another, usually a woman' and went on to further detail in its guiding principles that, amongst other factors, it may take place within same-sex relationships, against children, the elderly, disabled people and may involve women against men. The male representative from the CSU took great offence at this definition, stating that it discriminated against men. The local police wanted to move away from a gender-specific policy on domestic violence despite a number of policies being in place, like that of GLA which stated that women are more affected than men. Whilst we accept that women can also perpetrate violence, it became apparent that the police did not understand the gendered nature of domestic violence. Needless to say, this discussion was a rather heated one, reflecting the stalemate in which the forum is trapped.

Unsurprisingly, we have not had much success in developing corporate policy on domestic violence in the multi-agency forum due to, among other things, lack of leadership and commitment, irreconcilable perspectives on domestic violence, and a refusal to accept that it is a gendered issue. The forum appears to be unable to move beyond 'training needs' for members. Presentations by domestic violence forums from other areas and multi-agency data collection, none of which is channelled in any worthwhile direction, feature regularly on the forum's agenda. Whilst we sometimes go to these forums, we are frustrated with the lack of movement towards substantive changes in housing, social services and other policies.

The excuse of multiculturalism

In Southall, as in other minority communities, the police have from time to time invoked language and cultural and religious differences as reasons for non-intervention in response to Asian women's demands for protection against domestic violence. Consultation with community leaders takes place at formal and informal levels for a number of reasons, including the need to gain 'community' approval for police operations. Crimes committed against young Asian women are often 'non-crimed'. For example, forced marriages are often treated as if they were merely an issue of adolescence, cultural conflict or simply a private family matter. Specific police rationales for non-intervention have ranged from 'not wanting to offend Asian men' (although this is never a factor when enacting immigration raids or carrying out extensive stop-and-search practices) to recognising that 'older Asian women have a higher tolerance level'. Asian/ minority women are treated differently merely because they experience violence in a different cultural context. We have always been at pains to point out that all women experience violence in a cultural context and that differences of culture should not lead to a denial of civil rights for minority women. The dangers of multiculturalism are particularly acute for minority women in East London and in Northern England, where there is dominant religious leadership but no counteracting, progressive voices like that of SBS.

We strongly suspect that the need to 'respect' cultural differences in the resolution of marital violence was a factor in the police response to Vandana Patel (see above). It is well known that the police came to an informal 'arrangement' with a local Asian women's refuge that the estranged parties should meet to resolve their 'differences'. There is no evidence to suggest that Vandana Patel was given proper advice or a choice as to whether or not she wanted to meet her husband. It is our view that police recognition of equality was replaced by the recognition of cultural diversity only, which together with a routine trivialisation of domestic violence ensured that Vandana Patel had no control over her own life. In less extreme forms, this is an experience echoed by Asian women up and down the UK.

It is our view that the multi-agency approach accommodates a multicultural perspective more easily. The presence of mainly male Asian business, religious and political leaders in the local police consultative forums, such as that in Ealing, have helped to ensure that women are not included in notions of the community and that gender crimes within the community are rarely discussed.

The Macpherson report and its local impact

Not all our experiences of the local police have been negative. In a few exceptional cases, we have received excellent cooperation from the police. The benefit to the women is that they are listened to, are able to access the criminal justice process without fear of further violence, intimidation or humiliation, and achieve some measure of protection and justice. We prefer partnership to develop organically on a case-by-case basis which gives real meaning to the term, rather than in the mechanical approach adopted by multi-agency forums.

The response of the police is baffling to us since there is no consistency in their approach. They can be very good, usually in helping to collect the belongings of a woman who has escaped domestic violence or who needs to return to her home. Yet even here there is no guarantee.

We remain particularly alarmed by the fact that the right of women to advocacy by groups such as ours is being seriously undermined. The use of advocates was a key recommendation of the Macpherson report. It is not surprising that workers are often forced to quote the law and the Macpherson report. But when we do mention the Macpherson report at any but the highest levels, the response of police officers is 'Oh you're going to throw that at us now', or 'I don't care what the report says', or 'It's nothing to do with domestic violence.' It is all the more disturbing that some of the most serious failures are reflected in recent cases. In one case in 1999, our caseworker was asked to leave when accompanying her client to Southall Police Station to report a rape. The police argued that 'force policy' demanded that women make statements un-accompanied. Yet in other instances, workers have been allowed to support their clients when reporting to the police. Even solicitors attempting to get the police to institute criminal proceedings against perpetrators of domestic violence have been treated with contempt in some of our cases. Women have been criticised for having involved us in their dealings with the police. The police believe that the women have been 'influenced and pressurised' into taking action by SBS. Such responses reinforce our suspicion that the police exploit Asian women's ignorance of the services available and their low expectations of the police. What needs to be stressed is that Asian women's ignorance of services and of their legal rights is actually compounded by the police response. We have witnessed inaction, negligent action and even oppressive action by the local police in their response to the needs of such women.

In 1999, Amarjeet suffered a serious attack by her husband, who attempted to rape her and almost killed her. During the assault, in June, she managed to dial 999. Had the police not arrived in time, it is more than likely that she would have been grievously and even fatally wounded. She had been subjected to torture, violence and abuse nine months prior to this incident, and was not allowed to leave the home or make any calls. Amarjeet was taken to the local police station. The officer who initially attended to her explained that she should think about pressing charges but that it was prema-ture to make such an important decision. No other assistance was offered. She was advised to see a solicitor. The solicitors noted that she was covered in bruises and appeared to be depressed. They advised her to seek immediate medical assistance. They also advised her to return to the police, as she was determined to press charges. Within days, however, Amarjeet returned to her solicitors in floods of tears. She had been referred to the local DVU and had found the behaviour of the female DVU officer and the interpreter to be very negative. She complained that she had been made to feel that she was the guilty party. She had informed the DVU officer that she wished to press charges against her husband. However, the officer interrogated Amarjeet and refused to take her statement or press charges. She repeatedly asked Amarjeet 'What will you achieve by pressing charges?' Amarjeet informed the officer that she had no support in the UK and that she wanted justice and protection so that her husband did not assault her again. But the officer told her that she was talking 'rubbish'. Amarjeet felt very intimidated by the aggressive manner of the officer. With regard to medical evidence of the injuries she had sustained, the officer replied, 'How do we know you have suffered all of this? We were not present there.' The officer further asserted that the medical reports and the bruises could be a hoax or that Amarjeet may have caused the bruises herself. Amarjeet explained that she was not able to go back to India due to the shame she would be made to feel for the break-up of the marriage. The officer replied 'Well is that our fault now?'

The police kept insisting that Amarjeet had only gone to them due to pressure placed upon her by her solicitors, despite Amarjeet's repeated assertions to the contrary. Amarjeet's solicitor telephoned the DVU officer to seek an explanation for her behaviour, but no justifiable reason was forthcoming. The solicitor asked the officer to reconsider her refusal to take a statement from Amarjeet, and told her that in any interview they would like to be present. The officer refused their request to be present, declined to take a statement from Amarjeet and suggested that the solicitor was influencing Amarjeet. The solicitor asked to be put through to the duty officer. This request was denied and the officer disconnected the phone. The solicitor made a formal complaint regarding the officer's conduct and neglect of duty. They insisted that a different officer take Amarjeet's statement in their presence. Amarjeet then sought the help of SBS. The presence of a DVU did not guarantee a swift and professional response from the police.

Many of our cases show that women are routinely deterred even when they do have the confidence to press charges. The first question posed when women contact the police is, 'Do you want to press charges?' This question is asked in the absence of any prior encouragement or the giving of accurate information about what this entails, how the system will work and how victims can be supported in the face of reprisals or fear of further intimidation from the perpetrators. It is not surprising that in these circumstances women are reluctant to press charges, so fuelling the myth that women don't want to press charges. Such routine police failure cannot be summed up as a case of a few 'bad apples' within the police force which can be overcome by training and awareness. To some extent this was recognised in the Macpherson report – hence the finding of institutional racism. But the recognition needs to extend to other areas of policing too.

The list of cases of police malpractice continues, some of which are very serious indeed. In March 2002, SBS was alerted to a case by an advocacy project based in Hammersmith. A woman from Eastern Europe had reported domestic violence to the Hammersmith police and volunteered information that she was an immigration 'overstayer'. She was detained in a police cell. They then informed her that they had a 'duty to report her to the Home Office'. She was deported the same day. Nothing was done about the violence that she faced.

Perkash's case

As the Macpherson report was being written, SBS was helping an Asian woman, Perkash Walia, in her contacts with the police. Her ex-boyfriend, who also happened to be a practising priest at a Southall Hindu temple, had seriously assaulted her. Perkash suffered a near-fatal knife attack to her neck and a deep, six-inch knife cut to her thigh, as well as beatings, kicking and attempted strangulation. Witnesses to the actual attack called the police, who failed to apprehend the perpetrator although his whereabouts were well known, until he fled to India. The police did not carry out essential investigations or obtain crucial forensic evidence or witness statements. Working on the assumption that women who experience domestic violence 'waste police time', they merely went through the motions of an investigation.

Following a period in hospital, where she underwent emergency surgery, Perkash had to obtain her own photographic evidence of her injuries and collect crucial information on the whereabouts of her assailant and the witnesses. Three months after she was assaulted she had to retrieve her own blood-stained clothing from the scene of her assault to present to the police! Some twelve months later, when her ex-boyfriend returned to this country to resume his post at the Hindu temple, Perkash had to monitor his movements, alert the police and insist on his arrest, only to discover to her dismay that they had gathered no evidence except a cursory four-page statement that was taken from her a week after the assault.

It was at this point that Perkash contacted SBS to put pressure on the police to charge and prosecute her assailant. The case eventually went to trial, at which Perkash had to shoulder the burden of the entire prosecution case: it was simply her word against that of her assailant. Fortunately the jury chose to believe her, and her assailant was found guilty of causing grievous bodily harm, with the result that he was given a lengthy sentence of imprisonment. Perkash felt vindicated, because she had persisted and achieved some degree of justice in the face of police intransigence, and because the presiding judge at the conclusion of the case raised concerns about the police investigation. But she achieved her vindication despite rather then because of the criminal justice system.

The case highlights how Perkash's experience of domestic violence was compounded by police racism and sexism. Her experiences highlight just how institutional racism operates, not in a necessarily obvious way but in combination with gender discrimination. The police played on the myth that women in Perkash's circumstances do not wish to pursue criminal charges and on stereotypical assumptions of Asian women as passive, ignorant and unable to articulate their needs. They did not expect her to show courage and determination in pursuing justice. In due course, angered by the lack of action on the part of the police, Perkash Walia submitted a formal complaint directly to the Metropolitan Police Commissioner about his officers' litany of failures. She sought to compel those officers to account for their gross neglect of duty. The response on behalf of the Commissioner was all too familiar: the Metropolitan Police tried to avoid any investigation of the complaint by requesting a dispensation from the Police Complaints Authority (PCA) due to the delay on Perkash's part to lodge a complaint. It appeared as if the PCA would do the bidding of the Metropolitan Police.

Once again, Perkash had to shoulder the burden to take it further. With the assistance of a solicitor, she pointed out that any delay in her complaint was perfectly understandable: given the effects of the acute trauma of the assault she had suffered, she had wished to leave the whole episode behind her, and it was only when that proved impossible without some semblance of accountability in respect of the conduct of those officers that she proceeded with the complaint. She pointed out that, in any event, it was incumbent upon the PCA to ensure that an investigation of her complaint took place if it was practicable, as it certainly was in this case. And she pointed out the implications of Articles 1, 3 and 13 of the European Convention of Human Rights:[9] namely, that when individuals have been subjected to inhuman or degrading treatment there must be an official investigation; that this should be conducted diligently with a genuine determination to identify and prosecute those responsible; that, in the absence of such an investigation, legal protection of human rights would be ineffective in practice because it would be possible in some cases for some to abuse the rights of others with virtual impunity; that where fundamental values and essential aspects of private life are at stake, effective deterrents may be indispensable, and may only be capable of being provided by the criminal law; and that the ultimate effectiveness of a remedy may depend on the proper discharge by the investigating police officers of their functions and, therefore, on an effective official investigation of any complaint that such functions have not been properly discharged.

Following several months of fast and furious correspondence from Perkash's solicitor, and under the threat of a challenge in the courts, the PCA finally conceded that they would require an investigation of Perkash's complaint after all, albeit one conducted by the Metropolitan Police themselves. In essence, Perkash was being asked to have confidence in the very police force that had already victimised her twice over: first in their failure to investigate the assault upon her, and then in their attempt to avoid any investigation of her complaint into those original failures.

Eventually, under the threat of a further challenge, the PCA were forced to make a second concession, and Perkash was granted the right to have her complaint investigated by another police force. In late 2001, Surrey Police embarked on a thorough investigation of the police handling of the case. The outcome of the investigation and the ensuing PCA decision on the complaint is currently awaited; it is expected to recognise systemic failures on the part of the Metropolitan Police in the handling of Perkash's case.

Whatever the final outcome of the complaint investigation, Perkash's case has already been significant: it is the first time that a complaint against one police force about its handling of a domestic violence case has been handled by another police force under the supervision of the PCA. It represents a vindication of our attempts to ensure that the police should account publicly for their failures in their handling of such cases. Perkash's case should also serve as a warning bell against the overwhelming tide of opinion around us which assumes that the police have changed their practices on domestic violence.

In many ways, Perkash's case echoes the criticisms made of the police in the investigation of the Stephen Lawrence murder. Yet her experiences do not sit very comfortably within the boundaries of orthodox debates on racism and the police.

The 'carrot and the stick'

We are probably unique among women's groups in having a policy of encouraging users of our centre to submit formal complaints in every instance of domestic violence where there has been police failure to take effective action. We have become a thorn in the side of our local police, who are often exasperated by the need to deploy scarce police resources and staff to investigate 'trivial' problems that are largely to do with entrenched 'attitudes' in the force. In a pattern that is now predictable, upon receipt of the complaint the police will put enormous informal pressure on women, often in our absence, either to drop the complaint or to accept an informal resolution. Usually they convince the women that they will have 'appropriate words' with the officer(s) concerned. Needless to say, the problem with this approach is that it is shrouded in secrecy and there is no way of knowing what action, if any, was taken.

Given the hostility we face from our local police, we have found ourselves in the odd position of having to write to John Grieves, then Deputy Assistant Commissioner, formerly head of the Racial and Violent Crimes Task Force of the Metropolitan Police, in order to get the local police station to take action. The fact that we have had to go to the top is instructive: at the rank-and-file level the police still see domestic violence as a 'waste of their time'.

As a result of our policy of making formal complaints, the local police have from time to time asked us to build strong links with local community liaison officers to resolve the difficulties that we raise in our casework. But the problem is that there is nothing in place to ensure that women have similar lines of communication. Instead, our experiences show that they are fobbed off when they are not subjected to harassment and assault. The wider public who do not have cosy links with the police are entitled to the same immediate attention and service that we as an organisation are offered.

We are often told that it is 'better to reward officers for getting it right than beat them with a stick for getting it wrong'. This is a worrying response. The assumption behind such a statement is that we can expect the police to get things routinely wrong in domestic violence cases, begging the question as to whether such an attitude would be palatable to society at large in other areas of crime. SBS met with a similar response when it proposed an independent police complaints procedure at the Home Affairs Select Committee's inquiry into domestic violence in 1992. A representative of the Metropolitan Police Commissioner replied that the 'carrot approach is better than the stick'. The question of police accountability cannot be framed as one of either rewarding or punishing police failure or malpractice. The real issue is how far the police are willing to make themselves, their policies and their procedures open to public scrutiny.

Yet even where complaints have been investigated, not a single complaint made by our users or by us has been upheld to date. Although Perkash's case may represent an exception to this rule, we expect that the majority of complaints in these cases will continue to be dismissed. But this will not deter us for two important reasons. First, the process affords women themselves a glimpse of the machinery of police accountability at work or not. Second, it allows us as feminists to situate our demands within the wider movement for greater police accountability, thereby contributing to a wider analysis on policing.

In a panoply of cases where there has been police abuse of powers in relation to the black community and otherwise, the complaints system has singularly failed to be seen to investigate with total impartiality. And even in that rare case where a complaint is upheld, disciplinary action against officers is an exception to the rule.

The demand for an independent investigation of police complaints was perhaps at its peak in the late 1980s and early 1990s as a means of highlighting police malpractice. Ten years on, that demand has been won. The Independent Police Complaints Commission (IPCC) came into being in 2002 under the Police Reform Act 2002. The Commission will be set up in April 2004. It remains to be seen whether it will bring us any closer to greater police accountability. It needs to ensure transparency of the process at every stage, without which it will inevitably go the same way as its discredited predecessor – the PCA. Transparency of process is as important as achieving an independent investigation of complaints: justice needs to be seen to be done. In any event, we know that the scope of the investigations to be conducted by the IPCC will not include complaints about the handling of domestic violence cases. Such complaints will therefore continue to be handled within the police forces themselves, and the transparency of the investigation process will be all the more important in that context.

Conclusion

SBS has attempted to understand the nature of policing initiatives on domestic violence, including those on multi-agency partnerships, by viewing their development in the context of the policing of black communities and trends in policing generally. Our experience tells us that domestic violence multi-agency forums have not led to greater accountability on the part of the police. Instead, we would argue that multi-agency forums in particular, around which there appears to be a gathering consensus, have served as a useful smokescreen, diverting attention away from neglect of duty and even abuse of power by the police, especially in relation to black and minority communities and women. Even studies on multi-agency policing commissioned by the Home Office concede the point that, despite having some impact, the approach does not benefit everyone. Ethnic minorities and women, for example, do not receive an equal amount of police protection and/or are subject to an unequal degree of police coercion.[10]

Sadly, the wider women's movement has failed to be critical of multi-agency policing, with the consequence that there is an increasing separation between the groups who have developed good relations with the police and those who have not. Amongst the groups who are marginalised by this process of slow (albeit not conspiratorial) co-option are minority groups. This has profound consequences for the possibility of political alliances to challenge injustice. This point was disturbingly brought home to us recently. At a conference on domestic violence and Asian women's refuges, organised by the Newham Asian Women's project in 2001, a former worker from the National Women's Aid Federation made an extraordinary public attack on an SBS member who tried to voice criticism of the police during a debate on policing and domestic violence. The former women's aid worker was closely involved in a project with the police in Wales, and found herself in the peculiar position of vigorously defending the police. It was not her defence of the police so much as her castigation of us that took us by surprise, since her tone was in keeping with the hostility we have often encountered with the police themselves!

The Stephen Lawrence inquiry has created a space within which to engage in an open debate on the nature of institutionalised racism and policing and to develop effective strategies to combat it. Ultimately, any analysis of institutionalised racism must also address how police racism and incompetence compound the difficulties arising from women's experiences of domestic violence. Institutionalised racism rarely operates in isolation of other power relations, and effective strategies to address it will be flawed, and may even have a devastating impact on women's struggles for freedom, unless we understand the phenomenon in all its dimensions. It is in this context that the debate on 'police and race relations' needs to be rethought. Women are part of the community and must be perceived as such in any debate on police and race relations.

These are just some of the urgent challenges that we face in the post-Stephen Lawrence climate, not the least of which is the inability to move beyond the straitjackets of race and gender.

Notes

1. Adam Crawford, 'The Partnership Approach: Corporatism at the Local Level?', *Social and Legal Studies*, vol. 3, no. 4, 1994.

2. The concept was enthusiastically promoted by John Alderson, a chief constable and principal architect of community policing, serving in the Devon and Cornwall Constabulary between 1973 and 1982.

3. P. Gordon, 'Community Policing: Towards a Police State', in P. Scraton, ed., *Law, Order and the Authoritarian State*, Open University Press, Milton Keynes 1986.

4. Domestic Violence Units were set up as specialised units within police stations to deal exclusively with the issue of domestic violence. Many were staffed by female police officers and their job involved coordinating overall police policy and response to domestic violence in their area.

5. Lord Scarman's findings on the Brixton disorders (1986) led him to make the key recommendation to set up police liaison committees or consultative committees throughout the country. This recommendation was later enshrined in the Police and Criminal Evidence Act, 1984 (PACE). However, the legal framework for liaison committees was carefully circumscribed so that it did not dent police autonomy or power in operational or decision-making matters. L.G. Scarman, *The Brixton Disorders, 10–12 April 1981: Report of an Enquiry by Lord Scarman*, Cmnd 8422, HMSO, London 1986.

6. Minutes of Tottenham multi-agency domestic violence meeting, 11 October 1988.

7. Interview with an officer at Brixton Domestic Violence Unit by Rebecca Morley, 11 January 1991.

8. For more details of this meeting, see Southall Black Sisters 'Two Struggles: Challenging Male Violence and the Police', in C. Dunhill ed., *The Boys in Blue: Women's Challenge to the Police*, Virago, London 1989.

9. Article 1: the duty of member states to secure to everyone within their jurisdiction the rights and freedoms defined in the Convention. Article 3: the requirement that everyone's right not to be subjected to inhuman or degrading treatment should be protected by law. Article 13: the requirement that everyone whose rights and freedoms under the Convention are violated should have an effective remedy before a national authority.

10. T. Jones, T. Newburn and D.J. Smith, 'New Policing Responses to Crime against Women and Children', in their *Democracy and Policing*, Policy Studies Institute, London 1994.

9

Orange is not the only colour:

young women, religious identity

and the Southall community

Sukhwant Dhaliwal

But Southall the playground, the reviver: it's not right is it? Only if
you drift along there, tourist style, that's how it can look. You
don't take in the sad acres of cheap housing spreading away from
the main roads, the trash, and the broken cars. You don't bother
with unemployment, inter-community tensions, racism ... You're a
tourist – I'm a tourist – and you suck up all the bright lights and
the genius of the place, don't ask too much, don't get captious.
And like that, uncritically, Southall the Movie is simply fantastic.
That profusion out of nothing – the Bollywood videos, the temple
at the end of Margaret Road, incense-scented, the plugs for
Uzbekhistan Airways, the beautiful saris, the veg, the Glassy
Junction transformational boozer, Diwali, the thunderous rags-
to-riches Mercs and BMWs, SNOOP – the Ultimate Entertainment
Magazine, oh God, the sweet shops and restaurants, the traffic
jams, the drifting music, the cheap international phone calls.[1]

The *Guardian* applauds Southall for becoming 'a truly multicultural
community which is working hard to put racial tensions of the past
behind it', a sentiment corroborated by a Somali woman who is
anxious about being moved out of Southall. She likes Southall; she
feels safe here because 'everyone is a foreigner and we know how
each other feels'.

If you trek down past Southall railway station on to The Green
itself, you will notice that it has become a cornerstone of life for
the newly established Somali community, milling with Somali men,

cafés and barbers' shops. Southall has become a more ethnically diverse community with a growing refugee population that has fled civil unrest in countries like Somalia, Eritrea, Afghanistan, Sri Lanka, the former Yugoslavian states and parts of the Middle East. They have begun to take root and shape in their new home. Although my Somali friend is happy here, things are not so sparkly bright. One of our Asian clients said that she does not want her children to go to a school which is now 'full of Somalis'. When she was reminded that Asians had faced the same racism when they first arrived in Britain, it gave her food for thought.

Behind that 'profusion out of nothing' there is a darker side. Alongside the railway station there is freshly daubed graffiti. The first few lines read 'Raj Karega Khalsa' ('Khalsa rules' – a reference to the birth of Sikhism and the Sikh separatist movement for Khalistan). This has recently replaced appeals to join a debate on the failings of Christianity and the blessings of Islam. The reply reads 'Sikhs get out of Bharat. Hindustan Zindabad' and is painted in orange. These are potent visual symbols of an alarming growth of religious divisions amongst Asians in the area. We have been monitoring this rise in religious fundamentalism and the way in which it has impacted on the attitudes of young men, and its consequences for young women.

Some have argued that our preoccupation with the growth in religious identity is misguided. Many people have argued that religious identity per se is just another vehicle for expressing discontent with the state, or a reflection of concerns with what was happening 'back home', and that the post-Macpherson public meetings and the race riots of this decade are a clear indication of the existence amongst Asians of a sense of racial identity. This chapter considers how the resurgence of religious identity has had a lasting effect on political struggles in this country and, particularly, in Southall, on democratic, pluralistic and secular values affecting the struggles of women to assert themselves and their sexuality. In my job as youth worker at SBS, I have gone into schools and further education colleges to raise issues of racism, sexism and religious identity. I have used that experience to look at the gradual erosion of secularism.

Unique among Asian settlements in Britain, Southall has always been a pluralist community with a secular tradition. The major religions of the Asian subcontinent are represented: Hindus, Muslims, a small number of Christians, and Sikhs, who form the majority. A wide range of political opinion is also represented. Asians have been active particularly on the left. Southall residents placed themselves firmly on the map in 1979 when Asian and African-Caribbean migrants joined forces with white anti-racists and socialists to demonstrate against a meeting of the National Front at the local town hall. It was seen by locals as a proud moment of unity against racism, fascism and police brutality. This early period of settlement was also characterised by local workers' strikes that gave the struggles of Southall a clear class perspective. As Gita Sahgal noted in her article in *Refusing Holy Orders*, 'Political pluralism also ensures that opposition to the rise of fundamentalism comes from secular voices from within the community.'[2]

Since the mid-1980s, emotive demonstrations declaring the importance of religious over racial affiliation have resonated across Asian communities in England. There have been demands for the allocation of prime sites in order to establish centres of worship. In Southall today, religious buildings occupy prime sites while voluntary groups have been decimated. Many religious buildings carry the title 'educational and cultural centre', perhaps enabling them to secure state funding for that part of their work. Religious processions have become a mark of this new consciousness and a regular feature of Sundays in Southall, marking anything from the birth of Khalsa, to Eid, to Lord Krishna's birthday. Attendance at these processions is phenomenal and now far outnumbers relatively nominal figures at local anti-racist protests or demonstrations for workers' rights. In 1999, at the twentieth anniversary to mark Blair Peach's murder, there were fewer people on the demonstration to commemorate Southall's struggles against racism and fascism than there were on the procession marking the three-hundredth birthday of Khalsa.

The shift in emphasis from racial to religious identity has been both the cause and the effect of many developments in national and global politics. In part, the failure of the anti-racist left to mobilise disaffected youth and the multicultural funding policies of the metropolitan authorities in the 1980s have exacerbated religious divisions. Yet the resurgence of religion is also due to the development of a politics of difference spurred by nationalistic sentiments and movements around the world. South Asian countries have for a long time been walking a tightrope between secular and religious nationalisms. There is a complicated relationship between what happens abroad and how it is experienced amongst the South Asian diaspora across the globe. The emergence of a separatist Sikh movement and the 'Rushdie affair' in the 1980s became further catalysts in the rise of religious fundamentalism.

More recently we have witnessed a dangerous trend to conflate religious and racial identities. In the race riots in Bradford and Oldham, many of the youths involved saw themselves as Muslims rather than Asians, and sometimes even within that identity made a distinction between Bangladeshi Muslims and Pakistani Muslims. Similarly, at a conference entitled 'Race in Schools' in September 1999, Baroness Pola Uddin stated in her opening address that as a Muslim woman she hoped that Muslim parents were being consulted about religious education and PSHE (Personal, Social and Health Education) classes in their areas. She did not seem to be aware of the paradox that she continuously referred to herself in terms of religion despite the fact that the conference was about race. She asked if parents at a Tower Hamlets comprehensive had been properly consulted about the content of the sex education films to which their daughters were exposed. Ironically, it has been this kind of consultation that has led to girls, particularly from Asian backgrounds, being withdrawn from valuable sex-education classes. It is a shame that the baroness did not take the opportunity to exploit the real democratic possibilities behind the notion of parent power by challenging racism and racist expulsions within the education system as opposed to using it to limit the life choices open to girls.

It's just our Christmas, innit!

Southall has taken centre stage in the last ten to twenty years as the place to celebrate religious festivals. Past the permanent festival streetlights one can partake in the commodification and promotion of religious identities. You can buy bags, headscarves, hats, flags, and pencil cases amongst other things inscribed with khandas, oms and crescent moon motifs. More recently young people in Southall have fashionably combined religious bandanas and garments with chic high street labels. Fluffy dice hanging from rear-view mirrors in leather-interiored Ford Capris or Triumph Stags have been replaced by orange flags and orange fabric displayed in BMWs, Mercedes and Golfs.

Growing up in Southall in the 1970s and 1980s, I can recall the celebration of Diwali as an Asian festival of light, but Vaisakhi (a Sikh festival) celebrations appear to have become a regular feature in the last decade. Remittances by Sikhs in England to family members back home were directed towards funding the movement for a separate Sikh homeland and later rechannelled to fund new gurdwaras and schools abroad. I remember a Vaisakhi procession in 1995 in Southall. Young people at one of the largest Sikh gatherings I had seen were emphatically chanting religious and nationalistic slogans. A Muslim Somali tenant emerged from a house whilst this procession was passing and was confronted by a group of young Khalistani women and men, sporting orange bandanas. They turned on her and aggressively started to shout 'Khalistan zindabad' ('long live the land of Sikhs') at her. The clear intention was to intimidate. There were also fissures between some of the older generation and the young people, between moderates and right wingers. The procession appeared to be divided, with the quieter section at the front and the newly recruited Sikh youth federation at the back, dressed in orange or blue and vociferously demanding Sikh rights. And there were differences, too, between those who wished to be involved in a resurgent Sikh identity as a cultural experience and those who condemned the behaviour of young men carrying the Nishan Sahib, the Khalsa flag, in one hand and a bottle of beer or a cigarette in the other as they revelled in the streets in the evening. That same evening, I went with a friend to join young revellers on Southall Broadway. There was an exciting atmosphere, but it was brutally interrupted by police officers who arrived in riot vans and were wielding batons.

Post-procession revelry sparked clashes between two gangs known as the Chalvi boys (Muslims) and the Sher-e-Punjab (Sikhs). These clashes moved between Southall and Slough. The macho gang culture in Southall[3] did not fade away in the 1990s but reconstituted along religious lines: the Tooti Nung and the Holy Smokes were replaced by Muslim and Sikh gangs. Press reports refer to clashes between hundreds of Sikh and Muslim youth during the years 1995 and 1996. Out of revenge, both sets of youth attacked Sikh and Muslim property. However, what is interesting is that the attacks were orchestrated to coincide with religious festivals and were vicious expressions of hatred towards each other's community. One young Muslim man was attacked by sword-wielding Sikh youths, who sliced his arm; in 1996 a Sikh man was killed during a fight between Sikhs and Muslims. Such tensions and clashes have led to calls for the banning of all processions.

In this macho infighting, the policing of young women is never far off the agenda. In early 1996 a leaflet was being circulated, allegedly produced by a Muslim group called Khilafa, encouraging Muslims to marry and convert Sikh and Hindu women with the reward that they would go to heaven if they did. (No one really got to the bottom of who produced and circulated it. There were just as many allegations that the leaflet had been produced by Sikhs wishing to justify attacks on Muslim rivals.) The leaflets were contemptuous of Sikh and Hindu women and incited Muslim men to further violence in order, presumably, to protect the honour of their own women and therefore their respective communities.

During recent processions, however, there appears to be more of a party atmosphere, although even amidst all the 'fun and games' some women sense danger. The young people are clearly out to dance and revel in the streets, which are perceived to be a more acceptable venue than clubs. There is a greater presence of women with make-up and provocative clothing which might previously have been considered unacceptable. Such women, tattooed with religious insignia, also cruise in cars and wear bandanas.

In a television programme[4] intended to explore fifty years of a settled migrant community in Southall, Melanie Sykes could be seen celebrating Eid with a Southall family. She was shown cruising down the Broadway 'having a laugh with the girls', wearing her new Eid suit and laughing off the hoots and whistles from the lads huddled in groups around the Broadway. It is true that such processions become an excuse for flirting between the sexes. But whilst Melanie Sykes is 'having a giggle' with the girls, other women have to plan how to avoid harassment from the hundreds of young men who start their leching from the afternoon. The atmosphere in the evenings is also frightening for women, as festivities become an excuse for sexual harassment. I had to cancel a young women's support group meeting during one festival, when the young women complained that at a previous festival their attempts to reach the meeting were hampered by men in cars who stopped them at every opportunity.

Another recent trend has been the setting up of short-term, event-based, radio stations to whip up religious sentiment in order to bump up participation at festivals. One of these stations has become a permanent feature of people's lives. The host of a chat show dismissed claims by a woman caller that she was experiencing sexual harassment. He said that it is women who are at fault because they encourage men by giggling! Another woman caller complained about the problems she faced in marrying off her two sons because they wear turbans. The host felt that young women are becoming far too westernised and that they need to be brought back to their duties and reschooled in their religious beliefs. There is a great deal of pressure on parents and children alike to show they understand and adhere to tradition even though tradition itself is being rewritten every day. Radio stations, religious sermons and weddings are important sites for reproducing this sense of obligation and honour in the way they make examples of people. Yet it is important to note that whilst this is going on there are still attempts to build alternative identities. For example, the radio station British Born Asian (BBA) FM was set up by young Asians in Southall who wish to avoid sectarian, caste- and religious-based identities and reflect the fusion of different cultures in the music they play.

The other problem with these festivals, as one local teacher has argued, is that, unlike Christmas, they are distinctly exclusive. People of other faiths are not on the streets during these events. A cultural defence is sectarian when articulated as a religious identity. It is also noticeable that, even as they are expressions of religious unity, there are further splits along racial lines. Somalis, for instance, are not a visible part of the Eid festivities, which are Pakistani-dominated.

A woman and her God

Many of our women clients have found religion a source of spiritual comfort at times of stress, especially when they are escaping domestic violence. We recognise that the counselling we offer is not enough for many women. In the young women's support group that I had set up, women came from a variety of religious backgrounds – Sikhs, Hindus, Muslims, Seventh-Day Adventists, Evangelical Christians, as well as a number of women who did not associate themselves with any religion. One young woman orphaned in a civil war in Central Africa and abused by her brother, who was acting as her guardian, found that her church provided the kind of holistic support she needed, which we just do not have the resources to provide. The church befriended her over a long period of time, organised regular outings and events, and gave her daily spiritual support.

In Southall, religious institutions, such as gurdwaras, have played an important role in the life of the community, filling the often yawning gaps left by the social welfare system and lending support to progressive causes. For example, they have provided free food for many refugees and asylum-seekers and strikers at local trade disputes. They have become an essential stopgap for homeless families and single people not assisted by the council. Members of the gurdwaras in Southall have even made referrals to SBS.

There is a strong need for women in flight to feel that they have not lost contact with the community, which is often centred on the place of worship. Even women who have become outcastes and may be characterised as 'bad' in religious sermons will visit the temples and gurdwaras with their children. In other cases women who have lost contact with their community continue to keep faith with their religion. One long-standing client, who had fled violence from her husband during Ramadan, fell ill because of the combination of stress and fasting, yet she refused to break her fast. Her husband, whilst pretending to be an upstanding member of the Islamic community in public, had subjected her to years of sexual abuse that she regarded as 'sinful'. She wanted to reclaim her faith on her own terms and by herself, away from community leaders who had reinforced her oppression. Her prayers brought her peace and helped her deal with the stress of being a single parent. However, she was clear that her unity with other Asian women was very important. She understood that the religious texts that she read permitted violence against women and promoted the notion that men are superior to women and have rights of ownership over women. SBS has been very clear that ours is a secular space for women of all and no religions. We have never denied women the right to practise their faith, although we have also fostered an atmosphere where equal respect is shown to those who do not wish to believe.

Women like Kiranjit Ahluwalia clearly understand the pressure that religion brings to bear on women to stay in a marriage, even a violent marriage. In her speech in absentia to a public meeting in Crawley in 1990, to mobilise support for her campaign to be released from prison, she said:

> My culture is like my blood – coursing through every vein of my body. It is the culture into which I was born and where I grew up which sees woman as the honour of the house. In order to uphold this false 'honour' and glory, she is taught to endure many kinds of oppression and pain in silence. In addition, religion also teaches her that her husband is her God and fulfilling his every desire is her religious duty. A woman who does not follow this path in our society has no respect or place in it.[5]

Many women convert to other religions in order to escape from the oppressions of their own. A Hindu woman looked to her local priest for support when she was thrown out by her husband. When the priest sexually harassed her, she converted to Islam. Another client, Jaspal Sohal, converted from Sikhism to the Jehovah's Witnesses.

Failure to assert a secular ethos in the SBS centre could lead to the kind of situation one Asian women's refuge found itself in. It decided to establish a separate post for a Muslim worker to work with women fleeing violence. Discussions that ensued were largely about the fact that many of the residents were Muslim and that it was important for them to have access to someone who knew about their particular faith. This was because Muslim women fleeing violence were somehow projected as having a different dimension to their experience. Once the Muslim woman worker was recruited, however, she argued that Muslims experienced a greater level of harassment than other black people because they were Muslims as opposed to being just Asians. She therefore justified the need for a specialist post so that she could help these young women hang on to their religious identity without it being used against them. At around the same time, a separate refuge for Muslim women was established in London in 1989. In East London too, local Muslim councillors attempted to establish a separate centre for Muslim women even though there was already a prominent and long-established Asian women's group attempting to secure funding for a centre for all Asian women.

Taking the battle into colleges

An area of service provision that is always an important site of contestation is that of education. RSS, a fundamentalist Hindu party from India, runs camps in East London and elsewhere in Britain which give youngsters an 'appropriate education'. Anti-racists have also sought to address bias in the teaching of history and to challenge the ways in which the education system has reproduced stereotypes and racism. For the last ten years we have been working in schools around the borough. On several occasions we have been asked to facilitate debates at colleges and universities outside of the borough where issues around women's rights and identity have arisen.

Christian 'pro-life' campaigners and the Islamic group Hizb-u-tahrir were both known to have flooded freshers' fairs with their propaganda throughout the 1990s. The Islamic groups, for instance, came in many guises; their literature would sing the praises of an Islamic state and oppose the capitalist and communist systems. An Islamic state would be based on 'natural' rather than man-made laws, ones ordained by God and therefore morally pure and not subject to abuse. Some of the literature was highly inflammatory, encouraging anti-Jewish, anti-Hindu and homophobic sentiments. A key objective was to mobilise women and suggest that Islam provided true equality. The Khalistanis used similar tactics. However, Khalistani discourse is constructed mainly as a response to a perceived imminent threat to the preservation of Sikh identity: the focus of the Khalistani agenda has shifted somewhat from demands for a separate homeland, and the need to co-opt women has meant that the language has been somewhat modified.

In the mid-1990s, students began demanding separate religious or prayer rooms in further education colleges. Ealing Tertiary College was one such college: the Islamic society made demands for a separate prayer room; it also monitored women's dress as well as the attendance of Muslim students at prayer. As a concession, the authorities allocated different rooms for prayer on a daily basis.

It is inevitable that colleges and schools have witnessed religious gang violence given that religious identity has been constructed in opposition to the 'other'. In January 1995, for example, Sikh and Muslim youths clashed outside West Thames College in Hounslow. Around 150 youths were involved. They blamed each other for provoking the violence and the college authorities for not protecting them.[6] In response to the rise of such sectarian violence, a range of initiatives were attempted to promote tolerance and multiculturalism. These initiatives have involved secular groups like SBS. We organised educational sessions at a number of schools and colleges to promote unity and equality.

In March 1993, we hosted what turned out to be a heated debate amongst sixth-form students at Ealing Tertiary College entitled 'Religion does more good than harm'. Over a hundred students attended. We worked together with the students and stressed the importance of not using the debate to attack or defend any one religion in particular. When the debate was opened to the floor, it was soon dominated by the male members of the Islamic Society at the college. They perceived the debate as being an attack on Islam and were attending, as they saw it, in order to 'defend' their religion. Secularism was blamed for the ills of society and capitalism was cited as the root of our problems. We were also told that if women covered their bodies and behaved modestly then they would not be harassed or raped. The whole atmosphere quickly became intimidating to the women who attended. Some were singled out as examples of 'good' and 'bad' women. Despite this atmosphere, several women spoke against their arguments (challenging religious bigotry and the patriarchal underpinnings of religion) and the motion was defeated. Afterwards, SBS received telephone calls from Muslim fundamentalists, who accused us of being anti-Muslim and invited us to take part in a debate where the 'real issues' could be discussed. The young women who had spoken against the motion were also harassed by the Islamic Society. The unfortunate consequence of these tensions was that teachers at the college became reluctant to organise debates on religion.

Another sign of the growing importance of religion is the number of young Muslim women wearing hijabs, which has increased dramatically in the last decade. A local teacher told us that he first noted women wearing headscarves in the college in 1992. He has had many discussions with the young women about why they choose to wear the scarves. Their reply was that they were wearing them in order to preserve their purity as Muslim women. They stated that they felt freer than white women, who are stared at because of the way they dress. In fact, we have noted that in our local schools girls of all religious persuasions believe that women ought not to dress provocatively if they want to avoid harassment and rape. The teacher believed that his students identify more strongly with their religion than with their race, and when referring to 'our religion' what they actually mean is 'our patch' or 'our turf'. Interestingly, the students pick and choose which parts of their religion they identify with. Salman Rushdie was still a point of debate at this college almost fourteen years after the fatwa was issued. Although many students do not know the name of Rushdie's book or sometimes even his name, Muslim students still refer to 'that man' and believe that he ought to be in prison or killed. Many argue that Christian blasphemy laws do not protect Muslims

When SBS organised a debate on arranged marriages with A-level students in June 2001, the issue of mixed marriages became a focal point. The importance attached to the tradition of arranged marriages within the Asian community is partly about retaining cultural purity and ensuring that marriages are contracted not merely in the same religion but also within the same sub-sect or caste. After the debate, a member of the independent television film crew who filmed the debate for a documentary felt that the views expressed by students in favour of arranged marriage were racist because they opposed marriage across race. He felt that arranged marriage was a sectarian practice aimed at maintaining cultural, racial and religious or caste purity. Caste acts as a further divisive force within our communities. Caste is not necessarily equivalent to class position in this country but is an important feature of status and power relations between various sections of the community. It prevents women marrying below caste but not above caste. Although many Asian women of higher castes are involved in work traditionally assigned to people belonging to the untouchable or lower castes, such as cleaning and general labour (ironically, racism acts as a leveller), there is friction between these groups at work. At family and community levels, however, marriage restrictions and often the social spaces the different caste groups occupy remain clearly demarcated. Many of the gurdwaras in Southall have different caste affiliations. Different caste groups will hold different processions to mark the same festivals.

At the arranged marriage debate, students did not articulate the view expressed prior to the debate: that the practice of arranged marriages was inherently patriarchal. When one young man confused the term 'mixed marriages' with the term 'same-sex marriage', referring to 'batti men', the debate came close to slumping into homophobic hysteria. The sad truth is that Southall continues to be framed as a 'family' (heterosexual) space by politicians and councillors, in which 'sensitive' issues like homosexuality cannot be debated. In May 1999, for example, the Dominion Arts and Cultural Centre opened with a photography exhibition by gay artists Sunil Gupta and Polomi Desai. The exhibition, part of a wider theme, 'making visible the invisible', displayed images of homosexuality. It attracted much adverse publicity following comments from Piara Khabra MP that although he is 'aware of the rights of minorities' he did not feel that the display was the 'proper way to tackle such an issue in a "sensitive" community like Southall'. He claimed that 95 per cent of people expected to use the Cultural Centre would be 'disgusted' by the photographs and that the decision to exhibit them at the launch had been an attempt to push 'controversial ideas on to people'. Sexuality, therefore, to this day, remains a taboo subject.

Keeping God out of the classroom

Fundamentalist groups forcefully mobilise minority communities around the idea that religious affiliation is one's primary affiliation. The fight for religious equality, which began in earnest around the time of the Rushdie affair, was mainly articulated in terms of state funding of religious schools. This has been a particularly difficult issue to confront given that state racism has meant that minority religions are not granted the same equality that Christianity commands. When in power, the Conservative agenda of promoting the establishment of Christian schools and privileging Christian religion over others through the teaching of religious education and religious assemblies exacerbated the sense of injustice felt by minorities.

Under the present Labour government, although the number of religious schools established by ethnic minority religions has increased, there is a continuing disparity between funding of Christian schools and those of other religious persuasions. According to a newspaper article, the breakdown of faith state schools in England in 2001 was as follows: 4,716 Church of England, 2,108 Roman Catholic, 32 Jewish, 4 Muslim, 2 Sikh, 1 Greek Orthodox and 1 Seventh-Day Adventist.[7]

Discrimination against minority religion in the funding of religious schools was exposed in the way in which applications for voluntary-aided status from minority religious groups were rejected. The excuses given for such rejection centred on the fact that such schools were not necessarily viable and surplus places were available in other schools. Yet the argument about surplus places was bypassed when schools of Christian denomination required state funding to expand. In the early 1990s, the Conservative government also advocated greater parental choice in terms of both the ability of parents to withdraw their children from sex education classes and proposals for schools to opt out of local authority control and become grant maintained. Unsavoury alliances were built between religious organisations within minority communities and Baroness Cox's right-wing Parental Alliance for Choice in Education (PACE), which mobilised support for her private members' bill to secure government funding for religious schools, including those of minority religions.

The Education Reform Act 1988 fostered one religion above another by imposing Christian assemblies in schools, although schools with a multiracial intake could opt out. This allowed racists to create segregated schools under the cover of the right to a Christian education and more Christian schools. In 1988 PACE won a court case for parents of twenty-six white parents from Dewsbury to withdraw from a predominantly Asian school to attend schools where the students were mainly white.[7] Today in Oldham, Grange School is 97 per cent Asian while the nearby Church of England Blue Coat school is almost entirely white because admissions criteria demand church attendance from parents. As Polly Toynbee points out, while bussing children across race and class lines would be rejected as official policy, parents from all over Manchester bus their children into Oldham's 'good' Christian schools.[9]

The Labour Party was and is divided on the issue of religious schooling. Traditionally, Labour opposed religious schooling, arguing for a clear distinction between state services and religion. Many Labour councillors do not want to extend the principle of religious schooling to new schools (though few seriously argue to abolish state funding of religious schools). As Michael Durham comments,

> there is a deeper question brought into sharper focus by the Rushdie affair: would state funded Islamic schools serve to encourage Islamic fundamentalism, religious and cultural separatism? Faced with a choice between giving equal treatment to Muslims and promoting integration, councillors find themselves in a quandary.[10]

As the Labour shadow education spokesman, Jack Straw articulated a position that appears to have driven Labour once in government:

> We live today in a multi-faith society in which the minority faiths, once deferential and quiescent, are now seeking parity of treatment. In this controversy, which cuts across party lines, some say our education system should be entirely secular. This approach however is as helpful as suggesting that we should all have blue eyes, white skin and red hair and subscribe to one faith only ... since one key purpose of any educational system must be the establishment of a moral framework for children, religious leaders naturally take a direct interest in education ... the extent of the churches' involvement today is far more widespread than those outside the system think. One third of all state funded schools are voluntary aided or controlled.... A heterogeneous society like ours depends for its health upon a respect for differences, not upon the subjugation of minority cultures.

On concerns about the position of women in these schools he stated:

> Behind some of the opposition to Muslim and Orthodox Jewish schools lies the alleged 'oppression' of women. I think the best

judge of that are Orthodox and Muslim women themselves. The young women I have met in their schools have been remarkably independent of spirit, and Muslims and Orthodox Jews could reasonably point to their very low divorce rate and commitment to family life. One should be careful about judging other cultures entirely on the basis of one's own.[11]

Jack Straw later added that girls attending Muslim single-sex schools did better at maths and science than at other institutions. He also argued that educational standards at these schools could be ensured by tying them to a national curriculum, unlike in the past when voluntary-aided schools determined their own curriculum.

In a joint letter to the *Guardian* with Brent Asian Womens' Refuge, we accused the Labour Party of abandoning the principle of equality where black women are concerned and of delivering us into the hands of conservative men and religious leaders who deny us our right to live as we please. The point was that many Asian (Muslim and otherwise) and Jewish women did speak out against religious oppression but Jack Straw preferred to listen to community leaders instead.

We oppose separate schools on the basis that they foster an atmosphere of bigotry and apartheid. More centrally they seek to control the lives of women. We know that there will be no room for questioning or discussion of issues like contraception, abortion, sexuality, marriage, domestic violence and divorce. Women will be driven back into the home to be 'good' wives and mothers. In short through religious indoctrination women's lives will be policed. We call on all political parties to: cease state support for all religious schools; condemn and revoke the Education Reform Act which seeks to impose Christian assemblies and allows schools to opt out of state control; support a secular system of education based on equality for everyone in all communities.[12]

In December 1990, as SBS had predicted, Southall saw the combined effect of the Education Reform Act 1988 and the growth of fundamentalism when small groups of parents at two local secondary schools – Featherstone and Villiers – sought to change the status of these schools and create denominational (Sikh) schools. Some Sikh parent governors from these schools visited (predominantly

Sikh) parents and misled them into signing a petition ostensibly protesting against the council's plans to abolish sixth forms in these schools. This petition was actually calling for the schools to become grant maintained. Southall Black Sisters believed that the long-term aim was to ensure that these schools reflected the dominant Sikh culture or religion. The argument that girls attending colleges instead of sixth forms in schools would lead to loss of parental control was cynically utilised in an attempt to gain support.

The 'Save Our Schools' (SOS) campaign was set up soon after these petitions were presented to the governing bodies of these schools. In the SOS campaign, SBS and a number of other community groups, teachers, parents and students canvassed the parents in both schools to vote against grant-maintained status. In March 1991, Villiers High School voted by 93 per cent and Featherstone High School by 76 per cent against grant-maintained status. As a group working over the years to secure women's rights, we were relieved that parents, students, governors and teachers refused to turn the clock back. It was young girls who immediately recognised the hidden agenda. As one female student defiantly declared: 'We refuse to be locked up in our homes.'

SBS issued a statement addressing the fundamentalism and cultural chauvinism underpinning the campaign for grant-maintained status. Unfortunately, there was a reluctance by progressive groups within the SOS campaign to name, let alone debate in public, these vital but dangerous developments, in particular the implications for women. Around the country many other teachers and parents voted against disguised moves to establish religious schools through opting out. However, recently we have seen a dramatic expansion of fee-paying religious schools. And if Labour has its way, there will be a similar expansion in the state sector. The current Labour government came to power on a manifesto pledge to expand religious schools. David Blunkett reportedly wanted to bottle their 'ethos and success'[13] and has the wholehearted support of Tony Blair, himself a practising Christian. According to Polly Toynbee, this policy was placed on hold as a direct outcome of the 11 September events. There have been conflicting press reports on its future.

As Herman Ouseley stated in his report on Bradford after the riots in 2001, segregated schools have caused fragmentation along 'racial, cultural and faith lines'.[14] One possible reason for Labour party confusion as to the direction of this policy may be that for many parents and children alike this is an unpopular move. An *Observer* poll found that 80 per cent of the 6,000 people canvassed oppose the planned increase in faith schools.[15] A teacher at George Mitchell School in Leyton, East London, told a meeting organised by Asian Women Unite that when their students were surveyed about separate faith schools, 100 per cent were against this even though many of them have a strong sense of religious identity.

However, there is nothing to stop the expansion of private religious schooling. Private Sikh schools were established in Ilford and in Hayes during the 1990s. The Guru Nanak Sikh College was established in 1993 on the border of Southall and Hayes. The prospectus for 2001/02 states that the demand for the school came from parents concerned about 'drugs, indiscipline and declining moral standards'. It originally opened as an independent school with the help of a bank loan, teaching A levels at a time when local sixth forms were being dismantled. It now boasts that the first student at the college gained admission to Oxford University in 1998. Success meant that gradually the college extended its provision to the teaching of GCSEs. In 1998, the college was given a contribution from the local education authority and managed to extend its provision even further to primary school provision. In 2000 the college and school gained full voluntary-aided status. At present there are around 200 students at the college.

One of the management members of the school used a wedding held there as an opportunity to address guests about the school. He stated that children at the school started their day with a prayer and a religious assembly and spent the rest of the day learning the national curriculum. All their students learn Punjabi and are taught about the Sikh religion. The college prospectus for 2001/02 clearly explains the need to prove religious affiliation and commitment as part of its admission procedure, which excludes non-believers and non-Sikhs. He also boasted that the college had a vegetarian kitchen and that no alcohol or drugs could be found on the site. Despite state grants, the management member explained that a 15 per cent contribution was still required to cover the remaining costs, and he asked all present at the wedding to make a small contribution of anything between £20 and £50, which he said was 'not too much to ask of each person'. A congregation dripping in gold and guilt, primed by a man waving a £50 note, queued to make their donations which earned them moral respectability from the community. After his appeal, he announced that a twenty-minute collection brought in £700!

There are many reasons why parents choose to send their children to religious schools, even private ones. One woman told me she was sending her children to a Sikh primary school because it provided a 'cultural education' not available in state schools, and that as a second-generation Asian she was not equipped to provide it herself. One young woman explained to us how she voluntarily enrolled in the Guru Nanak Sikh college to do her A levels because of its outstanding reputation in A-level results. She was keen to focus on high achievement and, ironically, despite her parents' concerns, enrolled at the college. However, she soon found herself at loggerheads with the teachers, who raised issues about her behaviour – her head had been uncovered; she had breached strict rules of segregation; and they often felt that she was not dressed appropriately. The young woman also explained that despite the requirement to teach the national curriculum, the students were not taught sex education; teachers would always give them other tasks during these periods. Achievement levels, the rights of one community vis-à-vis another, the importance of religious identity, racism in state schools and, last but not least, the need to produce well-educated but homely, chaste and marriageable young women are all part of the attraction of religious schools. While some of these reasons may be understandable, the answer does not lie in setting up separate schools. More energy and resources need to go into ensuring that the state system accommodates a healthy respect for cultural diversity, while at the same time guaranteeing that girls do not lose out in its name. Schools in Southall are trying to reflect some of the pressing concerns of parents. They now offer Punjabi and Urdu as language options and encourage the teaching of Asian musical instruments in music classes.

At a local conference in 2001 on educational achievement organised by the London-based Black Training and Enterprise Group, young black people were asked to comment on careers advice and local youth services provision. A number of young Asian women said that they were not allowed to decide their own career paths. They were still fighting for the right to go to university, to live away from home whilst there, and to determine which career to pursue. Nor could they comment on local youth centres because they were not allowed to use these facilities, and were often questioned about being out in the evenings. Their parents did not trust them and were worried about what others in their community would say if their daughters went out, although their brothers were allowed to stay out as much as they wanted. Asian girls often bridge this gulf by living out 'double lives'. If social issues become the extracurricular activity and religious teaching becomes the core of the school curriculum at religious schools and colleges, how would these women gain access to information about society or broaden their choices?

In the work of SBS, we have consistently tried to get people to recognise that the experience of sexism cannot be seen as secondary to racism. Teachers at a local comprehensive called upon us in 1999 because they were concerned that many students were being negatively influenced by music that they were listening to – they were using abusive and sexist terms from this music in their relations with each other. The teachers were concerned that this was creating an environment in which certain views about women, how they behave and dress, and generally what they can and cannot do in their lives, were being taken for granted as the norm. We found that the most effective way to approach the issue was to draw parallels between the experience of sexism and racism, since racism was something we felt that the students would clearly identify with. We turned to a vital source of youth culture to drive the message home – rap lyrics! Interestingly, however, we quickly moved from debate about race to one about religion, a clear reflection of the way in which young people in the area see their identity. A young man pointed out that 'if you go down Southall Broadway you are more likely to get attacked if you insult someone about their religious background than if you said words like "bitch".' We continue to hear comments from boys such as 'but in our religion we don't allow women to cut their hair, or wear mini skirts or marry their boyfriends or have sex before marriage'. Unsurprisingly, the list for what girls cannot do because of their religion is always twice as long as that for boys. There will always be one erring male student who will say 'Nah man, my religion does not allow me to marry just any girl; she's got to be from my religion and caste.' The irony is that whilst many Asian parents do not restrict the freedom of boys by appeals to religion, many of the boys themselves, having exploited their freedom to the full, actually conform by marrying within their religion and caste.

Putting our own house in order

When we went to the school to address the use of sexist language and its impact on relations between boys and girls, teachers had warned us that the term 'refugee' had become a term of abuse. When we raised this, however, the students denied using the term in such a way. But another local teacher stated that in Southall the established Asian and African-Caribbean students are very anti-immigration, describing the situation as 'a case of pulling up the drawbridge behind them'. Eastern European students with asylum status, most of whom had little cash and were on voucher systems, were being bullied by children of established communities like the Asians. The Eastern Europeans often had a poor command of English and when they retaliated they were unable to defend themselves when disciplined by teachers. Often these students would spend the entire year at detention evenings after school for responding to bullying. Teachers have low expectations of them; they are stereotyped as being violent and deviant; most of them have low achievement levels. Teachers were reluctant to challenge the Asian students for fear of being called racist. This parallels the position of Asian and African-Caribbean students in Southall schools in the 1970s (a situation that gave rise to the development of Asian male gangs) and the continuing experience of minority children (especially Bangladeshi and African-Caribbean) around the country.

The hostility between Asian and Somali youth in Southall exploded onto the streets of Southall when a Somali youth was attacked by local Asians. A concerned school invited us in to debate the importance of black unity. We ran a session for 13- and 14-year-olds in 1996 on issues of race and religious identity. Many students did not identify with the term 'black' and were uncertain why we were called the 'black' sisters. We have attempted to work with young people in schools in order not only to gauge whether racism and gender inequality are still issues for them but to provide a space where they can debate difference and bridge their similarities. History is easily forgotten.

Given the extent of underachievement by Bangladeshi and African-Caribbean children in state schools, the call for separate, especially separate secular, schools for black children is hard to oppose. Recently Lee Jasper, the race advisor to the London Mayor,[16] advocated the establishment of black-only schools in order to counter racism within the education system. He encouraged the 'black community to avail themselves of the opportunity for funding available for independent state schools' for this purpose. He was referring to the Labour government's 'enthusiasm for religious and specialist schools rooted in local communities'. Instead of fighting the racism of state schools, the trend is towards exclusivity and segregation, which carries enormous dangers. Lee Jasper's argument that black-only schools would be an extension of other services like black day centres is, superficially at least, a seductive one. But there is a difference: unlike other black service provisions, which cater for special needs, schools are a vital building block of the kind of society we want to build. Segregation is not part of our vision. The present demand for segregated schools is the product of our histories, but our challenge is to reshape our present so that we can have a stab at a decent future. As the National Secular Society has stated, 'school provides the best, and sometimes the only, opportunity to teach tolerance, but only if children of all beliefs and cultures are educated together.'[17]

Conclusion

The horrific events of 11 September 2001, the retaliatory war against Afghanistan and the deeply unpopular war against Iraq have had a bruising impact on the Asian community in Britain. They have led to the dramatic rise of Islamaphobia, which expresses itself as hatred and fear of all Asians and Arabs.

September 11 has also been devastating for the struggle for unity within our communities. It is not only Nick Griffin, the leader of the BNP, who seeks to distinguish 'Muslims' from 'Asians', but Asians themselves. Soon after the attacks on the USA, many Asian − both Hindu and Sikh − listeners at Sunrise Radio in Southall put pressure on the station to ban the word 'Asians', because they did not want to be associated with the 'Muslims'. Some actually went to the trouble of putting up posters to make the distinction between Sikhs and Muslims after learning that Sikhs were being targeted in the USA because they wore turbans. They expressed concern that Sikhs and Hindus were being wrongly persecuted for the events in the USA as well as for the rioting in Oldham and Bradford.

Yet the problem is that resistance to racism and the struggle for unity have also become tainted by the phenomenon of Islamaphobia. Some sections of the anti-racist left have 'Islamicised' resistance by adopting a 'we are all Muslims' type of solidarity, and justify this as an attempt to prevent moderate Muslims from being driven into the arms of fundamentalists. However well-meaning this approach to racism, it is highly problematic for non-believers and women. The hastily enacted Anti-Terrorism, Crime and Security Act of 2001 introduces an incitement-to-religious-hatred offence. This is a difficult and complex debate. We believe that while we must tackle racism in all its forms, it is important to guard against seeking a religious solution to what is in essence the 'racist exploitation of religious differences'.[18]

We have much to do to repair the lasting damage. No easy answers are forthcoming. What we do know, however, is that we must stand together, offer secular solutions and tackle fundamentalism and undemocratic forces within our own communities at the same time as resisting racism in all its manifestations.

Notes

1. Charles Jennings, 'The Occidental Tourist', *Guardian* Space magazine, 4 November 1999.
2. Gita Sahgal, 'The Experience of Asian Men Organising', in Nira Yuval-Davis and Gita Sahgal, eds, *Refusing Holy Orders: Women and Fundamentalism*, Virago, London 1992.
3. Southall Black Sisters, *Against the Grain: A Celebration of Survival and Struggle*, SBS, London 1990.
4. *Southall Stories*, BBC2, 20 March 1999.

5. Kiranjit Ahluwalia and Rahila Gupta, *Circle of Light: The Autobiography of Kiranjit Ahluwalia*, HarperCollins, London 1997.

6. Patrick Sawer, 'Religion: Just an Excuse for Gang Violence', *Hounslow Informer*, 13 January 1995.

7. See 'Facts about Faith Schools', *Guardian Unlimited*, 14 November 2001.

8. Saeeda Khanum, in Yuval-Davis and Sahgal, eds, *Refusing Holy Orders*.

9. Polly Toynbee, 'Keep God Out of the Class', *Guardian*, 9 November 2001.

10. Michael Durham, 'The Religious Issue that Won't Go Away', *Guardian*, 14 March 1989.

11. 'Language Barriers: Commentary', *The Times*, 20 April 1989.

12. Letter to the Editor 'Drawbacks of Single-sex Schools' *The Guardian*, 22 July 1989

13. Toynbee, 'Keep God out of the Class'.

14. Quoted by Polly Toynbee in ibid.

15. Kamal Ahmed and Ben Summerskill, '80pc Are Against New Faith Schools', *Observer*, 11 November 2001.

16. Will Woodward, 'Black Community "Needs Own Schools"', *Guardian*, 20 June 2001.

17. Quoted in 'Facts about Faith Schools'.

18. Stuart White, 'Don't Legislate for Religious Belief', *Observer*, 7 October 2001.

Rama or Rambo?

The rise of Hindu fundamentalism

Pragna Patel

In most South Asian communities in the UK, fairly progressive, anti-racist and secular ideals that underpinned the adoption of radical black identities in the late 1970s and early 1980s were replaced by militant religious ones in the wake of the Rushdie affair. The growth of such religious identities, which is largely a political phenomenon, is only partly to do with the need to feel empowered in an increasingly racist world where anti-racist policies have failed to bring about equality. It is also a response to what is perceived to be the growing threat of 'Western secularism' and its 'corrosive' effect on minority cultures and traditions, especially in relation to the family. This latter tendency has, of course, gone hand in hand with official multicultural politics (see Chapter 1, 'Some Recurring Themes'). We have witnessed the impact of Sikh and Muslim fundamentalism on such communities as Southall, Bradford and Tower Hamlets, particularly in shaping male youth identity (see Chapter 9, 'Orange is Not the Only Colour'). Yet very little is said about Hindus, who are perceived to be a homogeneous group that has achieved economic and educational success, which in turn has led to a high degree of assimilation within the host community.

When Ayatollah Khomeini issued a fatwa against Salman Rushdie for the perceived blasphemy of his novel *The Satanic Verses*, and Muslim extremists publicly burnt the book in Bradford, SBS issued a public statement in support of Rushdie. We asserted his right to doubt and therefore to dissent against his religion and culture. We opposed the silencing tactics of both the state – the operation of blasphemy laws (which protected and privileged Christianity above other religions), and the crude, intimidating tactics of religious leaders who claimed to be the authentic voice of the community. We knew that if Rushdie could be silenced, women within our communities would be the next targets. We knew that religious fundamentalism demanded absolute control over the minds and bodies of women, and we should do what we could to oppose it. The ensuing debate made us very uncomfortable since it was largely polarised between those who saw themselves as liberal-minded, but condemned all of Islam as barbaric, and religious fundamentalists. Joining in the debate also were racists who pointed to Muslim fundamentalist protests as evidence of their view that a multiracial UK would lead to calamity.

Women Against Fundamentalism

The problem with the consequences of the Rushdie debate, however, was that religious fundamentalism in the West generally became synonymous with Islam. We felt that it was vital to show how the collapse of the Communist bloc and the triumph of the free-market ideal over socialist ideals fed directly into the revival of more militant and political forms of religious movements worldwide. Religious fundamentalism was fast becoming the counteracting force against American and Western imperialism and racism.

SBS therefore joined with women from a number of different ethnic and religious backgrounds to form Women Against Fundamentalism (WAF) in 1989 (see Chapter 1, 'Some Recurring Themes', and Chapter 12, 'Walls into Bridges'). We recognised that experiences of racism and the effects of multicultural policies would temper our experience of religious fundamentalism, so an analysis of British racism and anti-racist or multicultural policies was crucial to our discussions. State racism and the failures of much anti-racist politics were central to the critique that WAF was to develop. Some of the campaigns that WAF initiated included opposing the imposition of Christianity in state schools, including Christian assemblies; ending state funding of religious schools; supporting campaigns to end racist immigration and asylum laws; and combatting violence against women and other restrictions on women's lifestyles and choices.

One of the significant factors about WAF was that it was a group that understood the need to oppose religious fundamentalism and racism simultaneously. The demonisation of Islam by the West has led to a marked reluctance by the left to confront Islamic fundamentalism here, for fear of alienating Muslims and weakening unity against racism and class exploitation.

'We are Hindus first – not Asians'

As much has been written and said about Muslim fundamentalism and the forging of Muslim identity, this chapter will focus on the less well-known campaigns waged by SBS against the rise of the Hindu right in India and the creation of a specifically orthodox Hindu fundamentalist/nationalist identity in India and in the UK.

Political developments in India, especially since 1992 and the rise of the Hindu right – a nationalist and political movement devoted to creating a Hindu *rashtra* (state or nation) – has put paid to liberal notions of Hinduism as a tolerant religion capable of absorbing all religions and dissent and at the same time according equal respect to all beliefs. The reality tells a different story. The impact of the rise of Hindu fundamentalism on minorities in India and on the principles of democratic secularism enshrined in the Indian constitution has been truly terrifying to witness.

The violence unleashed by the Hindu right in India first targeted Muslims, who make up a significant minority, to seek revenge against purported historical (mythological) wrongs perpetrated by the Muslims against Hindus. This has gone hand in hand with a wholesale communalisation[1] of all public spaces and – perhaps most alarming of all – education and media. In schools, for example, entire textbooks have been rewritten, allowing no room to acknowledge India's diverse and rich cultural heritage.

The pogroms against Muslims were extended to Christians: nuns and priests have been raped and killed and Christian institutions ransacked and demolished. In one chilling case, in January 1999, a Christian priest, Graham Staines, and his two young sons were burned alive by a fanatical Hindu mob. Yet a judicial inquiry into the murders exonerated the communal organisations that orchestrated the violence. The Christian presence is seen as nothing 'but an anti-Hindu, anti-national conspiracy' and the lie that justifies such terrorism is that Hindus have long been targets of a missionary zeal to convert them to Christianity. These acts of terror are carried out by Hindu militants who belong to or are on the periphery of the main right-wing parties, often aided and abetted by police and politicians. The key players in stirring up communal violence are the Vishwa Hindu Party (VHP), Rashtriya Swayamsewak Sangh (RSS), and the Bharatiya Janata Party (BJP). The VHP is a rabid Hindu revivalist organisation that was mainly responsible for the Hindu *yatras* (marches) organised all over India in the late 1980s and early 1990s. Its main objective is to forge a mass Hindu identity based on anti-Muslim hatred. The *yatras* were particularly effective in stirring up communal riots because they were carefully orchestrated to take place in Muslim ghettos. The RSS claims to be a cultural organisation working mainly with boys and young men (and more recently women), yet its leaders in the past have aspired to emulate German nationalism under Hitler. Its central objective is to forge a militant Hindu identity by communalising the arenas of sports, culture and other extra-parliamentary spaces. The BJP is currently the ruling political party of India: its primary focus is to gain electoral dominance on the back of Hindu communalism. Collectively known as the 'Sangh Parivar' and also the 'saffron Taliban', BJP and other Hindu right-wing organisations have appealed to all Hindus to act in unison against what they perceive to be 'swamping' by India's minorities. In common with all majority religious fundamentalist organisations, they act as if they are a besieged minority.

The law has not been able to uphold the unequivocally democratic secular values of the Indian constitution. A series of controversial cases in 1995 legitimated right-wing Hindu ideology, 'Hindutva' (a way of life according to Hindu philosophy and principles), which underpins the search for a Hindu state. In the 'Hindutva cases', involving the prosecution of the elected representatives of the Hindu nationalists Shiv Sena and the BJP alliance government in Maharashtra, the Supreme Court of India delivered an ambivalent judgment on the meaning of secularism in the Indian context. These right-wing forces were found to be guilty of corrupt practices under the Representation of the People Act 1951, which prohibits appealing to religion in order to gain votes and prohibits incitement to religious hatred. Yet at the same time, the Supreme Court asserted that the very notion of Hindutva constituted a 'way of life', and that campaigning under this term did not violate the 1951 Act. The Court refused to accept the view that the term 'Hindutva' has come to be associated with Hindu fundamentalism or bigotry.

What is at stake ultimately is the struggle for the meaning of secularism itself. There is an urgent need to prevent it from being hijacked by the Hindu right, which seeks to disguise its attack on minorities by claiming to respect all religions equally. Nowhere is this more evident than in the attempt to impose a uniform civil code, which in reality is about forcing everyone to adhere to the right's notion of Hinduism.

These developments in India have had a profound impact on the Asian communities in Britain. The community here represents the full range of views – from liberal secularism to rabid conservatism – that is represented in the subcontinent. The communalisation process may not be so obvious here, but support for Hindu nationalism in the UK cuts across class and caste. Indeed, the affluent East African Gujarati community has played a substantial part in funding the Hindu right in India through temples and other organisations.

A turning point

In December 1992, the world witnessed a terrifying assault by Hindu fundamentalists on the Babri Masjid, a mosque in Ayodhya, North India. Hindus claimed that the site was the birthplace of Ram and therefore had a special significance for them. More than any other single event in recent years, it put paid to the idea that Hinduism is or can be resistant to the fundamentalist project. The widespread assaults, killings and rapes perpetrated on Muslims in India, following the destruction of the Babri Masjid, were widely perceived by many Hindus in India and in the Indian diaspora as legitimate in the 'war' against all Muslims and other minorities who dare to display disloyalty to the notion of a Hindu *rashtra*.

The last two decades in India have seen a dramatic increase in communal hatred and tensions. In 1977, there were 36 deaths due to communal violence; in 1980, the figure was 375; in 1983, the figure was 400; and in 1992 and in 2001, the figure ran into thousands. Muslims suffered by far the vast majority of these deaths.[2] In the aftermath of 1992, Hindu nationalist parties gained power at local, state and national levels. The new phase was marked by a particularly savage sectarianism. Its distinct features are: a right-wing ideology encompassing many classes and castes, including the army and the police; a thorough communalisation of arts and social activity and other social formations; the involvement of women in the right-wing movements, some in positions of leadership; employment policies favouring Hindus; and the widespread use of modern forms of communication such as videos and audio cassettes to forge a new mass Hindu identity.

Genocide in Gujarat

No words can express the horror that we witnessed unfold in Gujarat in February 2002 and after. Two thousand Muslims were killed, maimed, raped and tortured and hundreds of thousands of others left homeless and destitute, whilst many others had their property and business destroyed by Hindu thugs with the connivance of the police and BJP politicians at regional and central levels. Dead bodies of Muslims were dug up, and saffron flags were flown high over the land. The explosion of hatred into a cycle of terror and violence was not unexpected. Indeed many would argue that it was written on the wall ever since the Sangh Parivar orchestrated the *Ramjanambhoomi* movement in the 1980s that led to the destruction of the Babri Masjid.

The killings of fifty-eight Hindu *kar sevaks* (Hindu right-wing activists) at Godhra station on 27 February 2002, was the excuse that the Sangh Parivar needed to regain popularity following their waning political fortunes in a number of Indian states including Gujarat. The *kar sevaks* were on their way back from the site of the Babri Masjid, having responded to a call from the VHP to all Hindus to do their religious duty to build the temple, in defiance of court orders. Two of the train carriages occupied by the *kar sevaks* were set alight by angry Muslim mobs at Godhra after they were provoked by the *kar sevaks*, who bullied, harassed and assaulted Muslim traders at the station and passengers on the train, forcing many to shout 'Jai

Shree Ram' (victory to Ram, a Hindu greeting). Among those killed were a number of women and children. Instead of calling for a thorough criminal investigation, the Sangh Parivar called for revenge on the Muslims. The Gujarati press published unsubstantiated stories of Hindu women having been raped in large numbers by the Muslim mobs. This was to become a powerful justification of the mass rapes of Muslim women and children that followed.

The BJP-led coalition government praised Narendra Modi, the first chief minister of Gujarat in Indian history to be a member of the RSS, for showing 'restraint' in his handling of the violence! L.K Advani, India's home minister, dismissed Modi's cynical offer of resignation by arguing that Godhra was pre-planned by Muslims while the genocide was a spontaneous outburst by outraged Hindus. The effect was to endorse Modi and his policy of cleansing Gujarat of Muslims. Yet there was nothing spontaneous about the genocide of Muslims. Evidence points to the fact that the genocide was pre-planned and state-sponsored. It was followed by attempts to boycott Muslim traders. The lack of state response to prevent the genocide and even the Godhra tragedy – evidence suggests that the Godhra incident could have been prevented, since there was enough information in the public domain about the heightened tensions between Hindus and Muslims – amounts to nothing short of an abrogation of moral, political and legal responsibility for the welfare of all of India's citizens.

On a recent visit to the UK, the Indian historian Dilip Simeon suggested that what we are witnessing in Gujarat is a breakdown of the secular and democratic constitutional order and a blatant corruption of the rule of law by Hindutva forces, which had already marked out the state of Gujarat as the experimental laboratory for the installation of the Hindu *rashtra*. He believes that a gradual degeneration of political discourse is taking place and a creeping fascist movement and moral order emerging.

What also marks out this particular round of violence is the way in which Muslim women were brutalised in the most sadistic manner, even though women have always been the symbolic ground upon which community identity is forged. It is difficult to describe the violence without appearing sensationalist. But sometimes we must note every act of violence so that we can comprehend the reality. This point is especially significant for Indians of Hindu origin living in the West who see themselves as 'peace-loving' and 'law-abiding' citizens, unlike their 'barbaric' Muslim counterparts.

In Gujarat, women in large numbers were systematically raped and then torched to death. Mass graves revealed bodies of Muslim women. Testimonies from survivors in refugee camps talk of women being gang-raped, of having instruments inserted into their bodies, of sexual assaults, of vaginas and wombs being sliced open, and of being beaten up with rods and pipes. Pregnant women were cut open and fetuses hung up on three-pronged trishuls (swords which are meant to be religious but are turned into weapons and instruments of sexual assault). In one case, several eyewitnesses testified that a pregnant woman was raped, tortured, and her womb then slit open with a sword to disgorge the fetus, which was then hacked to pieces and burned with the mother. In another case a 3-year-old girl was raped and killed in front of her mother.

Beyond the use of rape in forging a patriarchal and pure community identity, Tanika Sarkar argues, the excessive nature of the violence perpetrated against Muslim women and children is part and parcel of the action–reaction discourse, where the aim of revenge is to 'outstrip the original offence' – past and present. The identification between killing and masculinity, she argues, is a strong and uniquely Sangh teaching. Whilst rape is seen as a religious duty fuelled by fear of virile Muslim male sexuality, the killing of babies and children is based on the fear of over-breeding Muslims who will one day outstrip Hindus in India.

Another significant element was the burning of Muslims – men, women and children – after they had been killed, which has been seen as forcing a Hindu cremation upon them. This was a mainly symbolic act aimed at removing any trace of Muslim presence. Above all it was, as Sarkar puts it, 'a kind of a macabre post-mortem forced conversion'.

Hindu mobs insisted that those Muslims who wish to return from the relief camp, run largely by NGOs, in the wake of the genocide could only do so if they swear allegiance to the Hindu India. Meanwhile the state has offered no protection or meaningful compensation to the survivors of the genocide.

'Hinduise politics and militarise Hinduism'

Perhaps the slogan 'Hinduise politics and militarise Hinduism', coined by the chief ideologue of an earlier ultra-nationalist organisation, V.D. Sarwarkar, in 1942, clearly demonstrates how the construction of the Hindu identity is to be achieved. This aim underpins the present Hindu nationalist movement. It involves a specific construction of the Hindu self: a masculine, aggressively communal self that is intolerant of other faiths and even other conceptions of Hinduism. Ironically, those who saw Anand Patwardhan's film *Father, Son and Holy War* will have noted how this specific form of masculinity borrows as much from Western constructions – the Rambo type – as it does from delving into Hindu mythology and reinventing mythical heroes such as Ram.

The call to women to take part in the 'war' against Muslims reveals major contradictions in the modern conception of the Hindu woman. They were encouraged to train in martial arts alongside men and so take on a masculine persona, but this specific construction relied on notions of women doing their 'duty' to their men folk rather than taking part as autonomous beings. The role played by women in the construction of Hindu identity should not be underestimated. Tanika Sarkar has provided an invaluable insight into how women are galvanised by the Hindu right wing: It is a very complex process which, she argues, equips them with a new self-empowering image but which does not impact upon patriarchal authority.[3]

Hindus in Britain

The destruction of the Babri Masjid in 1992, and the genocide in Gujarat in 2002, created schisms not only between the Hindu and Muslim communities in Britain but also within families. They had a chilling impact on me personally. I found myself forced to question the open allegiances to right-wing forces displayed by my relatives. It became clear that many Hindus sympathised with, if not directly supported, the cause of the Hindu right. The arguments, shouting matches and even silences revealed a schizophrenia as memories of partition (when India and Pakistan were separated by Britain in 1947 into two distinct nations) resurfaced, even though many had not directly experienced it, to justify the 'need' to take revenge against Muslims.

In the UK, Hindu revivalism has been quietly gathering strength, operating within a social and cultural milieu rather than in an overtly political way – a result of the multicultural politics which co-opts certain layers of the community. In the UK, the VHP (known as the World Hindu Council) has been instrumental in galvanising support for initiatives such as the movement to reclaim the site on which the Babri Masjid was built. The main aim of the VHP, which has members in Britain, the USA and elsewhere outside of India, is to unite the various Hindu interests so as to speak in one voice. The RSS, known in the UK as the HSS (Hindu Swayamsevak Sangh), operates cultural centres, but its primary focus is work with Hindu (male) youth. Like fundamentalists in all religions, the VHP in this country has turned to education to promote its agenda. A deeply disturbing development, for instance, has been the way in which the Hindu right has attempted to gain legitimacy by putting out materials on religious education in order to influence the school curriculum and multiculturalism generally. A leaflet entitled *Explaining Hindu Dharma: A Guide for Teachers* has been published without any awareness on the part of publishers of the anti-Muslim and communalist politics of the VHP. The text, although more measured in tone than that used in India itself, nevertheless propounds the notion that India belongs to Hindus only. It also contains conservative notions of womanhood and sexuality. The academic Parita Mukta has warned that, 'if due care is not taken, the RE world may well find itself implicated in the production and dissemination of knowledge by vested groups who form part of the new religious movements and who have a lamentable record on human rights.'[4]

Hindus have always organised along caste lines in the UK. Until recently, these divisions, at least at the political level, were submerged under Asian and black identities that prioritised struggles against racism. The aftermath of the Rushdie affair and the construction of a global Muslim identity and politics have, however, led many Hindus to forge a unity in order to achieve some measure of political power in Britain. In many respects, British Hindus are following the example set by Muslim communities, demanding an end to the so-called discrimination of Hindus. This demand was one of the driving forces behind the attempts to unify all British Hindus over the Watford (Bhakti Vedanta Manor) Temple affair in the 1990s. The temple was for a long time run by white convert Hindus and was largely regarded by Asian Hindus as an alien and 'inauthentic' development. However, demonstrations around the temple were organised by Asian Hindus, attracting thousands from around the country, creating a timely opportunity for the display of the militant face of Hinduism. The campaign to keep the temple open became the symbol of struggle against an 'unacceptable' threat from the British state to Hindu cultural and religious autonomy.

When the Babri Masjid was razed to the ground, Hindus in the UK made a number of important demands, set out in a series of press releases. The most important of these was the demand to be recognised as 'Hindus' rather than as Indians or even Asians. This was the first public assertion of a clear Hindu identity. Interestingly, while 'celebrating' the carnage that was perpetrated on Muslims in India, Hindus asserted their 'respect' for law as British citizens in this country. Hindu leaders were careful not to attack Muslims here directly, referring to them as fundamentalists instead and so differentiating between mythical notions of Hindus as essentially non-violent and civilised and Muslims as unruly and fanatical. In the face of (imagined) Muslim provocation in India, UK Hindus appealed for calm and for the right to be protected, presumably from Muslim retaliation, although this was never clearly stated.

The forging of a militant Hindu identity has borrowed not only from Muslim fundamentalist activity, but also from the Jewish experience in the UK. Many Hindus have attempted to emulate what they perceive to be the Jewish success story. Many Hindu leaders regard Jewish people as having integrated successfully into British society while still retaining their Jewish identity and a wider sense of belonging to Israel. Yet it is at this level that Hindu identity becomes especially problematic for women. Hindu fundamentalists have attempted to ban plays and films deemed to have caused 'offence' to Hindu religious beliefs. When the film Bhaji on the Beach was shown at a cinema in Nottingham in 1994, a group of predominantly Hindu men surrounded the cinema, intimidating women as they attempted to enter. The film is about a group of Asian women of many different religious backgrounds who, having experienced domestic violence and other restrictions on their lives, go on a day trip to a typical English seaside resort. In the process they rethink their lives and develop their own network of friendships and support away from the stranglehold of their communities. Clearly the depiction of strong Asian women questioning aspects of their cultural traditions was deeply threatening to the protesters.

In the USA, the Hindu right has set up an organisation known as the American Hindu Anti-Defamation Coalition (AHDC). It has campaigned, for example, against the night clubs and bars which form part of the Indian subculture for combining Hindu deities and art with 'liquor, smoking and dancing to the latest Western music'. The AHDC has organised petitions against what it perceives to be the 'misuse' and denigration of Hindu symbols. On other occasions, the organisation has pursued the American commercial world for offending Hindu sensibilities. Some companies have, for example, manufactured sportswear and even toilet seats which advertently or inadvertently use Hindu religious symbols in their designs.

Yet perhaps the most insidious development is the alliance that has formed in the USA between Hindu and Jewish extremists who are followers of Rabbi Meir David Kahane. Meir Kahane was the assassinated Israeli politician who advocated the expulsion of Arabs, many of whom are Muslims, from Israel. The two extremist organisations have come together largely because they share a common enemy – Muslims. Religious fundamentalist groups have often formed alliances with each other, but what is interesting in this case is that the members of both Hindu and Jewish right-wing groups have chosen to live in the USA and yet are actively engaged in the politics of constructing imaginary homelands from afar.

The alliance initially formed around a website, HinduUnity.org, run by militant Hindus in New York, which was shut down in 2001 by its service provider for being a hate site. The service provider had received several complaints about violence advocated by the Hindus towards Muslims. For example, the organisers of HinduUnity have urged all Hindus 'to stand up and take arms' against Muslims in India, urging them to 'Fight if you must! Die if you must!' The website is an official site of the Bajrang Dal, a fundamentalist Hindu movement which has been implicated in attacks on Muslims in India and was one of the prime movers of the destruction of the

Babri Masjid. The site is also known as the 'Soldiers of Hindutva'. But a few days later, the fundamentalist Hindu website was back on the Internet, having been rescued by the Kahane followers, who themselves have been under investigation for possible ties with anti-Arab terrorist organisations in Israel. The Kahane followers put the Hindus in touch with their own service provider. Both the Hindu Unity and the Kahane sites now have direct links to each other and have promised to advertise the other's events. In the annual Salute to Israel Parade on Fifth Avenue in May 2001, Hindus marched alongside Jews. In turn, in June 2001, Kahane followers joined in a protest outside the United Nations against the treatment of Hindus in Afghanistan by the Taliban regime. Members associated with the Hindu site have also written to American Congress members urging them to remove Kahane's political parties from the State Department's list of terrorist organisations.

Women and Hindu fundamentalism

In India the impact of Hindu fundamentalism has been particularly devastating for women in terms of the revival of the practice of sati[5] and the attempt to universalise Hindu personal laws. The VHP has been very vociferous in demanding that the Hindu personal code should be applicable to all. The BJP in opposition had been more guarded, arguing for a Hindu code under the guise of a uniform civil code. Worryingly, Hindus demonstrated in Ahmedabad against abortion, condemning it as 'murder', when Hinduism has never opposed abortion before. In fact the 'secular' Indian state has vigorously promoted it. The anti-abortion campaign also condemned working women and advocated that women should give up their jobs in favour of unemployed men. Such demonstrations form part of a wider anti-family planning campaign which views all international organisations, especially those run by Christians, as a conspiracy to eliminate Hindus in favour of Muslims and Christians.

Whilst in the UK Hindus have not been as vociferous on the issue of abortion or being governed by personal laws as have many Muslim leaders, their manifesto reiterates a commitment to family values which, in our view, amounts to obeying the rule of patriarchal law. The law in Britain, in relation to marriage, divorce and child custody matters, has become a particularly fertile ground for conservatives of all hues. Much of the day-to-day casework of SBS and other Asian women's groups bears witness to these developments – where the law and welfare system have become effective arenas in which conservative leaders attempt to assert the precedence of religious and traditional customs over rights and remedies laid down in civil family law. For example, we were involved in the case of a Gujarati Hindu woman who fled to a refuge with her daughter after facing violence from her husband. He applied for a residency and contact order, arguing that he would ensure that his daughter 'grew up within the Hindu faith' to strengthen 'her cultural and religious identity'. There was clearly an assumption that, as an Asian woman who had left her marriage, she was no longer a 'Hindu'. Had she not reconciled with her husband, due to her fear of stigma as a divorced woman, SBS would have been compelled to prepare an 'expert' report to show how Asian women do not shed all aspects of their identity simply because they question the abuse to which they are subjected (see Chapter 11, 'Shifting Terrains').

Our experience leaves us in no doubt that granting Muslims the right to be governed by Shariah or personal laws would set a dangerous precedent. Moreover, if India heads towards a thorough implementation of personal family laws, it is likely that this will have a significant impact on Asian women in the UK. As it is, the vigorous lobbying of politicians by Muslims for the implementation of personal laws in this country is being watched with interest by secularists and fundamentalists alike. It is inevitable that any concession granted by the state in respect of autonomy in this area of law will have an effect on all minority religions. Hindu fundamentalists have referred to ancient Vedic texts as their primary source of authority, and have called for all Hindus to follow 'pure' Hindu dharma and counteract anti-Hindu activities. It may only be a matter of time, therefore, before Hindus demand Hindu personal law.

Resistance

In response to these developments, SBS decided to join forces with a number of groups and individuals to oppose the rise of the Hindu right in India and prevent the communalisation of South Asian communities in this country. The campaigns have been watersheds in my own political development.

In the wake of the destruction of the Babri Masjid, and the burning of Hindu temples in the UK, SBS and Brent Asian Women's Refuge became involved in a loose coalition of predominantly Asian men and women from a range of political traditions and campaigning backgrounds – anti-racists, feminists, anti-caste Ambedkarites (followers of Ambedkar, a leading campaigner for the rights of untouchables or dalits in India during the 1960s), activists, academics, secularists and humanists. We came together in 1993 to form an anti-communal organisation – the Alliance against Communalism and for Democracy in South Asia. The main task of the Alliance was to support anti-communalist forces in India and to prevent communalism from breaking out in our communities in the UK. For many of us, this was not only a way in which we could voice our horror and opposition to developments in India; it was also an opportunity for feminists active in the fight against religious fundamentalism to seek support from other constituencies. The Alliance was effective in unsettling the confidence of those who were galvanising financial and other support for Hindu communalist forces in India, as they liked to pretend that their support from Hindus was absolute. Our campaigning was nevertheless difficult. We found that, in the larger Hindu communities of London, Leicester and elsewhere, there was widespread support for the VHP, the BJP and Shiv Sena.

The role played by Asian women in resisting Hindu fundamentalism in the UK has been vital, especially in revealing the interrelations between nationalism, fundamentalism and gender and in exploding the myth that Muslims are the only fundamentalists in Asian communities. We became involved with a number of confrontations with Hindu right-wing supporters. The response to us at meetings and social gatherings was to adopt aggressive and disruptive tactics in an effort to suppress us. The vociferous presence of women was felt to be particularly provocative, and we were labelled Muslim-loving prostitutes, outcastes, and women in the pay of Muslim fundamentalists or the Congress Party of India. One such confrontation took place at a *mela* (fair) in North London in 1993 organised by Kutch Leva Samaj, a Hindu caste community. The *mela* attracted thousands of Hindus and gave the appearance of being a cultural event, although it was presided over by religious figures, including some who openly supported the Hindutva movement. We decided to use the occasion to distribute leaflets advertising a forthcoming anti-communal public meeting organised by the Alliance. The leaflets appealed to all Hindus to uphold a humane vision of Hinduism espoused by the likes of Mahatma Gandhi.

We were made to seek permission from the organisers of the event. We were marched to the main podium by male stewards and told to wait, while they disappeared to consult with leaders who remained 'faceless'. They duly returned and, without giving reasons, demanded that we leave. The most we could get out of them was that they did not want to 'mix the social event or even religion with politics'! It was clear that our leaflets caused great discomfort to their leaders. With the aid of mobile phones, the male stewards kept in close contact with each other to monitor our activities. Finally, they forced us out of the grounds, having first tried, unsuccessfully, to confiscate our leaflets.

We then decided to distribute our leaflets at the gate, but were met with a hostile response. The stewards, including some women, hurried dignitaries and visitors in without giving them a chance to take a leaflet from us. Some stewards became apoplectic at the contents of our leaflet, screaming and lunging forward to assault us. They hurled abuse, calling us Muslim whores and bitches. They even threatened to rape us and to humiliate us by publicly stripping us. Boys as young as 11 mimicked the adults, threatening rape and making lewd gestures. They distinguished us from their wives, mothers and sisters to justify their acts of sexual aggression as being towards those who did not belong to them. (Though this logic does not apply, of course, when disciplining women within the family.) In Surat, India, Muslim women were raped by Hindu mobs, who videoed the event and distributed the tapes for public viewing.

Those members of the public who did take our leaflets were made to return them to the stewards at the gate. If they refused, stewards simply pulled the leaflets out of their pockets and tore them up. Very few people protested in the wake of what they perceived to be 'justifiable' control of 'troublemakers' by the organisers, although a few did try. The tearing up of our leaflets took on a ritualistic dimension. We were told that we were causing offence to

the public. Eventually, the stewards called the police, who duly arrived in a special riot-control van and threatened to arrest us for
breach of the peace! The police were bemused by the confrontation
but were clearly intent on upholding the rights of the organisers.
Our protests then took on a twofold struggle as we also remon-
strated with the police for failing to arrest or even warn the stewards
who had tried to assault us.

We were confined, geographically and metaphorically, to the
margins of the event and, by implication, the Hindu community.
But the most insidious aspect of the behaviour of the *mela* organisers
was that they became the 'thought police' and 'gatekeepers' of their
community. We came away bruised and angered by the experience
but also with strengthened resolve to fight the rise of Hindu fundamentalism. With the help of young boys, who had the task of looking after visitors' cars, our last act of defiance was to place our
leaflets on the windscreen of every parked car in the compound.
There were hundreds of cars and we had a field day.

This meeting that we were trying to advertise at the *mela* was
held on 15 August 1993, the forty-sixth anniversary of India's independence, and had been called to discuss the Hindu assault on the
Babri Masjid. The main speaker was Gandhi's grandson, Ramchandra
Gandhi, flown over from Delhi for the meeting. He is a practising
Hindu and freelance writer and philosopher. He appealed to those
present – largely Gujarati Hindus representing a range of castes and
religious traditions – to uphold the humane version of Hinduism
espoused by Gandhi and to create a *Bharat Parivar* (Indian family/
nation) rather than the narrow *Sangh Parivar* (Hindu) family/nation
espoused by the Hindu right, which in 1949 was responsible for
the assassination of Gandhi by the Hindu nationalist Nathuram
Godse. He considered it his duty to kill Gandhi for betraying the
'Hindu' cause by advocating the rights of minorities in India and
calling for the creation of a secular, multicultural India. The meeting
proved to be highly volatile. What was alarming was that the majority of those who attended, including women, were in complete
sympathy with the Hindu right in India, and indeed regarded rabid
fundamentalist leaders such as Bal Thackeray, the leader of the Shiv
Sena, as a hero. Bal Thackeray encouraged pogroms against Muslims
and aided McCarthyite-type activities. Shiv Sena cadres are active at

a grassroots level in trade unions, and when in government they fulfilled certain election promises and took a stand against multi-national corporations that resonated with those sections of the middle class who are facing economic decline. In Britain, Bal Thackeray and the nationalist vision that he upholds are popular among those Hindus who need to safeguard their own economic interests in India.

As we tried to hold a rational debate, we were heckled, intimidated and even threatened. Ramchandra Gandhi was listened to, however, partly because of who he is, but also because he spoke from within the Hindu religious traditions and was therefore less susceptible to the charge of being 'westernised'. But it was clear that he did not have much support. It was terrifying to witness people decrying Mahatma Gandhi as a 'traitor' to the Hindu cause. Many Hindus refer to him as an effeminate coward who was unable to stand up to the Muslims at the time of Indian independence.

The same Hindus, here and in India, praise the likes of Advani for having the 'guts' to stand up in defence of 'Indians'. 'Do you know what happened in Godhra?' shouted some BJP supporters at a recent anti-Advani demonstration organised by Awaaz and South Asia Solidarity Group in London in August 2002. Advani's supporters were attending a reception to honour him as a hero. They tore up our leaflets, which protested against his presence in the UK and demanded that all those implicated in the genocide be punished in accordance with the law. The assertion that 'for every action there is an equal reaction' is popular amongst certain Hindus in the UK. Revenge by 'Indians' is therefore deemed necessary to avoid emasculation.

In May 2002, in response to the genocide, Awaaz: South Asia Watch was formed. It is a loose secular network of individuals and organisations made up of anti-racist and feminist groups, socialists, Ambedkarites, Indian and Pakistani Muslims, Christians, Sikhs, Jains and people with no faith. Whilst some of us were part of the Alliance against Communalism and for Democracy in South Asia, others are new to the campaign. The aim of the network is to combat religious hatred, racism, religious fundamentalism and fascism in the UK and in South Asia. Although the focus is very much on keeping the memory of genocide alive, the network is equally committed to opposing the political use of religion to attack other minorities in South Asia such as Hindus and Ahmaddis in Bangladesh. Another urgent task that Awaaz is addressing is the monitoring of Hindu organisations in this country that are financially or otherwise supporting religious violence in India. Recently we demonstrated outside the offices of the Charity Commission to revoke the charity status of Sewa International, which raises fund for groups like HSS (Hindu Swayamsevak Sangh) in India.

Through campaigning, monitoring, research and dialogue, we also aim to contribute to the international effort to make those who perpetrated the genocide or were complicit in it account for their crimes in accordance with international humanitarian law, and to support secular democratic movements in South Asia and the UK. So far, Awaaz has engaged in a number of different activities, often in conjunction with South Asia Solidarity Group, which include an advertisement in the *Guardian* for witnesses to the killing of members of two British Muslim families; a picket of the Indian High Commission against the presence of L.K. Advani; demonstrating against Uma Bharati, India's minister for sports and youth; organising public meetings in Southall to raise awareness and lobbying of MPs, including the British foreign secretary.

In these grim times, SBS has begun the long and painful task of at least trying to ensure that Hindus in the UK are informed about the events that have taken place in India. Many Hindus are misinformed; others support what happened. But on the whole it appears as if the majority is in a state of mass denial. The problem is that many Hindus, especially women who have little exposure to different sources of information, have views which are largely informed by the Gujarati press. Some women admitted to feeling ashamed of what took place but do not know what really occurred. My mother, who was actually in Gujarat at the crucial time, gave me eyewitness accounts of burnt-out shells of auto rickshaws, stalls and homes belonging to Muslims, and spoke of her pity for the innocent Muslims, amongst the poorest in her village in the Kheda district of Gujarat, who were being attacked and driven out. It was heartening to hear her stories of the attempts by some Hindus to protect (often by hiding) and feed the Muslims. She was scathing about the 'bawajis' (VHP men in saffron), whom she described as 'troublemakers'. The problem, however, is that with the passage of time, when asked about the events again, what appears to dominate her perspective is not what she saw and how she felt, but the stories of the rape of Hindu women in Godhra and Pakistani Muslims infiltrating the border, illegally amassing weapons and fomenting trouble, thus leaving the Hindus with no choice but to 'defend' themselves. There is an urgent need to address this level of misinformation and denial or amnesia.

Each time religious hatred erupts in India, we despair as the task of opposing it gets harder and harder. But this time what has compelled many to put aside their differences, come together and oppose the Hindutva movement is the overwhelming sense of shame, and the need to ensure that our silence does not become complicity in the genocide that occurred.

Quietly but surely

The destruction of the Babri Masjid led to an articulation of 'Hindu' interests for the first time in Britain. Intellectuals and cadres alike are encouraged either to speak on behalf of a very class- and caste-ridden community as if with one voice, or to train fodder for the ongoing 'war' against Muslims. There is now a network of organisations called 'overseas friends of the Bharatiya Janata Party' which is dedicated to providing support for the BJP in India through fundraising, campaigning and other activities. At the opening of the biggest Hindu temple outside India, the Swaminarayan temple in Northwest London in the mid-1990s, L.K. Advani was the chief guest, along with the then home secretary, Michael Howard. The Swaminarayan Mission is a highly evangelical and affluent wing of the Hindu religion – sometimes described as the 'growth religion' in this country. It purports not to be involved in politics. The facts, though, speak for themselves.

In a recent radio interview, in Bradford, Hindu community leaders (belonging to the VHP) complained that the dominant Muslims had operated an ethnic cleansing strategy, driving all but a handful of Hindus away from the area. Whilst little factual evidence was presented, such statements show the levels to which Asian communities are now undergoing a process of communalisation. The reality is that Hindu fundamentalists, like their Muslim counterparts, are fighting for scarce resources and have campaigned vigorously to ensure that the British state does not favour Muslims above them. A familiar and depressing pattern of scrambling over scarce local resources is taking place in Asian areas around the country.

Hindus in the UK have continued to consolidate their new-found political identity, which has gone largely unnoticed because Islam has become the West's main 'enemy'. The Rushdie affair and the events surrounding 11 September are just two reasons why Islam and anti-Muslim racism will continue to dominate right-wing and left-wing agendas. In a recent debate on Islam in the *Guardian*,[6] it was asserted that, unlike many undemocratic Muslim states around the world, only India, with the second largest Muslim population in the world, actually guaranteed Muslims their rights because India itself was a democracy. Such ignorance about the rise of the Hindu right, with its assaults on minorities and secular and democratic principles, is astonishing and highly dangerous.

Conclusion

With the collapse of the Babri Masjid in India, I found that a wall surrounding some of my own guarded orthodoxies had crumbled. The recognition that I could be struggling for equal rights as part of a minority in this country and at the same time, whether I liked it or not, be a member of a majority − Indian − Hindu diaspora, which in the name of God was annihilating minorities elsewhere, was an important one. With the recognition came the need to take responsibility and do something to stop the deeply shameful and inhuman events that were unfolding in India.

At the conclusion of the well-attended public meeting organised by the Alliance in Wembley, a friend and colleague of Muslim origin broke down and wept. Many of those who had attended the meeting had been mobilised by Hindu organisations, and their virulent anti-Muslim abuse, devoid of any rationality, had left my friend feeling stripped off her humanity. I understood then the full significance of the struggles we have been engaged in. We pledged together to fight for the right to occupy and defend the secular space we had created for ourselves as feminists within SBS and Brent Asian Women's Refuge, even if we needed to rethink what to put in that space.

Notes

1. Communalism, a term and concept specific to the Indian subcontinent, refers to the construction of a community solely around religious identity and religious conflict. Communal politics is the politics of such a religious community posing as a monolithic bloc in opposition to those who do not belong and are therefore constructed as the 'other'. Like multiculturalism, communalism in India has homogenising tendencies, denying internal variations in religious practices across regions.

2. 'Communalism: Its Causes and Consequences', leaflet by Inqualabi Communist Sangathana (Indian section of the Fourth International).

3. See T. Basu, P. Datta, S. and T. Sarkar and S. Sen, *Khaki Shorts and Saffron Flags*, Orient Longman, Delhi 1993.

4. Parita Mukta, 'New Hinduism: Teaching Intolerance, Practising Aggression', *Journal of PCIRE*, Autumn 1997.

5. Sati is the practice in which a widow is expected to throw herself on the funeral pyre of her husband.

6. Thomas Friedman, 'Solutions Lie in Democracy, Stupid!', *Guardian*, 23 November 2001.

Shifting terrains:
old struggles for new?

Pragna Patel

We live in an age in which the law has become, it appears, the main arena for our struggle for freedom, equality and justice. This is perhaps unsurprising, given the nature of the capitalist values which underpin our legal, economic, political and social structures, and which account for the erosion of the welfare state. Many victims of both state and individually perpetrated wrongs turn to the law not because they believe that the law provides any panacea but because it appears to provide some semblance of deterrence and account-ability. In an age of states run by unchecked corporate and multi-national power, it is understandable that often the only effective way in which the abuse of power can be questioned is in the courts of law.

The law has always been a site of feminist resistance. Feminists have challenged the law to respond to women's lived experiences. In the process they have subverted many of the sacred concepts of liberal legal theory and its appearance of 'neutrality', 'equality' and 'objectivity' – much of which is based on male assumptions about a male world order. Similar critiques have also been made from the point of view of race and class, exposing the ways in which the voice of those who are the most powerless and marginalised in our society has been silenced by the law.

Feminists have creatively used the law to achieve redress in all sorts of different contexts. In India, a feminist lawyer took on the case of a young girl with mental health problems who was sexually abused by a worker at the care home where she lived. The lawyer decided to pursue a compensation claim against the institution rather than a criminal conviction against her abuser. She felt that nothing could be achieved by throwing a perpetrator in jail for a few months or even years, whereas a requirement to pay some kind of financial compensation could serve to deter continuing institutional abuse.

In the UK, some feminists have focused on the criminal law in cases of domestic violence precisely because historically the law and law enforcers (see Chapter 8, 'The Tricky Blue Line') have helped to construct violence in the home as a lesser crime to violence committed in public spaces. It is a newish strategy but one that has still a long way to go. We are beginning to explore the availability of civil law, in conjunction with human rights law and other international human rights instruments, to compel the criminal justice system to protect women from violence in the home.

Nothing, however, is straightforward. The successful use of the law by women has itself become the subject of counter-moves. In the USA, in the city of Torrington, Connecticut, for example, in 1982, a woman sued the city police and twenty-four individual police officers after suffering permanent disfigurement and partial paralysis following a series of severe assaults by her ex-husband, which the police ignored. She was awarded $2.3 million in compensatory damages. The result of her success was that the police were then forced to intervene in cases of domestic violence, mainly because the insurance companies, faced with the prospect of paying out millions of dollars in damage claims, pressurised the police to arrest violent perpetrators. For a while mandatory arrest policies were followed throughout a number of states in the USA. But then the backlash started. More and more police and public officials succeeded in claiming immunity from such legal actions and the status quo ante was re-established when, in 1989, a Supreme Court ruling held that the 'state's failure to protect an individual against private violence does not constitute a violation of the individual's constitutional rights'.[1]

In the UK, the case law in the area of suing state institutions for failing to protect women from domestic violence or other forms of abuse is far from settled. SBS has become an experienced casework and advocacy agency and we find ourselves driven to the law for redress because of the failure of internal community mechanisms to protect women or uphold their dignity. The passing of the Human Rights Act 1998, which incorporates the EHCR, was a particularly exciting moment for us since it opened up the possibility of utilising the Act – and the very language of human rights – to hold the state accountable for the policing and prosecution of crimes against women. Our efforts to contest women's rights as human rights within the law have gained enormous impetus from a worldwide feminist movement which is increasingly turning to human rights law. But in the process, as black women, we find ourselves facing new challenges: the dilemma of seeking reform of the law for women whilst not undermining civil liberties for the rest of our community and society is particularly pertinent, as is the need to avoid creating stereotypes which work against the interest of minority women. I am reminded of Anne Jones's words of caution, in her powerful book *Women Who Kill*, that the law cannot be peeled away to reveal an egalitarian core.[2]

This chapter looks at the experience of SBS in some of our more high-profile cases. It examines how the law has helped simultaneously to empower and to disempower the women we have worked with. The limitations of the law highlight the necessity for alternative feminist strategies to complement the use of the law, especially the human rights legal framework, in achieving our emancipatory goals.

The criminal justice system and battered women who kill

Since 1990, two women have defined our work in respect of the criminal justice system, especially in relation to spousal homicide: Kiranjit Ahluwalia and Zoora Shah. Their cases have illuminated how the law deals with the issues of gender and race. We have had to turn the spotlight on, among other issues, domestic violence, racism, culture, religion and the failures of the criminal law and the legal system generally to accommodate these issues. These interconnected themes run through a great deal of our casework, forcing us to push at the boundaries of the law so that it reflects more accurately the experiences of minority women. Both women killed their partners out of desperation. Their cases had many things in common but also fundamental differences that led to different outcomes, raising important questions about the law.

Kiranjit Ahluwalia is an educated woman who aspired to a middle-class lifestyle in her marriage. She had an impeccable record as a conventional wife. Her account of abuse in her marriage was accepted and she was finally successful in overturning her conviction for the murder of her husband. Zoora Shah, on the other hand, led a poverty-stricken and precarious existence. She was an uneducated woman forced to survive as an outcast, following the break-up of her marriage, on the margins of her society. Her unconventional lifestyle – she was not married to her abuser – coupled with her lack of status in her community has contributed greatly to her continued incarceration. Ironically, the outcome for both women, despite some gains, fits within the parameters of how the criminal justice system perceives women who kill – as either as 'mad' or 'bad'.

Kiranjit Ahluwalia: gender and justice?

'Today I have come out of my husband's jail
and entered the jail of the law.'

Kiranjit Ahluwalia suffered violence and abuse for ten years, ever since the start of her marriage. The final straw came when she discovered that whilst her husband beat her day and night, he was also having an affair with another woman upon whom he was lavishing gifts and attention. She felt humiliated but trapped. She had made numerous attempts to end the relationship, often appealing to her family and his for help. She had sought court injunctions to restrain him from further violence but fell under pressure to reconcile for the sake of maintaining family *izzat* (honour). She attempted suicide. At a point when the violence towards her escalated, she agreed to renounce all her desires and her very identity in an effort to please and keep her husband. In a letter to her husband which amounted to a charter of slavery, she begged him to return to her and in return she would give up things that she liked to eat and drink, stop visiting friends and relatives, and stop laughing.

On the fatal day itself, Kiranjit was assaulted by her husband with a hot iron and threatened with further violence. She made one last attempt to talk to him about their marriage. His indifference triggered a rage in her that had been building up for some time. She threw petrol and then a lighted taper at him whilst he slept. Then she ran into the garden with her son and hid behind a shed. Her husband died about a week later from severe burns. She was charged with his murder, tried and found guilty, and sentenced to life in prison.

From the start, the entire criminal justice system failed Kiranjit. The courts were not concerned with the violence she faced, nor why a woman would destroy the very things that society teaches her to value. Throughout her interviews with the police, Kiranjit was made to focus only on the immediate events surrounding the killing, despite her pitiful attempts to explain the history of her actions. Unable to control or even recognise her own story, Kiranjit allowed herself to be silenced, thereby sealing her own fate as a long-term prisoner.

We knew that there could have been a different outcome had the legal system been amenable to recognising her own and countless other women's experiences of domestic violence. Thus began our long journey to challenge the law's power to silence Kiranjit. We knew we had to find legal grounds to reopen her case, but at the same time we were aware that we would have to mount a campaign to educate the public about the injustice she had suffered. The search for grounds of appeal became a learning process for all concerned, a process which showed us both the possibilities and the constraints of the law as an arena of resistance.

Our main problem was overcoming the law of provocation as constructed – a partial defence to the charge of murder. Hitherto, it had relied on a demonstration of immediate retaliation to an incident of provocation and did not allow for the context in which a fatal action takes place to be examined. As it stood, the law was constructed to reflect male-on-male violence. Over the next two years, the lawyers were to develop three substantive grounds of appeal. They included the fact that the trial judge had erred in law when directing the jury as to how to approach the test for provocation. The two-pronged test requires the jury to apply what is referred to as the objective and subjective limbs of the test in order to decide whether a defendant was in fact provoked to lose her self-control and whether the provocation was enough to make a reasonable person act in the same way as the defendant did.

In directing the jury on the objective limb of the provocation test, the trial judge drew the jury's attention to the 'relevant' characteristics of the defendant to be taken into account when deciding whether a reasonable person would have done as Kiranjit did. These, he said, were Kiranjit's age, marital status, ethnicity and education. But nowhere in the closed checklist that he presented did he refer to her as a battered woman. This omission had major implications for the way Kiranjit's trial had been conducted, since it excluded the context of domestic violence in which her tragic actions needed to be situated. We argued that the reasonable person had to be someone who was abused in the same cultural circumstances that Kiranjit found herself. We submitted reports to show that Kiranjit suffered from 'battered woman's syndrome', a concept borrowed from the USA, which describes the inability of some women to leave an abusive relationship due to cycles of depression, despair and hopelessness. Counsel Geoffrey Robertson QC tried to avoid completely medicalising the debate by arguing that, in Kiranjit's case, the jury could have applied their common-sense understanding of domestic violence without the need for expert medical evidence. However, the court was only willing to entertain the notion of battering as a sufficiently permanent characteristic if supported by medical opinion in the form of psychiatric reports. Although the necessary medical evidence was lacking at trial, the Court of Appeal was clearly willing in principle to recognise battered woman's syndrome in the context of provocation.

But many of us in SBS were troubled by the implications of our arguments. The problem with the concept of battered woman's syndrome is that it reinforces an image of women as passive victims rather than as survivors whose actions are rooted in the harsh realities of their everyday lives. It seeks to legitimise the view embedded in the very construction of the law of provocation that men are driven by momentary anger, whilst women are driven by mental or hormonal imbalances for which the proper defence is the psychiatric one of diminished responsibility. The concept cannot explain why it is that when a battered woman kills, her action is ultimately one of survival. The view that the battered woman's syndrome is a permanent characteristic is equally problematic. Those of us who work with battered women are aware that once the violence disappears, more often than not, their personalities and characters change. Clearly the battered woman is a social construct and not a medical one. The syndrome is yet another route by which the criminal justice system seeks to 'privatise' the phenomenon of domestic violence, rendering women's actions born out of depression, but not rage, palatable to society. Yet, in spite of our misgivings, the need to free a wrongly jailed woman had to take precedence.

The second ground of appeal was the challenge to the subjective limb of the definition of provocation, specifically the requirement that the defendant experiences a sudden and temporary loss of self-control. Such a challenge had been mounted unsuccessfully in the case of Sara Thornton. The injustice of denying the defence on this ground is self-evident once the context in which the fatal actions take place is made clear. Many battered women cannot respond immediately, due to their size and strength, but above all, to their fear of retaliation. And when they do, it is when the assailant is asleep, inebriated or otherwise incapacitated. In the course of our campaign we tried to show that anger can express itself in a variety of ways and that many battered women are likely to 'store up' their anger as the provocation escalates. For the first time, in Sara Thornton's case[3] the concept of a 'slow burn' reaction to acts and/or words of provocation was addressed. The Court of Appeal, however, concluded that Sara Thornton was a cold and calculating murderer. Her appearance of outward calm following the killing of her husband did not fit the court's perception of a provoked woman. She was outspoken, articulate and daring. Her protests, ranging from her hunger strike in 1992, through to her open defiance of authority, all played a part in keeping her in prison for longer than necessary.[4]

The court in Kiranjit's case rejected this second ground of appeal. In the process, however, it made a significant concession to the feminist critique. Lord Taylor – the presiding judge – accepted the notion of a 'slow-burn' anger and declared that the time lapse between the act of provocation and the act of killing need not be construed as a cooling-off period as a matter of law. Instead, the matter should be left to the jury to determine. This shift in judicial interpretation was rightly hailed at the time as a major step forward.

The third ground of appeal involved the use of medical evidence, which pointed to the state of Kiranjit's mind at the time of the killing. Evidence of 'endogenous depression', indicating diminished responsibility, though available, had not been adduced at her trial. Fresh medical reports to show that she was depressed at the time of the killing were presented to the Court of Appeal. Unsurprisingly, it was this ground, which questioned neither previous decisions nor male power and authority, which secured Kiranjit's retrial at the Old Bailey in September 1992. The judge at her retrial made it clear that he had only accepted her plea of manslaughter on the grounds of diminished responsibility and not provocation. She was sentenced to three years and four months' imprisonment, exactly the time she had already served. She walked out of court a free woman.

When we began the legal challenge, we realised very quickly that we would not be successful without mounting a political campaign to release Kiranjit Ahluwalia. The campaign had to lay bare the gendered assumptions of homicide laws and the legal structures through which women's powerlessness has been entrenched. We had to raise social and political consciousness around the issue of domestic violence to enable the legal challenge to take place successfully. Raising consciousness meant politicising the issue of battered women who kill. Our slogans, 'Women's tradition, struggle not submission' and 'Domestic violence is a crime, self-defence is no offence' have since become the rallying cries of all feminists against domestic violence.

The campaign placed pressure on the judiciary to ensure that justice was seen to be done. But more importantly, it helped to counter some of the negative effects of the law's response. We needed to find alternative ways of ensuring that Kiranjit's experiences were not perceived to be just an 'Asian' woman's problem – thereby confirming the 'backward' nature of 'Asian culture'. The campaign was also crucial in building solidarity between women across communities and even solidarity between different constituencies, again to ensure recognition of the point that domestic violence affects all communities, for which all of society must take responsibility.

Morgan James Smith and the House of Lords

In 2000, the gains we had made in the Kiranjit Ahluwalia case and others were directly challenged in the Court of Appeal by the case of Morgan James Smith. Ironically, the case involved a man who had shot his former friend and successfully pleaded manslaughter on the grounds of provocation. He claimed that his depressive state lowered his powers of self-control, so that when provoked by his friend's behaviour – who stole from him – he retaliated. The Crown decided to appeal against the outcome on the basis that the interpretation of the law of provocation in particular blurred the distinction between the defences of provocation and diminished responsibility. At the Court of Appeal, however, the judges felt that decisions in a line of cases, notably that of Kiranjit Ahluwalia and Emma Humphries, had firmly established that depressive illness and the mental state of someone provoked into killing could and should be taken into account as a characteristic of a reasonable person when juries determined whether that person would have lost their self-control. The court therefore felt bound by its previous decisions. However, in so far as the distinction between provocation and diminished responsibility was blurred, the court felt it was necessary to clarify the issues by referring the matter to the House of Lords.

Referral to the House of Lords gave SBS the opportunity to make representations to it, outlining in particular the need to look into all contexts in which battered women kill, including the cultural contexts, so as to avoid the law's perception of women as a homogeneous category. The initiative was taken by Justice for Women, who approached SBS and the civil rights group Liberty in seeking leave to make third-party interventions to the court as interested parties. There was a further irony. We realised that, if successful, we would be defending the concept of the battered woman's syndrome in what would be a comprehensive discussion of the law of provocation.

The final judgment was favourable on a three-to-two majority. The judgment gave rise to two significant outcomes. First, the House of Lords accepted the fact that groups like ours had a right to make representations to it. We had been encouraged by the example set by Amnesty International when it intervened in the Pinochet case. Although only written representations were accepted by the House of Lords, the final judgment was influenced by the representations made by all of us. In the wake of the Human Rights Act, third-party interventions in courts are now a more frequently used strategy with which to give voice to those who would not otherwise be heard. The second significant outcome was the fact that the House of Lords decided that the law of provocation should remain. Furthermore, it accepted that women can lose their self-control out of fear and depression as well as anger.

Zoora Shah

'I had become a bed mattress for all the men in the community.'

The case of Zoora Shah has been our toughest challenge yet. Despite the gains made by Justice for Women and SBS in the cases of Kiranjit Ahluwalia and Emma Humphries, the court was not prepared to be stretched further, especially in its understanding of her cultural background.

Zoora Shah came from Mirpur in rural Pakistan in the 1970s following an arranged marriage. Her husband, who had subjected her to violence, abandoned her and her young children while she was pregnant with her third child. She was befriended by Mohammed Azam, a drug dealer from the criminal underworld of Bradford, when she was totally isolated and destitute. Living in squalid rented accommodation in often racist environments and abandoned by her brothers, Zoora allowed Azam to arrange a mortgage on a house. Although Zoora made the repayments from her benefits, factory work earnings and savings, Azam, a married man, used the fact that the house was in his name to enslave her sexually. This sealed her reputation as a 'prostitute', which she had already acquired by virtue of the fact that she was a divorcee, living on her own without a man in a conservative community like Bradford.

Azam used Zoora for sex as and when he pleased, including in the cemetery where she had buried two other children who had died at childbirth. Azam possessed firearms and threatened to use his contacts in the criminal world to find her if she tried to run away. He also often threatened to throw her and her children onto the streets. Azam tried to get her to smuggle drugs from Pakistan for him and when she refused he assaulted her. When Azam was convicted of dealing in heroin and sent to prison for ten years, he tried to pimp Zoora to male inmates about to be released. Her house had become a prison, and she could not free herself from Azam's control.

Zoora was too ashamed to report the reality of her situation to her GP and social services, with whom she was in constant touch. She was therefore unable to avail herself of what little state help existed for abused women. In her desperation, Zoora turned to community leaders for help – including Azam's brother, who was then leader of the Bradford Council of Mosques and had been in the forefront of the anti-Rushdie campaign. But he did nothing. The records of Zoora's GP and social services show that she suffered from depression and illness throughout her married life and relationship with Azam. She had countless abortions, viral and kidney infections and suffered from anaemia and malnutrition. She worked for pitifully low wages looking after disabled children. Zoora then turned to the only people who were willing to help her – other men who were either criminals or had contacts with the criminal world, who seized their chance to exploit her acute vulnerability as a single woman.

In the last phase of her relationship, Zoora felt less and less able to tolerate Azam's sexual demands on her. But the final straw came when she feared that he had sexual designs on her daughters. Zoora finally snapped by administering arsenic, bought in Pakistan. She did not care whether he lived or died. Zoora was charged with a number of offences including murder. She refused to give evidence out of fear and shame. She was ashamed of what she had become in the eyes of the community and could not bring herself to reveal details of her sexual history in public. Bound by the all-powerful notions of honour and shame, she therefore chose to remain silent in the hope of saving the honour of her daughters. Zoora was found guilty on all counts and given a life sentence with a tariff of twenty years.

Race and justice?

Although race was not a component of the legal challenge in Kiranjit's case, in my view the original trial judge's summing up was a muddled understanding of her racial background. He said:

'the only characteristics which you specifically know that might be relevant are that she is an Asian woman, married incidentally to an Asian man…. You may think she is an educated woman. She has a university degree.' It is not too difficult to see that, in the judge's mind, her education and her Asian background stood as two polarised and mutually exclusive opposites. Whilst not forming a plank of her appeal, this compelled us to explain, in the form of a specialist report, the specific cultural context in which Asian women like Kiranjit live. We attempted to explain how culture does have a bearing in terms of the strategies available for Asian women to escape violence. But we had to walk a tightrope. Whilst not wanting to construct Asian culture as some monolithic and static phenomenon, problematic or pathological, we needed to spell out exactly how Asian women can be constrained by their families and communities.

Zoora Shah's case represented more difficult challenges. What complicated matters was that Zoora did not lead a 'normal', 'passive' existence as a 'victim' of violence, but tried to retain some control in an impoverished world inhabited by male predators. Unlike Kiranjit, Zoora did not have anyone to support her or even verify her story. Even her brothers initially distanced themselves from her.

Unlike Kiranjit's case, race and culture formed a small part of the legal arguments put forward by Zoora's barrister, Edward Fitzgerald QC. The main arguments centred on the fact that hers was not a premeditated act despite the use of poison as a tool. The main ground of her appeal was comprehensive new evidence, including her own story and reasons why she had remained silent at her trial. The other important ground was based on medical opinion that she was suffering from diminished responsibility at the time of the fatal attack. We submitted her medical notes, which were a contemporaneous record of her depression, and her various illnesses, statements from new witnesses who spoke about her depression and psychiatric reports which concluded from the medical notes available that she was severely depressed at the relevant time. The court was not even remotely interested in what we believe was to them a story too 'alien' to grasp in all its complexities. The court ignored the wealth of evidence which independently supported her account of utter destitution and despair. Zoora lost the appeal to overturn her conviction for the murder and attempted murder of Mohammed Azam.

One of our main concerns with the court's handling of the case was the rejection of expert evidence from a well-respected psychiatrist trained in cross-cultural psychiatry, Dr Lipsedge. He gave evidence on the ways in which notions of honour and shame affect women in Asian communities. Instead, the court substituted its own opinions about Zoora's cultural background and her lifestyle, guided by a conservative psychiatrist for the Crown – Dr Rix, who had no experience of gender issues within Asian communities. He presented Zoora as a cold and calculating woman – especially because she chose to stay silent at her trial, acted in contradictory ways and had an ambivalent relationship with her abuser, whom she regarded as both her saviour and her destroyer. The court's attitude was not altogether surprising since it was presided over by Justice Paul Kennedy – not known for his liberal views on race.[5]

The judgment was littered with ill-conceived misconceptions about women's responses to violence and the cultural contexts in which this is experienced. It made sweeping assumptions about the codes of honour and shame – which bind many Asian women to submission – bordering on racially gendered stereotypes. The court said,

> This appellant is an unusual woman. Her way of life has been such that there might not have been much left of her honour to salvage and she was capable of striking out on her own when she thought it was advisable to do so, even if it might be thought to bring shame on her to expose her to the risk of retaliation.

Zoora's story of surviving by her wits in an all-male, criminal world in absolute poverty was deemed to be 'incapable of belief'.

Fragrant or flagrant?

In the eyes of the Court of Appeal, Zoora was the flagrant author of her own downfall, unlike Kiranjit, who fitted the classic stereotype of the fragrant, passive Asian wife who tolerates her oppression. Zoora had lied at her original trial, albeit to cover her shame and dishonour. When, on one occasion, Zoora smashed the windscreen of a car belonging to a man whom she suspected had been sent by Azam for sex, the court interpreted this as the act of a 'strong willed woman'. She was, after all, a woman who had been labelled a prostitute. The court did not seek to enquire into how she acquired such a reputation – that her status as a prostitute in the eyes of her community was sealed when she was abandoned by her husband, regardless of the reasons. It betrayed a complete absence of awareness of the intertwined issues of culture, gender and power within minority communities. As Susan Edwards succinctly points out, 'Gender and ethnicity are at the very gravitas of the circumstances in the case against Zoora Shah who could not speak and when she spoke could not be heard'.[6] Without giving reasons, the court conveniently ignored the evidence presented by the psychiatrists (including one for the Crown). In seeking to justify such wholesale rejection of Zoora Shah's case, the court hinted that the psychiatrists had simply been duped by Zoora's clever manipulation!

The failure of the appeal was devastating, especially for Zoora's children, who had experienced the transition from childhood to adulthood far too quickly and without their mother. They took some comfort from the fact that following recommendations from Lord Chief Justice Bingham in 2000, the home secretary reset Zoora Shah's tariff at twelve years. Whilst this decision was disappointing – we had hoped for her imminent release after eight years in prison – the reduction in tariff nevertheless represented a major achievement in the circumstances. Basing his recommendation on the rejected evidence that we had presented to the Court of Appeal, Lord Chief Justice Bingham stated: 'There is considerable material apart from Zoora Shah's own evidence to show that she was' suffering from 'some kind of depressive illness and … that her social situation was of the most stressful kind imaginable. She had suffered from some kind of abuse from the victim.' Lord Justice Bingham appears to have rejected the description of this case as a 'particularly callous and premeditated murder for material gain'. On the contrary, he stated that 'this was the conduct of a desperate woman threatened with the loss of her home and with destitution in what remained for her a foreign country'. We felt vindicated. The decision, however, shows us that obtaining justice is still, in such an advanced democracy as ours, akin to playing the lottery.

The legal system's response to these cases reveals a complex matrix of racial, class and male power which disempowers women like Zoora. The law's ability to resist our challenges to its power raises vital questions about the nature of our legal victories.

Multiculturalism and the law

Zoora Shah's case highlights vital questions of how multiculturalism is played out in law. One burning question that arises is how far we can expect the law to be tolerant of diversity but at the same time accommodate the constraining effects that culture and religion can have on women. Such a question becomes even more pertinent when we consider the fact that much of the judiciary has yet to overcome its prejudices in relation to psychiatric evidence, which is often perceived to be little more than psycho-babble, let alone grapple with nuanced approaches to race and culture.

Kiranjit's and Zoora's powerful critiques of their own specific circumstances, culture, religion and of their experiences of domestic violence gave the lie to the stereotypical assumptions about Asian womanhood constructed by the law. The need to guard against race and gender stereotypes whilst working within the framework of the legal system proved to be our major preoccupation in both the cases.

Yet herein lies our dilemma. Whilst the overriding priority is to do what is in the best interest of the individual client, a critical analysis of the content and direction of change is crucial if the law is to be divested of its patriarchal, race and class power. In the interest of the client, we may have no choice but to reinforce stereotypes on both race and gender questions, as we did, perhaps inadvertently, in Kiranjit's case in presenting her as a virtuous, long-suffering, battered wife held back by a conservative community. However, the same stereotype worked against Zoora Shah.

The law prefers neat and simple categories. What makes the position of minority women vis-à-vis the law more precarious is that what little autonomous voice they do have is mediated through those who claim to be the 'representatives' of the community. Zoora was at a major disadvantage because her reputation as a woman without 'honour' – painted as such by the brother of the deceased

– preceded her to the court. Thus the process serves to further
marginalise women like Zoora who are in law only permitted one
reality – a one-dimensional reality.

Culture as an excuse?

In the course of undertaking these cases, we often asked ourselves,
'Should we not be troubled by the invocation of culture to explain
Kiranjit's and Zoora's actions, especially when in other domestic
violence contexts, involving Asian men who kill their partners, we
have denounced them for using culture as an excuse?' We had to
think hard about how and why we felt justified in using culture in
this way.

At first glance it appears as if we are being selective in our use
of cultural arguments. However, there are major differences, largely
to do with the contexts in which the cultural arguments are made.
Cultural traditions have always oppressed women while liberating
men. It is not surprising, since it is men as religious and community leaders who decide what the values of the community are.
When men argue 'My honour was at stake. She needed to be killed
because she had committed adultery', they use culture to justify
their acts of violence. No one asks the man why he could not have
simply walked away; after all there is no stigma attached to a man
leaving his home. Women, on the other hand, face very real consequences if they find themselves transgressing the norms of their
community, whatever the reason. It is important to understand why
cultural values keep a woman silent and close down her options.
The balance of power within a marriage and in the community is
important to understand. Women use culture to explain the constraints, both real and psychological, that keep them in an abusive
relationship, whilst men use culture to maintain power and control.
Disallowing culture as an excuse to an act of aggression does not
water down the principle of equality in the law: it recognises and
counterbalances the social, cultural and religious factors that create
inequality in the first place.

From the evidence available, it appears that men have received a
more favourable treatment in the courts when making cultural arguments. The case of Shabir Hussain, who mowed down his sister-in-

law, Tasleem Begum Saddique, in 1995 while she waited for her lover is a case in point. He drove his car over her body three times before speeding off. His defence on appeal, when he pleaded guilty to manslaughter on the grounds of provocation – that his sister-in-law's behaviour had dragged their family honour through the mud – successfully overturned his conviction for murder.

The campaign to free Zoora Shah

The loss of the Court of Appeal case meant that we had to turn our attention to the question of Zoora's tariff – the minimum amount of time she must serve in prison as a life-sentence prisoner. Challenging the Court of Appeal's decision required finding new evidence so that the matter could be referred to the Criminal Cases Review Commission. But new evidence would prove hard to come by since we had left no stone unturned in preparing the case for the Court of Appeal. The home secretary, Jack Straw, refused to meet the family and hear representations from them or their supporters. We enlisted the support of prominent Muslim clerics and religious institutions, as Jack Straw was more likely to pay heed to those whom he considered 'leaders' of their communities. The outcome was useful because the contacts we made are important in continuing the discussion about domestic violence and community responsibility – an area which has been somewhat neglected in our drive to get the state to accept responsibility. It is only now that we realise that an exclusive focus on the law can leave the wider questions about community obligations towards women, at best, only tangentially addressed. We would not have attempted a community-based strategy as a substitute for the challenge to the law, but we recognised that a change in legal and state perception of Zoora's predicament would only come about if we also engaged the religious leadership.

Zoora Shah received support from many organisations and MPs. Indeed the chairman of the jury at her original trial wrote to us stating that if he and other members of the jury had been in possession of what was now known about Zoora Shah's background, their decision might have been very different. He also wrote to the home secretary in support of our campaign. Eventually, following a hard-fought letter-writing campaign, which also included presenting a petition with thousands of signatures to the home secretary, Zoora Shah was set a tariff of twelve years.

The campaigns around Zoora Shah and Kiranjit Ahluwalia reveal some of the successes and failures of direct action as a tool for change. In Kiranjit's case, the political climate was such that we were still able to mobilise vast numbers of women. We had to call on the Court of Appeal to open the entire public gallery when her case was being heard because women were spilling out into the corridors and streets. Around the time of Zoora's appeal hearing, we could not even contemplate holding the weekly demonstrations that we had organised during Kiranjit's case. Lack of political activism forced us to look more to the media to raise the issues in Zoora Shah's case. But by then, the issue of battered women who kill had lost its 'sex appeal' in the media. We managed to get some attention, ironically, by tempting journalists with a story about Bradford, domestic violence and even religious fundamentalism – all of which had the potential for racist coverage. But the need for media coverage was crucial for us since we needed to put pressure on the judiciary. To our relief, some of the coverage in the English-language media was sensitive and respectable. The main coverage, however, came from the local media. Local radio stations in West Yorkshire kept faith with the story after we lost at the Court of Appeal. And such coverage was significant in reminding us of the power of the local media in galvanising support and raising awareness in the community. In Bradford the case of Zoora Shah became a cause célèbre – local radio coverage was able to reach Asian households in a way that we would never have been able to, because of the gatekeeping functions of religious leaders in communities like Bradford. We think that it played no small part in the support shown to Zoora's children when they collected signatures in support of a reduction in their mother's tariff.

Multiculturalism versus feminism

Following trends in the USA, some academics in the UK, with a few notable exceptions,[7] now consider it fashionable to talk about the gender deficit inherent in the multicultural approach in Western democracies. The debate, which is not new to us, is often couched in terms of the insurmountable tension between feminism and multiculturalism. To put it crudely, in the USA a number of voices have argued that multiculturalism should not be encouraged since women in minority communities are denied their rights by their cultures.[8] Recognising the group rights of minority communities, they argue, does not guarantee women's rights within them. They point to the prevalence of forced marriages, female genital mutilation and even wife-killing to argue that minority cultures are harmful to women because they are still rooted in patriarchal value systems which have diminished in Western societies. In response to such views, feminists, including those from minority communities in the USA, have argued that to reject multiculturalism is to encourage racism. Some, however, go further in warning against the use of cultural arguments in law to explain actions by women such as those who kill their violent spouses, as there is a danger of reinforcing notions of minority communities as 'barbaric' or 'backward'.

Both views sit uncomfortably with our experience. It is not sufficient to reject multiculturalism because in the struggle against racism it is still viable in promoting tolerance for diversity and in recognising the rights of minority groups, to which we as women also belong. Our identities and experiences are not shaped by gender alone. On the other hand, the women who come to our centre reveal the problems inherent in the multicultural approach in which the struggle for equality has become subsumed under the struggle for recognition of diversity. Women do face oppression in the form of forced marriage, dowry deaths or honour killings, all of which are often justified in the name of cultural difference. We are acutely aware that in the absence of democratic internal community mechanisms, there can be no substitute for resorting to the law. Women do not get a fair hearing, let alone justice, when they turn to the community for help. Whilst women continue to experience many setbacks in making the law accountable to their needs, nevertheless it represents a safety net without which they would be worse off.

The problem with the academic debates on multiculturalism and feminism is that the struggles by women in minority communities are completely ignored, as if activism has nothing to offer such debates. Yet without an awareness of these political struggles, there is real danger that important insights of how to negotiate the mine-field of race and gender politics will be lost. The reality is that black women's activism has both illuminated the problems women have had in negotiating their rights within their communities and in the wider society as well as pointing towards possible solutions. The solutions do not lie in either steering clear of the law or placing one's entire faith in a legal system which allows the space for per-sonal laws or versions of 'community justice' to become entrenched.

The real concern we have with the law, however, is that it either ignores difference altogether or, in its effort to reflect cultural sen-sitivity, adopts multicultural norms which actually reinforce the patriarchal values of our community. A number of our cases, espe-cially in respect of rights within the family, demonstrate the poten-tial of the law to be differentially applied. In one case, a woman of Muslim origin had been made to endure a protracted and painful battle to retain custody of her daughter following a breakdown in her marriage due to her husband's violence and her refusal to con-form as a traditional Muslim wife. Her ex-husband refused to grant her a divorce, thus forcing her into cohabitation with her boy-friend, also a Muslim, which in turn led to a community outcry. Inside the courts, however, the battle over custody of her daughter took an unexpected turn. The presiding judge failed to make a final decision based on a recommendation made by a court welfare officer that the child's interests were best served by remaining with her mother, who was the prime carer. Instead, the judge allowed him-self to be distracted by the husband's arguments that, in child cus-tody and matrimonial/family matters, the Muslim community is guided by Shariah. Introducing experts who were Muslim theolo-gians, the husband argued that according to Shariah laws, his wife was an adulteress and transgressor and should therefore return her child to him. He also argued that the ostracisation faced by the mother would affect his daughter's well-being and moral and reli-gious upbringing. Such arguments clouded the court's notion of justice and equality for the woman and for the young child, whose fate depended on the outcome of theological debates on the position of women in Islam rather than on rights enshrined in civil law. In the end, child custody was not granted to the father because he was imprisoned for a criminal conviction for violence.

The case raises some alarming possibilities about the future development and implementation of secular civil law in relation to women and the family in the minority communities in Britain. In classic multicultural, non-interventionist style, the judge appeared to allow Muslim personal law to supersede the civil rights of the woman. The assumption is that all members of the community uniformly interpret personal laws, and that the self-appointed religious leadership is widely accepted. The consequence is that women are excluded from the construction of the minority community in legal discourses. The actions and views of women are rendered deviant, whilst those of the community leaderships are accepted as 'authentic'.

The ultimate danger of such rulings lies in the construction of minority women as the property of their families and communities. Such constructions in turn feed into a wider social and political culture which disenfranchises many minority women from their citizenship rights, demarcating the boundary of community and the right to belong.

The law needs to accommodate both differences between communities and differences within communities and yet ensure that justice is delivered equally. Admittedly this is a difficult task since we require the law to reflect cultural pluralism but at the same time ensure that individual freedom is not undermined. We may rely on the use of expert reports, encourage judicial training and so on in an effort to minimise the risk of constructing and reinforcing legal notions of minority cultures, but because they remain strictly within the parameters of the law, they are bound to be at best only partially successful.

Since Kiranjit's and Zoora's cases, we have often been requested to provide expert reports in other cases involving Asian and minority women. It is impossible to avoid some generalisations about minority cultures and women's role within them irrespective of how many provisos we insert in such reports. This dilemma has helped us understand that we ought not always look to the law to find answers to the paradoxes that we encounter in the law. We need to mount effective challenges to the law's power from the outside, through for example the creation of effective alliances between women of different backgrounds but with common agendas. (See

Chapter 12, 'Walls into Bridges'). In our campaign on forced marriages, we have resisted the 'exoticisation' of the issue by insisting that the debate, and indeed the legal and policy responses to it, be framed within the general debate on domestic violence and women's human rights. This helps to avoid the view that the majority culture is superior since women who are pressurised into a marriage against their will require the same response as those who experience domestic violence.

Human rights

In the last two years or so, SBS has been particularly preoccupied with trying to use the newly enacted Human Rights Act in our casework. One very positive outcome of the enactment of the Human Rights Act is that the culture and language of the discourse itself has had a liberating effect on our thinking and our work. For example, using the language of human rights and compassion for other human beings was crucial in our campaign to win support from the Muslim communities in the Zoora Shah case. Of course this did mean that our feminist discourse was compromised but not to the extent that we felt uncomfortable (see 'Walls into Bridges').

We have used the human rights framework to highlight the failure of the state at all levels in ensuring that women enjoy the fundamental human right to live free from violence. More specifically, the Human Rights Act allows us to challenge the state for abuses that take place in the private sphere – the family. The break in the public/private divide which demarcates the boundaries of permissible state intervention is vital if we are to gain recognition that all forms of violence against women are a violation of human rights. And yet it is precisely the family or private arena which has proved immensely difficult to prise open in terms of applying the Human Rights Act in the UK, as is shown by the cases of Assa Devi Padan and Nazia Bi.

The Act allows for greater scrutiny of the state and its responsibility in eliminating gendered violence. In effect this means that the state must not only refrain from acts of violence against women but also put into place effective measures which prevent harm against women. Human rights discourse has become especially significant in our struggles against the effects of multicultural policies, which allow the state to operate and implement differential standards of justice and equality.

We have used the Human Rights Act in areas where legal challenges are otherwise difficult. The criminal justice system and coroner's courts, which, through inquests, investigate deaths resulting from suspicious circumstances, have had the spotlight of human rights turned on them.

Suicide: the hidden crime

In a number of cases where Asian women have committed suicide, we have intervened either on behalf of the deceased's family desperate to get to the truth, or as an interested third party. The latter is necessary where there would otherwise be no one to represent the deceased. One direct effect of the Human Rights Act is that we are more and more confident in intervening in cases to give voice to those who would not otherwise be heard. This is not, however, a straightforward process. It has been difficult to persuade the courts to recognise women who run refuges or resource centres for battered women as experts in the way those from the medical profession are recognized. For those of us who work with minority women, such recognition is even harder to come by since it is easy for the courts to accept the charge that is often levelled against us by community and religious leaders – that we are women who are influenced by 'Western' notions of liberation, who therefore undermine the fabric of minority cultural life.

The Human Rights Act nevertheless has provided us with the language to redefine domestic violence in the context of suicide as a violation of human rights and is proving a useful tool in interrogating the reality behind suicide statistics, as in the case of Assa Devi Padan (see Chapter 6, 'Sad, Mad or Angry?'). Assa had been married for twenty-three years; during that time, according to her daughters, she had been subjected to physical and sexual violence. However, in June 2000, following an argument with her husband arising from his decision to leave her, she killed herself. At her inquest we made the following submission: where there was evidence of torture and inhuman or degrading treatment relating to the circumstances of a death, then the failure of the inquest to investigate such evidence effectively constituted a breach of the fundamental human rights of the deceased. Such a failure also breached the rights of her family, who we argued had a right to put questions before the coroner's court to ascertain the circumstances in which Assa died. Under the Act, it was incumbent on the state, through the inquest process, to ensure that those who are culpable of crimes which led to Assa's death were punished under the criminal law.

In the case of Nazia Bi the High Court declined to apply the full rigour and implications of the Human Rights Act – or, indeed, other international human rights standards – to the coroner's decision not to resume an inquest into her death and that of her daughter Sana (see 'Sad, Mad or Angry?' for details). We had sought to challenge the coroner's decision on the basis that it represented a failure of the state to inquire fully into a suspected deprivation of life in circumstances where it was not the state but private individuals (i.e. her husband and possibly his family) that were at fault. We argued that just as the state is required to take positive steps to prevent ill treatment or fatal violence in circumstances where it has knowledge or ought to have knowledge of its occurrence, the state is also obliged to investigate such conduct in its aftermath in order to secure the identification and prosecution of the perpetrators and to prevent any recurrence in the future. In the course of the challenge, counsel on behalf of SBS argued that formal affirmations of rights to be found in international treaties or conventions and resolutions such as the Convention for the Elimination of All Forms of Discrimination Against Women, 1979, (CEDAW), which the UK has ratified, and the United Nations Declaration on the Elimination of Violence Against Women (General Assembly resolution 48/104 of 20 December 1993), ought to have been taken into account by the coroner when reaching his decision. These instruments require states to prohibit all gender-based discrimination and ill treatment that has the effect of impairing the enjoyment by women of fundamental rights and freedom; to take reasonable and appropriate measures to prevent violations of these rights; and, to this end, exercise due diligence to prevent, investigate and punish acts of violence against women, whether those acts are perpetrated by the state or by private persons. But the High Court emphatically rejected this proposition on the basis that such declarations were not part of domestic law and that the coroner did not err in law when exercising his discretion not to resume the inquest.

The High Court's decision represents a setback to our efforts to ensure that the Human Rights Act should be available to allow full scrutiny of acts of abuse in the private sphere. Case law has established the right of individuals to invoke the Human Rights Act in circumstances of abuse in the private sphere which the state knew about but did nothing to prevent. However, it does not extend as yet to circumstances of such abuse outside the knowledge of the state altogether. Our challenge clearly represented a leap too far for the courts. Had Nazia Bi been failed by the police when she telephoned them hours before she died, the coroner's decision might have been subjected to a different kind of judicial scrutiny. As it was, given the facts of the case, the court found that the coroner had exercised his discretion appropriately, having taken into account the criminal and judicial investigations into her death that had taken place, even though we argued that those investigations were inadequate and had not led to a full trial.

The outcome raises a number of questions. The notion that international declarations on human rights are not applicable unless they are incorporated into domestic law is plainly bewildering. What, then, is the point of such instruments? How can they ever be relevant to domestic law if the judiciary does not have the courage to draw on them for inspiration? Such instruments are passed and ratified in order to strengthen the protection a victim has against violations of her human rights. Yet the law is evolving in such a way as to prevent issues such as violence against women from being included within human rights discourse. Similarly, the inability of human rights law to reach into the private sphere, where most violence against women and children occurs, results in denying those who are powerless the mean of obtaining justice.

This leads to a fundamental point about the development of human rights law as we have witnessed it so far. It has been observed that denying the applicability of human rights to the private sphere can paradoxically lead to a situation where it comes to be perceived merely as 'a tool against the weak rather than a shield against oppression'.[9] For our part, we are all too wary of how the Human Rights Act will be used in the UK. As can be seen in other countries with comparable legislation on human rights, we suspect that in respect of the right to family life, in particular, the Act will be used by those who wish to maintain oppression as much as those who seek to challenge it.

Our legal challenges around the issue of suicides and Asian women took place largely in the absence of any wider political campaign, which we believe was partly responsible for the negative outcome in Assa's and Nazia Bi's cases. The sad reality is that the struggle to highlight the hidden truth behind many suicides committed by Asian women is being waged mainly within the four walls of the courtroom. Activism is essential to bring the values that we wish to create within the legal system alive. The Human Rights Act cannot be made to work for women until and unless there is the political will to do so. This in turns depends on political struggles, which create a culture of human rights that we do not yet have in this country. Whilst the coroner in Assa's case did invite the legal representatives to make submissions about the remit of coroners' courts on suicides to a Home Office Review, we are aware that it will take more than a few submissions to change attitudes.

Conclusion

The more SBS has had to engage with the law, the more it has dawned upon us that the law cannot, by its very nature, do more than occasionally provide an empowering tool by which women can seek some semblance of justice. The law silences the truth in many ways – this was driven home to us by the case of Zoora Shah in particular, leading us to the realisation that truth and justice are not unproblematic terms. We are acutely aware of the limitations of the law, reflecting as it does the wider values of society. When those sitting in judgment belong to a mostly unaccountable elite, important questions about how the Human Rights Act will be implemented with regard to minority women arise. Balancing group and individual rights raises difficult issues, which require careful handling by the legal system. So far the results suggest that the law has not been able to reflect cultural diversity in such a way that women's human rights can be guaranteed.

Then there is the problem with what we feel to be a perceptible shift in feminist struggles in this country – including our own, where the battleground appears to have shifted from the political to the legal arena. We live with the legacy of Thatcherism, and the political climate we face is such that the law has become the main arena for struggle. It seems as if feminists are turning to the law because we no longer have the time or resources (or even the will?) to engage in long-term political struggles. The law provides a quick fix. But is it a justice which will last or even be recognisable by the streams of women who walk through our doors?

Notes

1. See Anne Jones, *Women Who Kill*, Gollancz, London 1991.
2. Ibid.
3. In February 1990, Sara Thornton was tried for the murder of her alcoholic and violent husband. She attacked him whilst he lay in a drunken state. At her trial she put forward a defence of diminished responsibility but it was rejected because she did not fulfil the requirement that she was suffering from an 'abnormality of mind'. She appealed against her conviction, arguing among other things that the court did not consider the defence of provocation. The Court of Appeal rejected this argument on the grounds that she was not provoked.
4. In 1996, following a second appeal and trial, Sara Thornton was finally freed.
5. Justice Paul Kennedy was the chief prosecutor in the celebrated case of the Bradford Twelve in the early 1980s. This case concerned twelve Asian youth who were prosecuted for defending their community from racial attacks which were ignored by the police. A nationwide campaign was launched under the slogan 'Self Defence Is No Offence', and they were eventually found not guilty.
6. Susan Edwards, 'Beyond Belief: The Case of Zoora Shah', *New Law Journal*, 8 May 1998.
7. Floya Anthias and Nira Yuval Davies have over the years made important contributions to the debate on multiculturalism, especially from the point of view of the impact of multiculturalism on gender relations. See, for example, *Racialised Boundaries: Race, Nation, Gender, Colour and Class and the Anti-racist Struggle*, Routledge, London 1992.
8. Susan Moller Okin has argued that multiculturalism and feminism represent a clash of cultures which are irreconcilable. 'Is Multiculturalism Bad for Women?', *Boston Review*, October/November 1997.
9. Andrew Clapham, 'Opinion: The Privatisation of Human Rights', *European Human Rights Law Review*, Sweet & Maxwell, London 1995.

Walls into bridges:
the losses and gains
of making alliances

Rahila Gupta

Although the concept of autonomous organisation has been central to the women's movement since the late 1970s, we found ourselves still explaining and asserting the importance of autonomy for the creation of a feminist politics, particularly to the anti-racist left in *Against the Grain*.[1] The idea that autonomous organisation – autonomous from your oppressor – provided a safe space in which to build confidence had come to be widely accepted in the women's movement. From the mid-1980s, however, this concept of separate development was adopted by groups crystallising around identities of race, class, sexuality, disability or age which came to be defined more and more exclusively, leading headlong into the cul-de-sac of identity politics and its attendant problems of isolation. It was a cul-de-sac that we have always steered clear of because we had recognised early on that successful campaigning needed the widest possible support. Marie Mulholland of Women's Support Network, an Irish women's umbrella group based in Belfast, believes that

> alliance building is also [necessary] to try and provide another way of people relating to each other [other] than in hierarchies of oppression.... And in some ways it's about creating some kind of level ground in which everybody can have some space together. It's about trying to get beyond or circumnavigate the kind of competitiveness of needs and agendas that goes on when people are marginalized. And also to get beyond that one-dimensional view of identity.[2]

The identities we choose can either limit or increase the potential for alliances. But whatever identity we choose, it must be clearly thought-out because, as Julie Bindel of Justice for Women says, 'it has not always been easy to involve ourselves in coalitions if the other groups do not have a strong sense of their own identity'.[3] We have found this to be true where other Asian women's groups, whose political agenda may be similar to ours, have steered clear of working with us cooperatively because they have felt threatened by the possibility that we would dominate the proceedings. We have always felt that it was a lack of certainty in what they wanted to achieve and who they were that made alliance building with them difficult.

Ten years ago we were talking about reaching out to both women of different ethnicities and to the anti-racist movement. The key difference between then and now is that the chasms that we have been willing to cross have become wider and deeper. This chapter is about the process of doing politics, the means rather than the ends. This process is about making alliances and about seeking support from unlikely quarters. What do we mean by alliances? What alliances are possible in Blairite Britain where the notion of building 'communities of interest' is all the rage? How different is an alliance with organisations that broadly share our values from courting limited and temporary support from organisations whose agenda may otherwise be anathema to us? And does the process of working with others transform the politics of the members of that alliance? At its simplest, no campaign for change can be successful without alliances. We cannot develop a strategy for change unless we understand how power operates in society, and alliances enable you to understand how power works horizontally as well as vertically. And within the alliance, it is the terms of the power relationship between the participants that dictate the final outcome. Of course, many campaigns can become bogged down in the attempt to build an alliance and never get to an end goal. Or they adopt such a broad-church approach that their values are compromised or differences are glossed over, as in the case of some anti-racist organisations which sought the support of religious organisations in the campaign against racism. Or the goal itself may become so watered down that the whole campaign becomes pointless.

In *Against the Grain*, we looked at the hilarious consequences of trying to organise a national march in 1986 protesting against violence against women. The leaflet was burdened with thirty-eight demands, ranging from the end of state violence, to sexual abuse, to medical violence – every interest group wanted its particular area of work to be reflected in the demands. Although the time and energy costs of alliance-building are high, a significant by-product of the process is the creation of a political culture based on inclusivity rather than exclusivity. This is critical in our fragmented times, when to talk of a feminist movement or anti-racist movement is to see things through rose-tinted glasses. That is not to say that the notion of a broad movement does not remain a dearly held aspiration. When public horror at the war against Iraq could bring a million and a half people onto the streets of London in February 2003, the largest march ever in the history of Britain, we know we are in the presence of something new. This has been made possible by the coming together of groups as disparate as the Muslim Association of Britain, the Socialist Workers' Party and secondary-school children – a volatile combination on the face of it. As Mark Steel, one of the speakers at a Brent Stop the War meeting in April 2003, said, the left has to learn how to work in this atmosphere of inclusivity, having for so long talked only to itself. The ground for the anti-war protests was laid by the anti-globalisation movement, which had been criticised for a lack of direction. Despite the fears that had been expressed that the centre would not hold, with its ragbag collection of groups ranging from anarchists to peace-loving veggies, the anti-globalisation movement has forced multinational corporations – which have made even nation-states go weak at the knees – to sit up and take note of the new mood. Ten years ago we could not imagine an effective response to growing multinational power. We were locked into single-issue campaigns. Sivanandan, director of the Institute of Race Relations, believes that a wider political culture is beginning to emerge which opens out to all and goes beyond fighting for the personalised rights of individuals and groups to taking on the power of governments and multinational corporations.

Historically the process of coming together, of opening lines of dialogue, differs from the umbrella groups of the past because it is informed by a new awareness today, one in which we have both seen the immobilising impact of identity politics and understood the strangulation and the invisibility of marginal groups – their lack of power which led us down the path of identity politics in the first place. Nira Yuval-Davis attempts to provide a theoretical framework for this process of coming together, which she calls transversal politics or dialogical politics 'in which the different participants remain centred in their own position whilst imagining how the world is seen through the eyes of the other participants in the dialogue'.[4] She goes on to say that 'Transversal politics aims at providing answers to the crucial theoretical/political questions of how and with whom we should work if/when we accept that we are all different as deconstructionist theories argue.'[5]

There is a recognition that differences are important but that these should encompass, rather than replace, notions of equality. It assumes a commonality of values. Does that result in us talking to the converted, or in taking a broader view of what constitutes commonality, as the left has been attempting in the last few years? How do we enlarge our constituencies? A key limitation of transversal politics is that it does not provide any strategies on how to work with those with whom there may be very little common ground. Nira points out that lack of decision-making mechanisms and lack of accountability are also weaknesses of transversal politics. According to an example she cites, if feminists decide in a particular social context to take up cudgels against forced sterilisations, even if this puts them on the same side as the Catholic Church, they would not become their transversal political partners.[6] But what language would we need to evolve to make that tactical alliance in order to win that particular battle?

In the case of Zoora Shah (see SBS Timeline), we went even further: we actively courted the orthodox, religious Muslim establishment. We recognised that support from them, the 'community leaders', would weigh heavily with the home secretary, Jack Straw, when we made our representations to him to reduce her tariff of twenty years. Apart from anything else, it represented our own maturation in understanding the processes and using the levers of change. Does this evolution define us as post-modern feminists, if there is such a thing? Nira Yuval-Davis summarises the tactics used by Muslim feminists in Iran in dealing with orthodox Islam: 'the piecemeal approach of post-modern feminism enables co-operation around specific issues without making generalised claims for women's rights or women's equality.'[7] In a sense, that is what we have been doing in attempting to get support for Zoora on the grounds of compassion without reference to women's rights. We began to understand that the religious establishment is no more a homogeneous monolith than we are. We were guilty of the same degree of reductiveness as the state is when it constructs black communities as homogeneous under multiculturalism. We began to exploit the differences between castes and subcastes, between the educated and the illiterate, the rural and the urban, to further our cause. If the Council of Mosques leadership in Bradford could not support the case of an abused woman, it did not preclude Rafique Malik, secretary of the Lancashire Council of Mosques from casting the first stone. He argued that 'We have a religious duty to speak for the right cause. There is a clear edict in Islam that we must hate the offence, not the offender. If there is any doubt when someone is sentenced to life and there was in Zoora's case – extreme provocation – then this is a major ground for mitigation.'

Dr Ghayasuddin Siddiqui, leader of the Muslim Parliament, recognises 'the downward spiral of powerlessness' that traps women like Zoora. He condemns the 'village culture and mentality' of Muslim elders who refuse to take on the issue of domestic violence even though it threatens to tear apart their own homes. The Muslim Parliament was in search of a constituency – it was seeking to attract young Muslims, including women. Dr Siddiqui felt that until the religious establishment was convinced that the problem of domestic violence exists, any initiatives to tackle it might be doomed to failure. A number of prominent individuals, like Dr Zaki Badaawi, the principal of Ealing Muslim College, made supportive noises but were unable to carry their committees with them when it came to lobbying Jack Straw to free Zoora Shah. Ealing Muslim College has a Shariah council and runs a reconciliation service. Dr Badaawi believes that a culture of reconciliation is necessary but recognises that this can cause difficulties for women if they are facing violence within the marriage. Dr Badaawi supports Zoora Shah on the basis of her extenuating circumstances. He says, 'Of course, we cannot give a blank cheque for women to kill their husbands. Because divorce is available in Islam, we feel that a woman can come to us if she is being ill-treated rather than kill her husband.'

Out of the 600 or so Muslim organisations that we contacted, only a handful supported us. One of the reasons is that, for liberals and fundamentalists alike, supporting Zoora Shah is tantamount to accepting that patriarchal power relations exist within our communities. Zoora did go to the president of the Bradford Council of Mosques, Sher Azam, who happened to be the brother of the man who was abusing her and whom she killed, but was offered no support. Even today, with a change in leadership, and personal factors out of the equation, the Bradford Council of Mosques sees no redeeming feature in Zoora's case. Such a divergence of views perhaps lay behind the reluctance of their umbrella organisation, the British Council of Mosques, to take a stand on the issue. Organisations like the Islamic Tarbiyah Academy lent cautious support to the campaign by signing the petition to free Zoora Shah, while pointing out that in an Islamic state she would have paid for her actions by being stoned to death. However, even in Pakistan, the courts acquitted Hidayat Bibi for the murder of her husband and a policeman because they conspired to rob her of her 'honour'.

We received some support for Zoora from the Muslim religious establishment on the basis of the racism of the British state and the criminal justice system – that they would have been more lenient towards a white woman facing the same charges. The language we used to draw them into dialogue was very carefully constructed. On the plea that Islam was essentially humane and compassionate, we argued that they should support a woman like Zoora in her campaign to be freed. We knew we could not win that cooperation using the feminist language of choice and autonomy. Nor as feminists could we argue on behalf of an entire group of women who are subject to violence, but only on behalf of one individual who had suffered enough.

Does that process change us or does it, as we would hope, lead to a shift in the understanding of the established orthodoxies? Domestic violence has become part of the agenda of the religious establishment. There has been public condemnation of domestic violence and forced marriages. Of course, the methods of dealing with violence have been containment and conciliation. And their analysis lays the blame for domestic violence firmly at the woman's door – either she demands too much or as a mother does not bring up her sons differently – the latter argument having been made by Dr Badaawi.

Strictly speaking, our contact with the Muslim religious hierarchy belongs to the same category as our contact with the Women's Institute – it represents too great a chasm. We were not in alliance with them but were seeking limited support on a single issue. However, part of the process of seeking support was similar to that of working in an alliance. We had to bear the differences in mind at all times and negotiate our way around them. We had to walk on eggshells. The Women's Institute (WI), the Townswomens' Guild (TWG), Justice for Women (JFW) and SBS organised a joint petition for limited and specific changes in the law of provocation as a result of the high-profile cases of Kiranjit Ahluwalia and Sara Thornton. The WI gathered 43,000 signatures, while we managed approximately 2,000. The need to win their support speaks for itself. Interestingly, when we asked the WI and the TWG for support on our campaign against the one-year immigration rule, they said that their members would not agree. The process of working together on a single issue did not transform their politics. It could be argued that such transformation only takes place in a long-standing alliance.

However, even with long-standing allies, like Justice for Women, a predominantly white women's group, we find significant differences of opinion that show that perhaps transformation is more a hope than a reality. Take the time when JFW tried to use immigration laws to exclude undesirables. Mike Tyson was seeking permission to come to Britain to fight in a boxing match in 2000 and JFW mounted a legal challenge against the government's decision to give Tyson a visa on the grounds that, as a serial rapist, he represented a real threat to women here. Although their legal moves failed, the case received a lot of media publicity. We opposed this course of action because we have always campaigned against the immigration laws as they are racist and have been used against black people. We felt that a more appropriate course of action would have been to organise demonstrations against Tyson once he was here. We felt that as allies and as black women we should have been consulted about these moves even if they eventually decided to take that route unilaterally.

We began working with Justice for Women when they organised a demonstration outside the High Court in support of Sara Thornton when she lost her appeal in 1991. By then we had been campaigning on behalf of Kiranjit for nearly two years. Black and white women, rich and poor, lesbians and heterosexuals, able-bodied and disabled women came together to support our campaigns. Such unity and energy was perhaps unprecedented. The issue of domestic violence was propelled onto the national agenda, and highlighted within and outside minority communities. More importantly, though, the joint campaign to release Sara Thornton, Amelia Rossiter and Kiranjit Ahluwalia, battered women from a range of backgrounds who had killed their husbands, implicitly and explicitly made the political point that domestic violence affects all women. Amelia was in her seventies, Sara was middle-class and articulate, and Kiranjit was an Asian woman. Amelia was the first to be released in April 1992 after three years in prison. Her case fitted the classic definition of provocation. She stabbed her husband a number of times in a fit of frenzy, having endured his violence for many years. When Kiranjit won her appeal, Justice Taylor in his judgment liberalised the interpretation of the law of provocation in a way that would benefit all women caught up in the criminal justice system. There had been no other campaign in which we were involved where victory would be felt across race – and that in itself was an incredible fillip to our self-confidence.

Although both campaigns were about battered women who kill, and although we shared our analysis of patriarchy and male violence, SBS were always very conscious of the role played by race in complicating matters for black women. This is an issue that Julie Bindel of JFW does not completely take on board when she attributes the success of our alliance to the fact that we shared a single analysis of male violence – that we agreed on patriarchy and did not blame the state, poverty or racism. 'The two groups built up a working relationship based not only on a single issue but within the single issue, a single analysis', says Julie.[8] For example, we wanted to ensure that any changes that we may demand in terms of the law should not have a detrimental impact on black men, like Satpal Ram,[9] who were in prison for having killed in response to a racial assault.

The alliance between JFW and SBS came close to breaking down over a discussion of changes in the homicide law. The groups broadly shared a reservation regarding the current homicide laws: that 'diminished responsibility' – the defence most easily available to women pleading guilty to manslaughter rather than murder – pathologised women. SBS had argued that the law of provocation should be more extensively used by women and should reflect the different ways and the different contexts in which women kill. JFW opposed any widening of the definition – that was to risk allowing more men to take advantage of it, while the courts, patriarchal institutions that they were, would continue to be hostile to women defendants. They argued for a more gender-specific law – the notion of preservation for women and children who had experienced domestic violence. However, even with self-preservation, some medical evidence would be required, and the danger of pathologising women was still inherent in that. Also, by logical extension, one could argue for a new race-specific law, if there was going to be one for domestic violence, so that men who had been victims of racial violence could argue provocation. SBS felt that existing homicide laws should become inclusive of all experiences. For issues affecting black women we have never really had the support of white women. Immigration law is one area, forced marriage is another, where we have had mainly the support of Asian women's groups.

The rise of religious fundamentalism in our communities has, however, threatened the alliances that can be forged with other Asian women (and Asian men). Yasmin Alibhai-Brown makes an eloquent plea to black communities to come out of their ghettos, to unite with white communities as the only way forward[10] – yet she identifies as a Muslim not as an Asian, which is an atomised rather than a collective identity. Whilst there has been a disturbing rise of Islamaphobia in the West, particularly since the American attacks, it is important to see that there are greater things we share as Asians and as black women. Within SBS, maintaining alliances between ourselves as South Asian women has not been difficult because we have always emphasised the secular ethos of the group. It has not been difficult to put into practice because women readily understand the commonality of their experiences as women. Language, food, films, as well as concepts such as shame and honour, are some of the common strands of the fabric of our lives. In debates about domestic violence or religious oppression, women are readily able to identify with each other's predicament. They negotiate their differences and arrive at a common stance against domestic violence in solidarity with each other. Cynthia Cockburn sums this up well in her discussion with Pragna Patel and Marie Mulholland,

> I think what you do is to make available what you might call a 'secular' identity, a way of avoiding the specific narrowing and fixing identities with which people are addressed by the state, by mainstream political forces, or by community or religious leaders. You provide a space where they can complain and be critical about their situation, redefine their sense of who they are, but without having to deny their belonging.[11]

That is why we are suspicious of developments such as the setting up of refuges for particular religious denominations like those for Muslim women. Do their experiences vary greatly from women of other denominations? Or is the real reason for setting up such refuges an attempt to contain the issue of domestic violence, to ensure that women return to the marriage after a period of respite without challenging the status quo?

The fatwa against Salman Rushdie was a wake-up call. We had noticed the way in which religious fundamentalism had been creeping up in our communities and we realised that we needed to take action. We organised a meeting of white and black feminists from a range of political traditions, ethnic and religious backgrounds. This culminated in the founding of Women Against Fundamentalism (WAF) in 1989. Although the catalyst had been Rushdie and the fatwa, the group was united on the need to tackle and make visible all religious fundamentalisms, partly to challenge the demonisation of Islam by the state and the liberal intelligentsia and partly to develop a common understanding of and an effective strategy to fight reactionary religious forces in all our communities. WAF was the perfect example of transversal politics in action:

> All feminist politics should be viewed as a form of coalition politics in which the differences among women are recognised and given a voice, without fixating the boundaries of this coalition in terms of who we are but in terms of what we want to achieve.[12]

WAF shot to prominence in the wake of the Rushdie affair because the media were caught up in a feeding frenzy and were keen to cover the issue from every possible angle. WAF's position represented the third way (a term forever blighted by Blair), one that had not been articulated by others, resisting both racism and religious fundamentalism. WAF carried out a number of different campaigns against Hindu, Catholic and Jewish fundamentalism, none of which received the same level of publicity. As a result it became identified with being anti-Islamic in some sections of society and especially the anti-racist lobby, who saw it as feeding into Islamaphobia, exactly the opposite of what WAF wanted to achieve. Pragna Patel described WAF as 'one of the most thoughtful and effective alliances of black and white women we've ever been involved in'. It included Jewish, Protestant English, Catholic-Irish and Asian women of various religious backgrounds. Pragna says in the discussion on inclusive movements in *Soundings*,

> Obviously given the composition of WAF there are horizontal
> differences of power among us in relation to power. But what's
> made it possible I think to deal with the internal differences and
> inequalities, is that we've looked first and foremost at the role the
> British state is playing in demonising certain minority communities.

The common values of secularism, feminism and socialism also held the alliance together. Through this alliance, SBS joined with African Women's groups to denounce female genital mutilation and organised a joint demonstration against a local authority (Brent) which attempted to legitimise it as a cultural and religious practice that ought to be tolerated.

We wanted to extend the work that we were doing in WAF, especially around Hindu fundamentalism after the destruction of the Babri Masjid in 1992 (see Chapter 10, 'Rama or Rambo?', for further details). We joined forces with certain sections of the anti-racist movement which had been conspicuous by its silence and discomfort around the issue of religion, to form the Alliance against Communalism and for Democracy in South Asia. Most of the tensions that arose in that alliance came from the view that gender was not a prominent issue. As women who had formed WAF and had analysed gender, religious fundamentalism and state response in some depth, we felt that our perspective was being ignored. Obtaining recognition from the Alliance that one of the major repercussions of communal identity was the impact on gender relations was an up-hill struggle. In fact when we were out distributing leaflets for a meeting on Hindu fundamentalism at a religious Hindu *mela*, and being threatened and abused by the organisers for doing so, the men in the Alliance deserted us, saying they did not feel capable of taking on such hostility! Forget solidarity with women; they were not even motivated to 'protect' us according to the patriarchal code of chivalry. On the whole, it was a group of people who were immersed in an anti-racist culture. We were seeing the beginnings of Islamaphobia at that time. While members of the Alliance could see that Muslims were victims of Hindu extremism, they would not condemn Muslim fundamentalism despite the secular values to which we were committed as a group. Many in the Newham Monitoring Project (NMP), an anti-racist organisation in East London, were embracing Islam as a militant anti-racist identity.

It was an issue that divided Asian women's groups as well. For instance, Newham Asian Women's Project (NAWP) never joined WAF. We felt that some members of NAWP were uncomfortable with WAF's position and were confused about which struggle to prioritise, women's rights or anti-racism. NAWP has been one of the London groups that has consistently supported SBS by turning up and mobilising for a number of our campaigns. However, we have never really worked in alliance with them on any particular campaign. It may be that their focus has been on service provision rather than campaigning, although recently through their Imkaan initiative (see Chapter 3, 'Taking or Giving Refuge?') they have become more active in developing policy. Other Asian women's groups, who were firmly entrenched within their religious identity, did not see religious fundamentalism as a threat; furthermore they differed from us on a number of key issues around domestic violence. We were particularly concerned about their involvement when mobilising against the Home Office Working Group on Forced Marriage and its insistence that reconciliation should be one of the remedies available to women escaping violence.

SBS found itself in an isolated position, especially when arguing that the Home Office should not recommend mediation as one of the ways in which to deal with estranged parties, because it can be so unsafe for women. SBS sought the support of other women's groups for the submission it made to the Home Office in March 2000. At a meeting with women's groups to discuss the submission to gain agreement, we were worried that women working within a specific religious denomination would not support us on the issue of reconciliation. We were also expecting some women's groups, like 'Our Voice' in Bradford, to support the use of immigration controls to help women escape forced marriage – for example, by reporting the marriage to the authorities as one of convenience and calling for the extension of the probationary period in order to deter men from entering the country through forced marriage (see Chapter 4: 'It Was Written in Her Kismet'). We have also been surprised at the amount of confusion on the issue, especially among white women, where the link between forced marriage and domestic violence is not recognised or understood. However, there was a strong and unexpected consensus among the thirty-five women's groups present – predominantly secular Asian and other black and minority women's refuges and resource centres. The initiative also received support from white or mixed-race women's aid groups, including national bodies such as National Women's Aid Federation of England and Scottish Women's Aid. SBS argued that forced marriage had to be addressed by the state. It had to mainstream the issue and incorporate it in its national strategy on violence against women and children. Also, there should be national minimum standards of good practice within a human rights framework. This included opposing the practice of mediation and reconciliation in situations of abuse, such as forced marriage.

The reluctance to discuss and challenge reactionary forces within the black community has remained a feature of the anti-racist left. In the wake of the Stephen Lawrence affair, Southall Monitoring Group (now known as The Monitoring Group), lawyers and a number of campaigns for racial justice for individuals came together to build a national civil rights movement. However, it did not include people who were fighting other forms of injustice – a missed opportunity. To be effective it should have been a broad coalition confronting different forms of oppression. A civil rights movement, in this day and age, should be made up of people who feel disenfranchised on grounds of gender, race, disability, sexuality and so on. The challenge was to create a framework of demands that met all those different needs. As Pragna Patel said in the discussion in *Soundings*,

> And if those demands, which would be about transformation of power, were met, everybody would benefit, not just one section of society at the expense of others. I can't even begin to imagine what such a collective set of demands would look like, but they would inevitably include devolving power from state to local level, they would be about transparency in decision making processes, about equality proofing ... and looming large in all of that, accountability within state institutions.

Even the use of images of Martin Luther King on the publicity material showed that the organisers were caught in a time warp, when there were different social and political forces at play. In addition, the movement was not led from within but from above by lawyers. However, there was one positive outcome of that initiative: it linked up disparate groups around single-issue campaigns, tragic stories of individual families, some of whom, like the refugee families, were particularly isolated, and provided support for them.

We were not invited to speak at the meeting to launch the National Civil Rights Movement in March 1999. We wanted to raise the case of Perkash Walia (see Chapter 8, 'The Tricky Blue Line'), which was a perfect illustration of police incompetence, racism and sexism, but we had a major struggle to get some space. The campaign was not run in a democratic way. Participants had to submit what they wanted to say in writing beforehand and it could be vetoed. Besides they could participate in the discussion only if they had signed up to the aims and objectives (i.e. they had to be members), but as this was the launch meeting of the group, those aims and objectives should have been thrown open for discussion. The aims and objectives were mainly to do with racial justice and police brutality. There was no space for the experiences of black women. After a great deal of lobbying, Sukhwant Dhaliwal was given an opportunity to address the meeting *without* signing up to the aims and objectives. Among other things, she said: 'If we are talking about institutional racism within the police force, we are also talking about the right to protection and justice for black women who report domestic violence.' We were unable to shift their agenda, although many of the participants agreed with our position. And eventually, at the end of the day, we signed up because we wanted to be kept informed of developments so that we could play a part in the movement in whatever way we could.

One of the alliances that we have failed to make is with working-class struggles by Asian women, although they have often been on our doorstep in Hillingdon and Heathrow. They have waged long and heroic struggles, either fighting for union recognition or at the forefront of the battle against privatisation and casualisation of labour, from the Grunwick strike of the late 1970s to the Hillingdon Hospital cleaners and the Lufthansa Skychef dispute of the 1990s. The fact that many working-class black women are concentrated in low-paid jobs with poor conditions of work has made them prominent in labour disputes. Black women have led these struggles, often without support from or in direct conflict with their trade unions, which have failed to represent their interests. Women within South Asia Solidarity Group, for example, have used these struggles to mobilise black women, particularly on the issue of racism. SBS have also attempted to make links with black women during these disputes. However, our approaches were both misunderstood and unwelcome to some, but not to all, of the strikers. For example, we went to the picket line to show our solidarity during the Hillingdon Hospital strike. One of the Asian women strikers, when she realised that we were from SBS, turned around and said 'I don't want to leave my husband'. Whilst we had not specifically come to recruit feminists, we had come to make connections and build alliances. These connections were not made by some of the Asian women strikers, particularly the shop steward, who would say at meetings that theirs was not a race or sex discrimination dispute, but one of labour. She was keen to underplay the issue of racism and sexism for fear of delegitimising their struggle.

The challenge for black feminism is therefore to draw in more working-class black women, to make the wider connections between the oppression of race, gender and class. How do we transfer the mobilisation and activism of black women from the shop floor to their political participation in the struggle against racial attacks on the streets and male violence in the home? Whilst we recognise that the economic independence of women helps to tackle the problems of racial and sexual oppression, the economic determinism of some socialists and feminists has failed to recognise the dynamics of patriarchy and racism. Indeed, groups like Black Women for Wages for Housework emphasise the role of economic independence at the expense of other factors in the oppression of black women.

We found also that where there is a union involved in the struggle, even if it is as big as the T&G and the Skychef dispute, they feel threatened by the involvement of groups like ours. The Skychef dispute began in 1998 when 75 per cent of workers, most of whom were women, voted to go on strike against the new 'flexible working practices' that the management were planning to introduce. They were all sacked although they had followed the correct legal procedures in agreeing to strike action. During the course of the strike, there were a number of areas in which the women felt let down by the union – some practical and easily resolvable like the provision of facilities on the picket line. Other concerns were to do with not being consulted or kept informed about developments, especially on their individual cases at the industrial tribunal. Throughout the two-year dispute, it was the women who kept the picket going, attending meetings up and down the country to seek solidarity from other sections of the trade-union movement, and yet they were underrepresented in the strike committee and the support group meetings. The men regularly praised the commitment of the women and admitted that the strike would have collapsed without them, yet saw no contradiction in the fact that they were barely represented at the organisational level.

We tried to play an intermediary role between the union and the women but they attempted to cut us out of the picture. Having first invited us to join the support group, they then kept us outside the door on the grounds that the proceedings were confidential and let us in when they were discussing social events. The support group consisted of a couple of trade-union officials from the strike committee and a motley collection of Trotskyite and communist groups. The role of the group was to raise funds and awareness and mobilise public support for the strike. The union was very defensive towards the support group, believing that it was out to undermine it. Although we agreed with some of the support group's criticism of the union, we had a very definite and specific interest – that of supporting the women in terms of whatever needs they articulated. We had neither the resources nor the desire to undermine the union (whether that was the agenda of the other left groupings, we were not able to determine). We got tarred with the same brush and were excluded. At the anniversary of the strike, a barbecue picnic on the green outside the factory was organised for supporters. The level of mutual suspicion between trade-union officials and the support group was so high that we found ourselves feeling we had betrayed one side when caught talking to the others.

Even in this context, the gender and race intersection proved uncomfortable. Showing our solidarity with the strikers, we stood shoulder to shoulder with men and women – and listened uncomfortably as the men on the picket line swore at the women scabs reporting for work, calling them rundis (prostitutes). But when the police threatened to arrest the men for not speaking English – they wanted to understand the swear words that were being used so they could arrest the pickets for abusive behaviour – we defended their right to speak in their own language and demanded to know which law prevented people from doing so and accused the police of racism.

In some ways, our failure to establish links with these struggles was more to do with our exclusion from local Southall politics, where the anti-racist and trade-union organisations view us with suspicion and do not seek our support for alliances they may have formed on specific issues. For example, in the Skychef dispute, different organisations lent support to different factions within the struggle and we did not have the patience or time to deal with this sectarianism. When our MP, Piara Khabra, made a number of racist remarks about the presence of Somalis in Southall,[13] eleven local organisations got together and responded in the local press but did not seek to include us in their action.[14] We are in the ironic position of being fêted as a national organisation doing important work, asked for advice and lobbied for support, yet sections of the very community in which we are rooted carry on as if we did not exist. We are invited by organisations, like Outrage, who are outside our locality and our specific constituency to show solidarity with them, for instance, at that brief moment of unity when the nail bombings ripped apart the heart of the gay and black communities. At a memorial service organised by Outrage, SBS made a statement of solidarity which, among other things, asserted: 'We have come to build bridges to each other in order to tear down the walls of bigotry.... Fear is their weapon but courage is ours.' And courage is needed to bridge some of the chasms that we must confront.

Notes

1. Southall Black Sisters, *Against the Grain: A Celebration of Survival and Struggle*, SBS, London 1990.
2. Marie Mulholland, 'Transversal Politics', *Soundings* 12, Summer 1999.
3. Julie Bindel, 'Neither an Ism nor a Chasm', in *All the Rage: Reasserting Radical Lesbian Feminism*, Women's Press, London 1996.
4. Nira Yuval-Davis, 'Gendering Ethics', paper presented at a conference on Women and Ethnic Conflict, Leeds, June 2000.
5. Nira Yuval-Davis, 'Women, Ethnicity and Empowerment', in K. Bhavnani and A. Phoenix, eds, *Shifting Identities, Shifting Racisms*, Sage, London 1994.
6. Yuval-Davis, 'Gendering Ethics'.
7. Yuval-Davis, 'Women, Ethnicity and Empowerment'.
8. Bindel, *All the Rage*.
9. He was released in 2002.
10. Yasmin Alibhai-Brown, *Who Do We Think We Are? Imagining the New Britain*, Penguin, Harmondsworth 2000.
11. 'Inclusive Movements/Movements for Inclusion', *Soundings* 12, Summer 1999.
12. Yuval-Davis, 'Women, Ethnicity and Empowerment'.
13. Phil McCorkell, 'Overwhelmed by Immigrants', *Southall Gazette*, 6 July 2001.
14. 'Stop Racist Seeds from Sprouting', Letters, *Southall Gazette*, 20 July 2001.

Black feminism in the twenty-first century: the age of women?

Hannana Siddiqui

In July 2000, SBS celebrated its twenty-first anniversary. The celebrations aimed to mark our achievements and take the British Asian feminist movement, if it can be called that, forward into the twenty-first century. But will the new millennium mark the coming of age of both SBS and the black women's movement in the UK? In the 1980s, SBS was one of a number of radical black women's organisations which were active up and down the country, but in the last decade the picture has changed considerably: the mantle of leadership of British Asian feminists, especially concerning the issue of domestic violence against Asian women, appears to have fallen on SBS by default. In the 1990s, we have seen the growth of organisations with an emphasis on service provision rather than campaigning, and the development of women's groups whose agenda has been the promotion of religious values through the provision of welfare services.

Within the broader context, we appear to be operating within an ethos where feminism is seen as outmoded whilst anti-racism is all the rage. Many now talk of 'post-feminism', as if women have all 'made it' in a world of sexual equality where there is nothing left to fight for. Sexual equality means women can go out to work and men can stay at home to look after the children and the home, girls are achieving better than boys at school, and women can enter the priesthood. 'Girl Power', symbolised by the Spice Girls and other female stars, is often regarded as having revolutionised young women. Post-feminism reflects gains made by successful middle-class, mainly white, women: a hollow victory with no insight into the needs of, or solidarity with, the disadvantaged and dispossessed. The ladette phenomenon – aggressive and competitive young women – has also been laid at the door of feminism. Following the horrific attacks on 11 September 2001, television evangelists accused feminists, among other 'deviants', of causing the tragedy.

If the *Guardian* Women's Page coverage of International Women's Day in 2001 is anything to go by, it also believes feminism in Britain is dead: two pages full of women's struggles everywhere in the world other than in the UK! If the state of feminism can be assessed by its icons, then what do we conclude from glamorous icons such as Shere Hite, Camille Paglia and Oprah Winfrey, as compared to the intellectuals of the 1970s and 1980s such as Dale Spender and Angela Davis? Lifestyle politics, preoccupation with the body, diets and tips on improving personal relationships seem to be the order of the day rather than women's rights and empowerment. British feminism has few leading icons and much of our thinking is influenced by feminists in the USA. It is the disjuncture between real lives and success-ful women who are icons that creates the 'emptiness' of many intellectual analyses of where women are at or leads to assertions that feminism is dead.

'Who needs men?'

Indeed, it is argued by some that the transformation has been so profound that it is men who need to be saved. It has always been part of the strategy of the establishment to make exaggerated claims on behalf of any movement that challenges the prevailing status quo so as to mobilise against it. However, Geoffrey Wansell takes the argument to a laughable extreme:

> To put it bluntly, it is an extraordinary transformation in the power of young women – at the expense of men. Yes, the sex war has got very hot indeed, so hot that the 21st century is already being hailed by social historians as the Age of Women.[1]

Geoffrey Wansell fears that the 'genderquake' is not just bringing about equality, it is actually 'feminising' society itself. The crisis of masculinity is so disturbing that 'the only things boys do better than girls are committing crimes – and suicide', states one consult-ant psychiatrist, Dr Sebastian Kraemer, in the article. Wansell points to biological weaknesses in men, which makes them more vulner-able than women, and to changes in the labour market and the education system favouring women. He quotes Dr Madsen Pirie, president of the Adam Smith Institute, who says that the old exami-nation system played to male strengths, namely 'risk-taking and grasp of the big picture', whereas the modern coursework-based system places more emphasis on female qualities of systematic preparation in modules, worked on consistently over time. Dr Pirie asks:

> Ultimately, we have to ask ourselves what sort of society we are producing if we feminise the entry qualification into its leadership positions. If we select the methodical over the risk-taker, male or female, and the systematic in preference to those with insight, will Britain still be capable of meeting the challenges the world throws its way? While the country might be more peaceable, more sensi-tive to the needs of its citizens, and more efficient in applying itself to the detail of good management, we ask if it will still be as inventive and creative. Will it still produce penicillin and the hovercraft? Or will it produce civil servants?

While claiming that women are doing better than men in almost every area, Wansell manages at the same time to be deeply insulting to women. At work, Wansell argues, although men still dominate the 'commanding heights of government and the boardroom ... the majority of men on the factory floor and office corridors are seeing their lives transformed for ever', as they now have to compete with women and not just other men for jobs, promotion and pay rises. However, 'men, even the so-called "new" men, still tend to define themselves primarily by the masculinity of their job, rather than by their role as a father and husband'. As a result, Wansell states, 'The self-esteem of the adolescent male is fragile at the best of times, but the genderquake had weakened it decisively – so that boys are being left bewildered and confused about their role.' As for women, Wansell says, 'With the advent of embryo fertilisation and the removal of the stigma on a woman of bringing up a child alone, it is hardly sur-prising that some women's magazines have started to ask: "Who

Needs Men?"' But in this bleak new world, Wansell clutches on to the straw that women's 'maternal drive' will make the pendulum swing back to a focus on family life.

Some female commentators, too, have argued that feminists have gone too far. Jane Fonda donated £9 million to a Centre for Gender and Education at Harvard University.[2] She feels that after decades of an educational philosophy which tried to empower girls with self-belief, it is now time to switch the emphasis to boys. The problem, according to her, is that young boys are conditioned to be 'manly and strong' from an early age. While we can certainly lay claim to the successes of feminism, that it may have forced men to redefine and reconsider their roles, we cannot by ourselves have brought on a crisis of masculinity. Many of the communities of young men that have been the focus of such analyses have suffered from poverty and unemployment, aggravated by racism. We presume that is what Bea Campbell meant when she was interviewed on radio in the summer of 2001 about the race riots in Northern cities – which she attributed to the crisis of masculinity.

The growth of the 'men's movement' and awareness-raising groups may point to the fact that there is a small crack in the veneer of patriarchy. Traditionally, it is the powerless sections of society that come together to fight from a position of strength. The formation of groups like Families Need Fathers is perhaps an indication of men's new-found vulnerabilities. The organisation has sought to undermine the gains women have made on the issue of male violence against women. This group argues that men, too, suffer domestic violence and are discriminated against in the legal system when, for example, applying for child custody or contact. Men's groups have attempted to establish their own services, and even set up a refuge for men in Southall – which closed down when it was underused and remained empty or was used by violent men who were forced to leave the matrimonial home when their partners had won injunctions against them! It is also instructive to look at the situation in the USA, which often influences what happens in the UK. In the USA, the Million Man March organised by the Nation of Islam in 1995 excluded women and focused not only on the issue of racism but also on black masculinity and male superiority.

However, much of this discourse on post-feminism and the crisis of masculinity does not provide an insight into the lives of millions of women like Yasmin, who form the backbone of our work and campaigns.

Real women and real lives

Yasmin works part-time as a cleaner at Heathrow Airport. Her husband is unemployed and receives benefits for the family. They have six children. Yasmin ensures she comes home in time to do the shopping, cooking, cleaning and caring for the children. Yasmin's husband often demands money from her, and if she refuses he beats her. At other times he beats her for no apparent reason. Yasmin speaks little English and has not been able to obtain a better-paid job. She has asked the council to transfer her and the children to another property, away from her husband, but has not received a suitable offer in a year. The last offer was unsuitable because the accommodation was too run-down and the estate had a reputation for racial attacks. She is not sure if the council will make another offer of housing. Yasmin has refused temporary accommodation because it would be too disruptive for her children, who are settled in the local school. She does not want to be too public by going to court. Yasmin has not told her family about her application for a housing transfer because they want her to stay with her husband. They say she must make her marriage work for the sake of her children and culture. Yasmin has also been told by her local priest that women should stay with their husbands and not go out to work because of the need to look after children. Does Yasmin not have anything left to fight for?

'Post-feminism' has little relevance to women who come to SBS. Sexual oppression continues to impact on the daily lives of women, often compounded with other forms of inequality including poverty and racism. Even where women have made progress – the right to work – we still have the spectre of low, unequal pay and poor conditions in addition to the main responsibility for the home and the care of children. Recent research on women in the workplace shows that there are plunging levels of satisfaction with work because of the lack of support structures at home and at work. A report by the Equal Opportunities Commission published in August

2001 found through an analysis of employment tribunal cases over three years that 90 per cent of staff who were victims of sexual harassment lost their jobs; most of these were young women and tended to be in low-paid occupations such as shop workers, factory workers, carers and office staff. It is believed that only one in twenty 'victims' pursues a formal complaint.

While the legacy of Thatcherism and the excesses of individualism, only marginally challenged by New Labour, remain with us, the need for a political women's movement is as crucial as ever. Sisterhood perhaps never existed, and there is certainly no cogent women's movement today. The case of Yasmin, however, shows the urgent need for women to unite on a common agenda and give solidarity within and to other movements for liberation, equality and justice. This is important in an era of new threats and challenges, including professionalisation, globalisation, the rise of religious fundamentalism and other undemocratic and reactionary movements.

Backstreet girls

Sometimes I think of us as women who live on the backstreets of Southall, partially hidden from the main thoroughfares, chipping away at the status quo. But the reality is that despite our location we are being recognised for our work and have entered mainstream consciousness. We *are* visiting the main roads: at times taking a step forward, at other times a step backwards. This is symptomatic of the wider black women's movement – except we all seem to be chipping away alone, with no collective battle plan. There is little unity between Asian and African-Caribbean and other minority women, or, for that matter, with white women.

Black feminist groups struggle to ensure that their demands are recognised and adopted in mainstream policies, particularly on domestic violence, and that progress is not undermined by other corporate and political priorities. Despite our marginalisation and the fact that we have opted for piecemeal reform, like white feminism, we must not underestimate our victories. The provision of services for black women, the few that do exist, has made a real difference, often with very little support from the state. Domestic violence has a higher profile in the community and larger numbers of people are prepared to stand up and condemn it. However, certain aspects of violence, like female genital mutilation and forced marriage, and other taboo subjects such as prostitution, rape, incest, and sexual orientation are still controversial subjects. Outside the community, the issue of forced marriage, and more recently that of Asian women and domestic violence, have become increasingly 'popular', so much so that even white women are setting up initiatives to tackle them. However, some of these are more about 'saving' Asian women, and competing for funding, rather than supporting and giving Asian women leadership in their own struggle to save themselves!

The wider women's movement feels that it has made progress in domestic violence, and most feminists are less openly critical of the state's response to the problem. Indeed, they have to work closely with the police, the Home Office and other bodies to influence policy. While there have been positive developments, leading to a greater recognition of the problem of domestic violence – even feminist language and demands have made some inroads – co-option and compromise have also watered down the agenda and isolated black and minority women.

White feminists are becoming more vocal about other areas of violence against women which have not been addressed by agencies and policymakers. Recent work has involved influencing policy, such as the Sexual Offences Review in the Home Office, and public campaigning through groups like the Campaign against Rape and in the legal arena. Prostitution and trafficking in women are the new battleground, attracting public criticism of the police, the Crown, the judiciary and the government. Women have long been active around rape and other forms of sexual violence and have lost none of the radicalism of their original agenda. However, even this area of work is devoid of an analysis of the intersection of race and gender shaping the experiences of trafficked women. There is no adequate analysis of why women from Eastern Europe or Africa are selected for prostitution and other forms of sexual oppression. This is not to say that black women have adequately tackled this pressing area of concern adequately either. Although Black Women Against Rape (BWAR) have been campaigning on rape, they reduce women's experiences to economic exploitation and racism only. They do not seek to understand how sexual oppression, poverty and racism are simultaneously experienced by such women. We too have not been active on the question of rape, partly due to limited resources and partly because rape and sexual abuse are still taboo in Asian communities. Black women need to become more active, particularly as we witness a new and growing phenomenon of international trafficking in women into prostitution. African girls aged 14 have gone missing from care homes following their arrival in this country as asylum-seekers. They are brought into the UK via Italy, where they are coerced by human traffickers to work in the sex industry. In 2001, SBS came across cases of Asian women being brought into the UK as exotic dancers, where they too were subject to sexual harassment and pressure to enter the sex industry by their promoters. In addition, many black women are driven into prostitution in this country as a result of poverty. Prostitutes in particular have been subject to vigilante action by Asian men in areas such as Bradford and Birmingham.

The entry of so many Labour Party women into Parliament at the last two elections yielded few results at first. Their publication Living without Fear[3] fell short of a long promised national strategy on violence against women. However, our arena of struggle is increasingly within the legal and social policy field, which aims to take on the shortcomings of the state, yielding gains slowly. Due to growing demands, the government is now beginning a consultation on domestic violence; we hope to ensure that black women's needs are fully represented and integrated into any initiatives that may result.

What of the future?

As we enter the twenty-first century, where are we heading? The main threat to women's rights has been the growth of religious fundamentalism in the last decade. And with 11 September and the wars on Afghanistan and Iraq, it threatens to occupy centre stage in world politics in a way that it has never done before. It has suited the West, especially the USA, which fostered regimes like the Taliban as a bulwark against Communism, to ignore their internally oppressive and undemocratic practices as they have ignored the abuse of human rights by other dictatorships that they have supported. And America under Bush, in a 'crusade' against the attackers, has adopted a God-sodden rhetoric which would make Osama bin Laden blush.

Bush and Blair's great concern for women's liberation from the Taliban when invading Afghanistan was enough to make us blush!

The new economic world order has thrown up opportunities as never before for us as women living in the West to show solidarity with women's struggles worldwide. The successes of the anti-capitalist protesters in the cities of Europe and the USA represent an opportunity for us to make connections with other struggles that we have always talked about. Many of us still have our roots in the Third World and have sought opportunities to connect with struggles there. Michael Hardt and Antonio Negri argue that those who are exploited by global capital have 'a greater potential for commonality among each other', that even though the new system is more elusive than its predecessor, 'it, also, simultaneously creates more potential for wider co-operation and connections between people, which are the preconditions for liberatory movements'.[4] They depart from the traditional view that America is the HQ of the new global economy, which is controlled by the IMF, World Bank or a few multinationals. Hardt argues that there is no central place of power. It is 'a smooth space ... both everywhere and nowhere. Empire ... is a non-place.' In an interview in the Observer, he makes an analogy to the seamlessness of the Web: 'The organising principle is similar to the principle of the internet – it links the internet age to the way power functions as a distribution network.'[5] And as proof of this claim, he points to the unequal development of economies in both the North and South where there are pockets of Third World in developed nations, and pockets of wealthy elites in many impoverished countries.

The heroic intervention of Women in Black UK in the Palestinian struggle points to the way in which activists in the West can and should intervene in other struggles. In August 2001, members of Women in Black went to Palestine to act as human shields to protect the Palestinians against Israeli tanks. They slept in the homes of Palestinians in Bethlehem; they acted as witnesses to the torture of Palestinian prisoners; they monitored and contested abuses of human rights; they defused violence and challenged Israel's ethnic cleansing programme. This is the kind of opportunity afforded to us by the globalisation of the struggle. This is very similar to the idea that has been floated by the American feminist Eve Ensler, who is looking to mobilise funds and women to sign up to an international women's peace corps, to be ready to take direct action at hotspots around the world and, by their mass presence, to avert the worst excesses of a brutal regime. The vitality and mobilisation of the 'stop the city' and green movements are also new areas where black women need to make connections and alliances.

It is also likely that the old arguments of biological determinism, which were used to validate not merely differences between gender but also the power imbalances that flowed from difference, will raise their heads again. And this time they will come with even greater scientific proof, derived from the mapping of the human genome. There has always been a hunger for the simplistic and comforting notions of fixed sexual essences which identify crude oppositions between women and men in the battle of the sexes. We have already seen crude attempts to isolate the genes for violence, shyness and homosexuality. Who knows what gene will be discovered that makes black women the way we are. And we will have to fight on that ideological battleground shoulder to shoulder with feminists like Lynne Segal, who says, 'As human beings, we are never in any way at the mercy of biology. We are always able to do with our biology what the cultural and social and personal resources available to us allow.'[6]

What of the future? The strength of black feminism lies in political activism and alliance-building between black women's groups and white feminists (see Chapter 12, 'Walls into Bridges'). Many black women have called on SBS to provide some leadership and cohesion to the movement, whether it be to give guidance on good practice to deal with domestic violence or to raise wider common political issues concerning black, particularly Asian, women. One Asian woman, a senior civil servant, admitted to us that in the past she had kept her distance from SBS because she thought we were too radical. Disillusioned with lack of change, she now wants us to establish a network of radical black women! In late 2001 we received an unexpected grant from Atlantic Philanthropies to enable some of this representation and alliance-building work. In 2002, we organised a number of regional meetings bringing together over a hundred Asian, African, Caribbean and other minority women and women's groups to consult, network and campaign on gender violence. In 2003, an umbrella organisation, of which we are a member, Asian

Women Unite!, organised a conference to mobilise and politicise Asian women. Working with Asian Women Unite! and established groups like Newham Asian Women's Project, Imkaan, Forward and Akina Mama wa Afrika, dealing with black women's health and female genital mutilation; and Kalayaan, which deals with overseas domestic workers, most of whom are black or minority women, also has the potential to make wider links. These and other initiatives will help to consolidate and build a stronger black feminist movement.

Perhaps the millennium will witness greater solidarity between black and white feminists in the international arena. Our hand will be further strengthened if, as black women, we can gain the support of the wider anti-racist and progressive movement. In our struggle for women's human and civil rights, we have always argued that women's rights are as important as racial justice; that struggles against all oppressions, including race, sex or class, can be waged simultaneously. Only by doing this can we hope to build a strong, progressive human and civil rights movement. Rather than rights for a few, we must have rights for all.

Mainstreaming our concerns is crucial if we are to have our voices heard, difficult as that task may be. Our common agenda has to be that of empowering black women, especially working-class women. We cannot fail to have noticed that behind every successful white woman there is an army of black, Eastern European and other migrant women doing the housework and child-care, thereby allowing white feminists to believe that they can have it all in the age of post-feminism! As black women we cannot rest until the fruits of feminism have been shared equally, and all women are free to follow their dreams. Perhaps then we can call this century the 'Age of Women'.

Notes

1. Geoffrey Wansell, 'Genderquake', Daily Mail, 21 April 2001
2. Richard Morrison, 'Who'd Be a Boy?' The Times, 15 August 2001.
3. Cabinet Office, June 1999.
4. Michael Hardt and Antonio Negri, Empire, Harvard University Press, Harvard 2001.
5. Ed Vulliamy, 'Empire Hits Back', Observer, 15 July 2001.
6. Lynne Segal, quoted in Dave Hill, 'The Truth about Men and Women', Guardian, 11 December 2000.

About the contributors

Sukhwant Dhaliwal was born and brought up in Southall. She has been extensively involved in the anti-racist and feminist movements, and worked at SBS for a total of four and a half years (three and a half years as youth/caseworker, about six months as a researcher and a few months doing schools work and helping with the immigration campaign). She is currently studying for an MA in social research at Goldsmiths College, University of London.

Rahila Gupta has been a member of the management committee of SBS since 1989. She is a political activist, freelance journalist and writer. Currently a member of the writing team of BBC World Service drama *Westway*, and a writer-in-residence at Bromley-by-Bow Centre, she has contributed short stories and poems to many anthologies. She wrote *Circle of Light* (1997) with Kiranjit Ahluwalia.

Muneeza Inam joined Southall Black Sisters in the early 1980s. She helped to set up Brent Asian Women's Refuge in 1984. Over the last decade she has worked in many housing projects and more recently in an Asian women's refuge run by a housing association. In her own way she has always tried to follow the example set by her father, which was to question and challenge all orthodoxies.

Anita Johal worked for Southall Black Sisters for four years. Through SBS she became involved in the black feminist and anti-racist movement, having contact with groups such as Women in Black, Interights and Amnesty, and becoming involved with campaigns such as Free Satpal

Ram and Amina Lawal. Her main interests are music and film and she has recently revived a need to be creative through DIY and mosaic.

Poonam Joshi has campaigned on issues of race/gender and discrimination for over thirteen years. She studied for an MA in development studies at SOAS before qualifying as a family/criminal lawyer with Winstanley Burgess solicitors. She started as a volunteer with SBS in 1996 and joined the MC in 1997. Her research and campaigning involvement with SBS has been mainly on the one-year immigration rule campaign.

Meena Patel joined Southall Black Sisters as an administrator/caseworker in 1987, becoming joint co-ordinator with Hannana Siddiqui in 1999. Her knowledge of accounts and administrative skills have contributed to the efficient running of the organisation. She has also developed the organisation's work in child support, mental health and counselling for women who have faced domestic violence.

Pragna Patel is a founder member of Southall Black Sisters. She was responsible for turning the organisation from a purely voluntary group to a funded centre with paid staff in 1982. She worked for SBS until 1993, when she left to train as a solicitor, although she still serves on the MC. She has contributed articles on gender and race issues to a number of anthologies and journals.

Hannana Siddiqui has worked on issues of race and gender for twenty years. She has been at Southall Black Sisters for sixteen years, advising and supporting survivors, participating in campaigns and undertaking local and national policy work. She is currently a joint co-ordinator. She has also contributed political essays to a range of publications.

Index